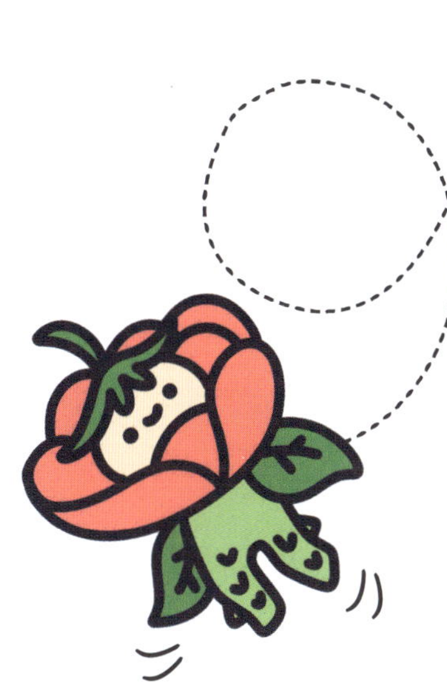

How to Draw

CUTE STUFF WOODLAND WORLD

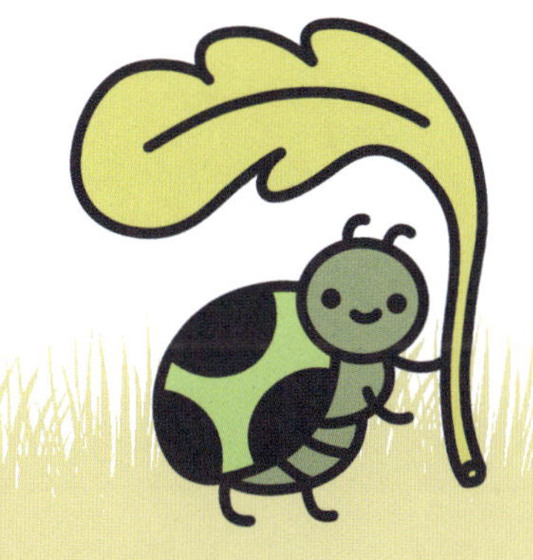

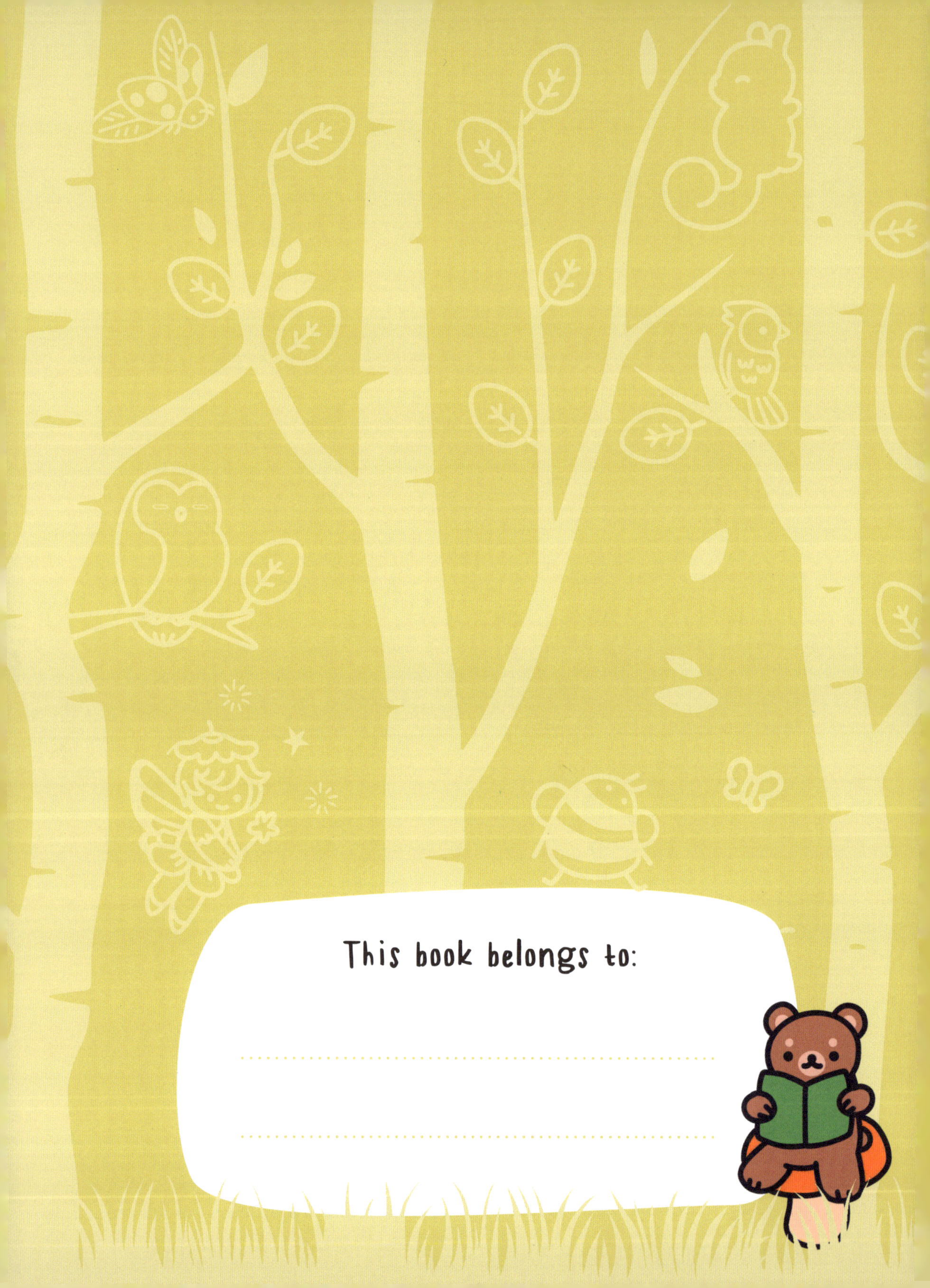
This book belongs to:

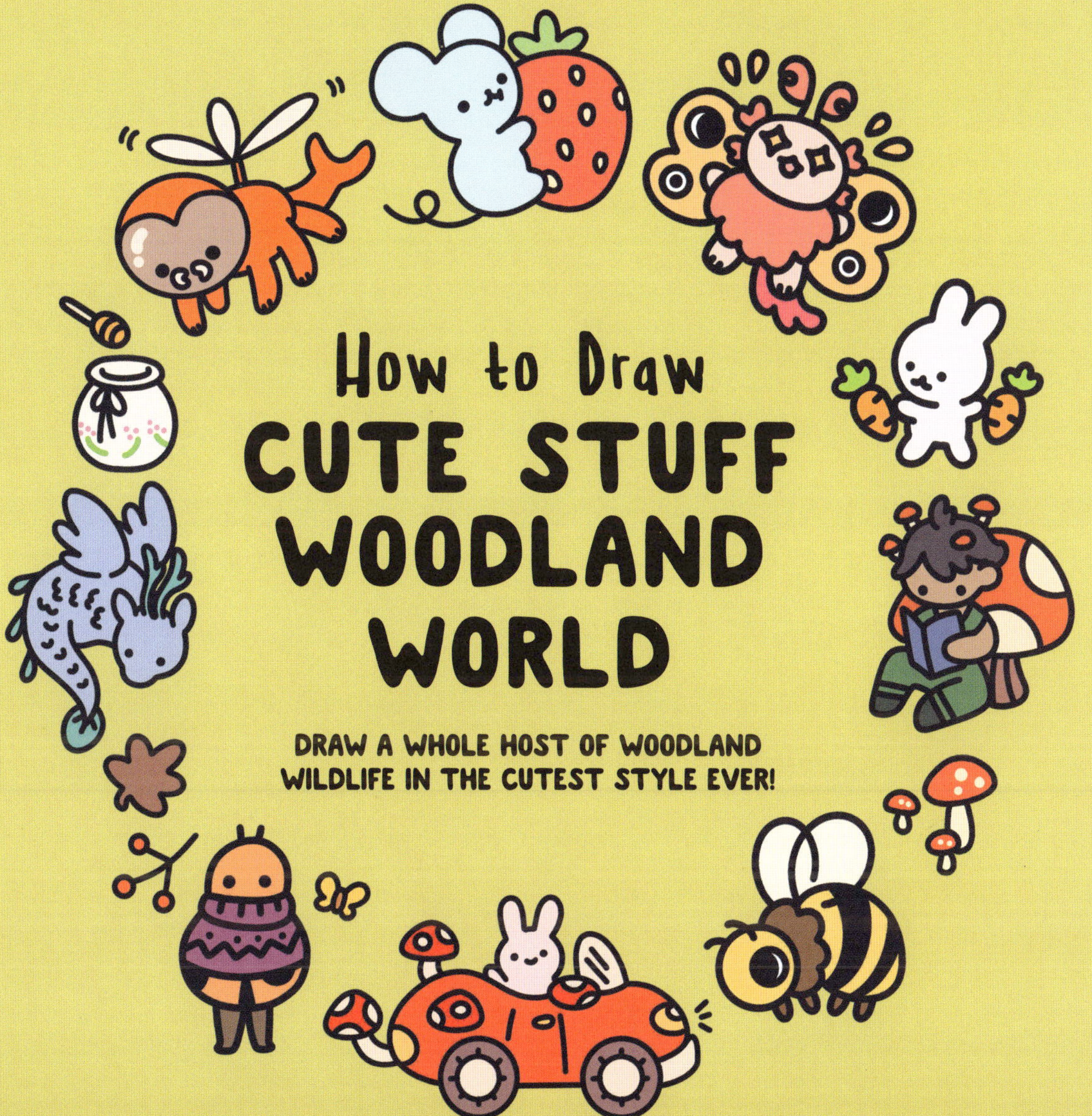

How to Draw
CUTE STUFF WOODLAND WORLD

DRAW A WHOLE HOST OF WOODLAND WILDLIFE IN THE CUTEST STYLE EVER!

Angela Nguyen

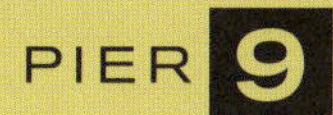

First published in Australia and New Zealand by Pier 9, an imprint of Murdoch Books, in 2023

An imprint of Quarto
1 Triptych Place, London, SE1 9SH
www.quarto.com

QUAR.422399

Murdoch Books Australia
83 Alexander Street
Crows Nest NSW 2065
Phone: (61 2) 8425 0100
www.murdochbooks.com.au
info@murdochbooks.com.au

Murdoch Books UK
Ormond House
26-27 Boswell Street
London WC1N 3JZ
Phone: (44 0) 20 8785 5995
www.murdochbooks.co.uk
info@murdochbooks.co.uk

ISBN 978-1-76150-003-9

Printed in China

10 9 8 7 6 5 4 3

A catalogue record for this book is available from the National Library of Australia

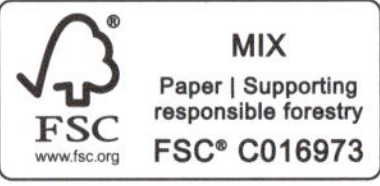

CONTENTS

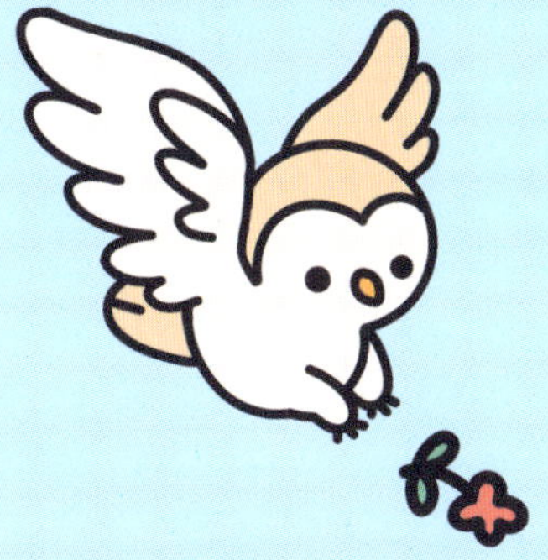

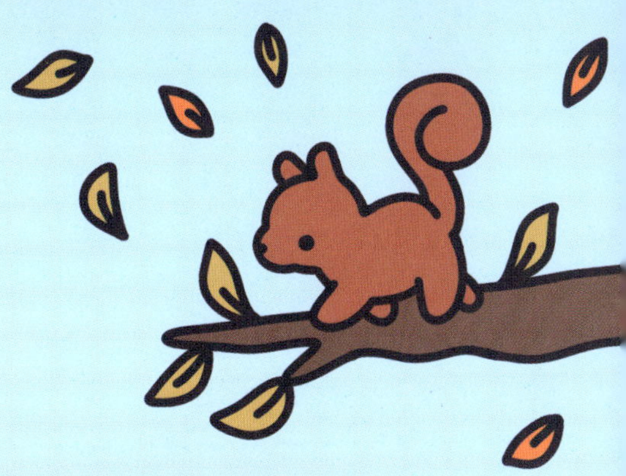

Chapter three
FOREST CREATURES 48

Chapter four
THE NATURAL WORLD 90

Chapter five
FOREST LIVING 114

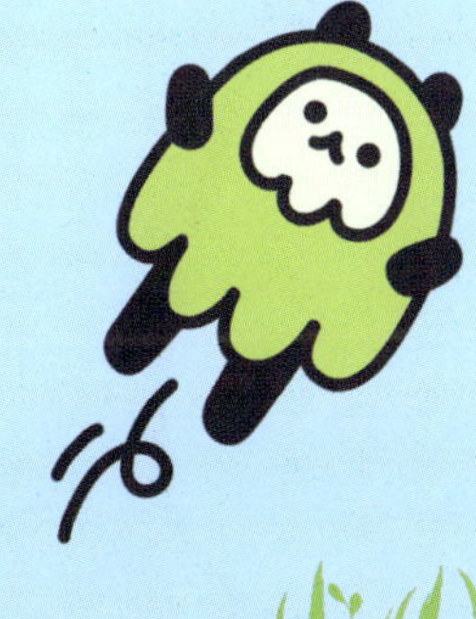

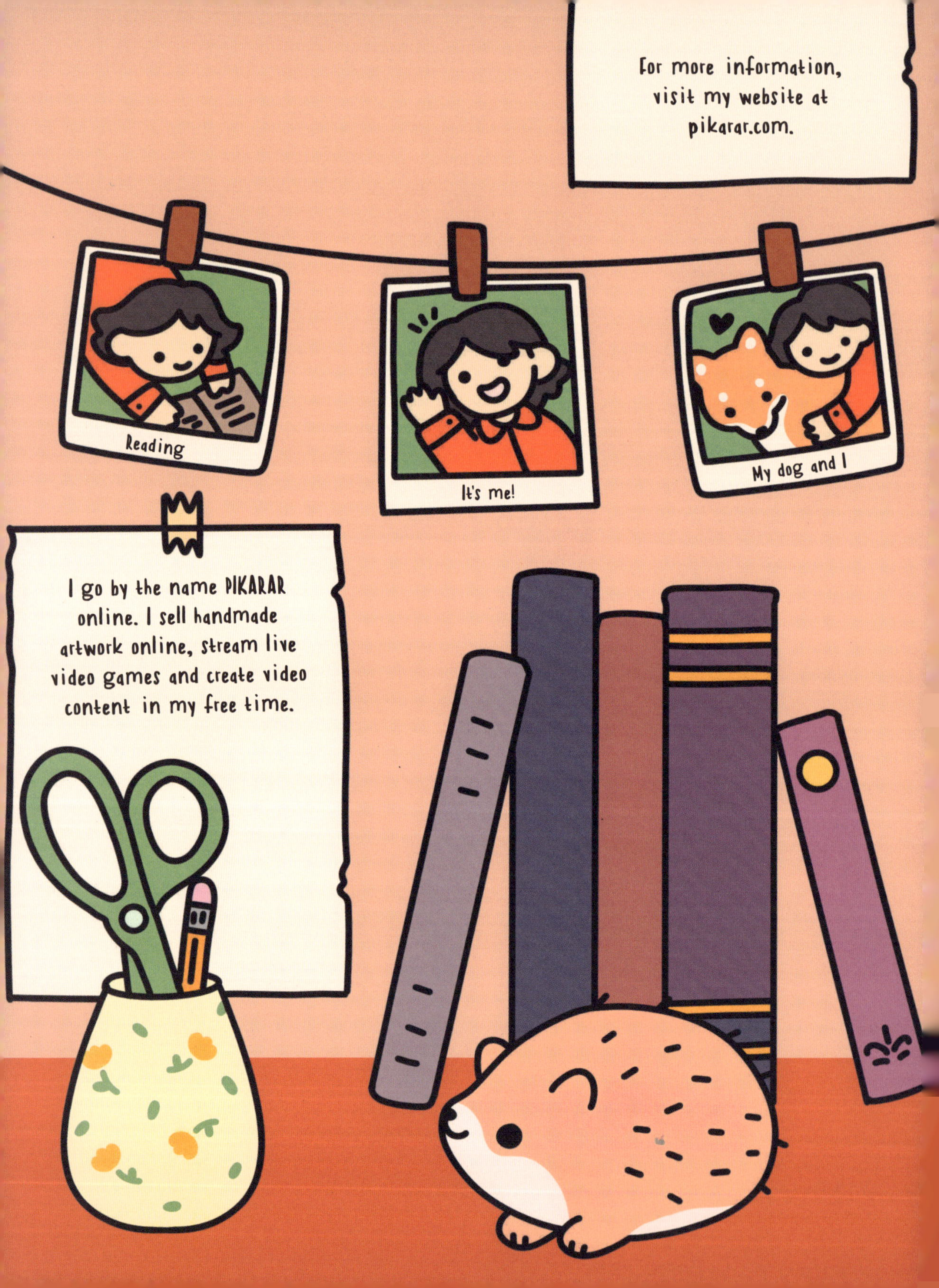

For more information, visit my website at pikarar.com.

Reading

It's me!

My dog and I

I go by the name PIKARAR online. I sell handmade artwork online, stream live video games and create video content in my free time.

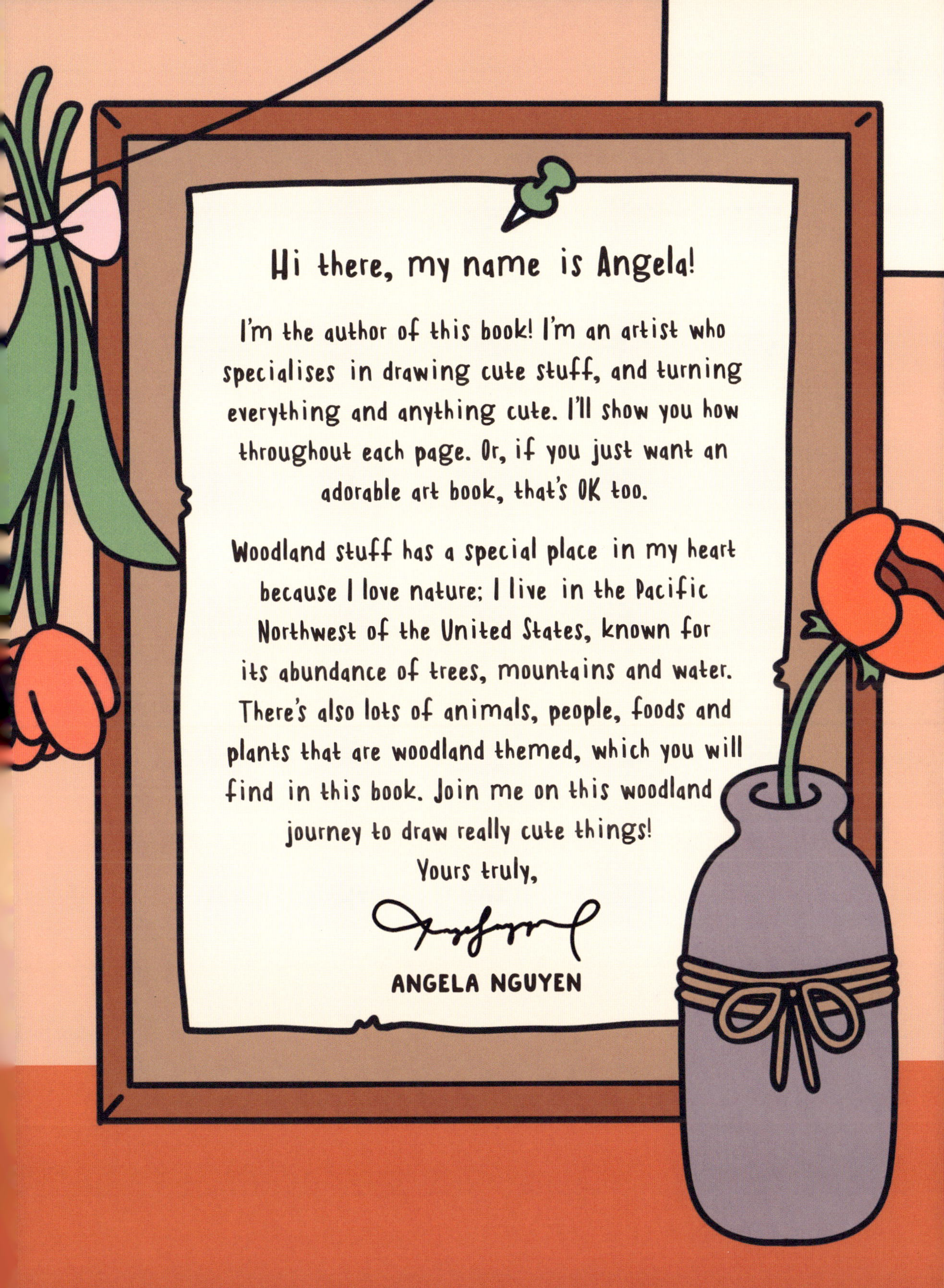

Hi there, my name is Angela!

I'm the author of this book! I'm an artist who specialises in drawing cute stuff, and turning everything and anything cute. I'll show you how throughout each page. Or, if you just want an adorable art book, that's OK too.

Woodland stuff has a special place in my heart because I love nature; I live in the Pacific Northwest of the United States, known for its abundance of trees, mountains and water. There's also lots of animals, people, foods and plants that are woodland themed, which you will find in this book. Join me on this woodland journey to draw really cute things!

Yours truly,

ANGELA NGUYEN

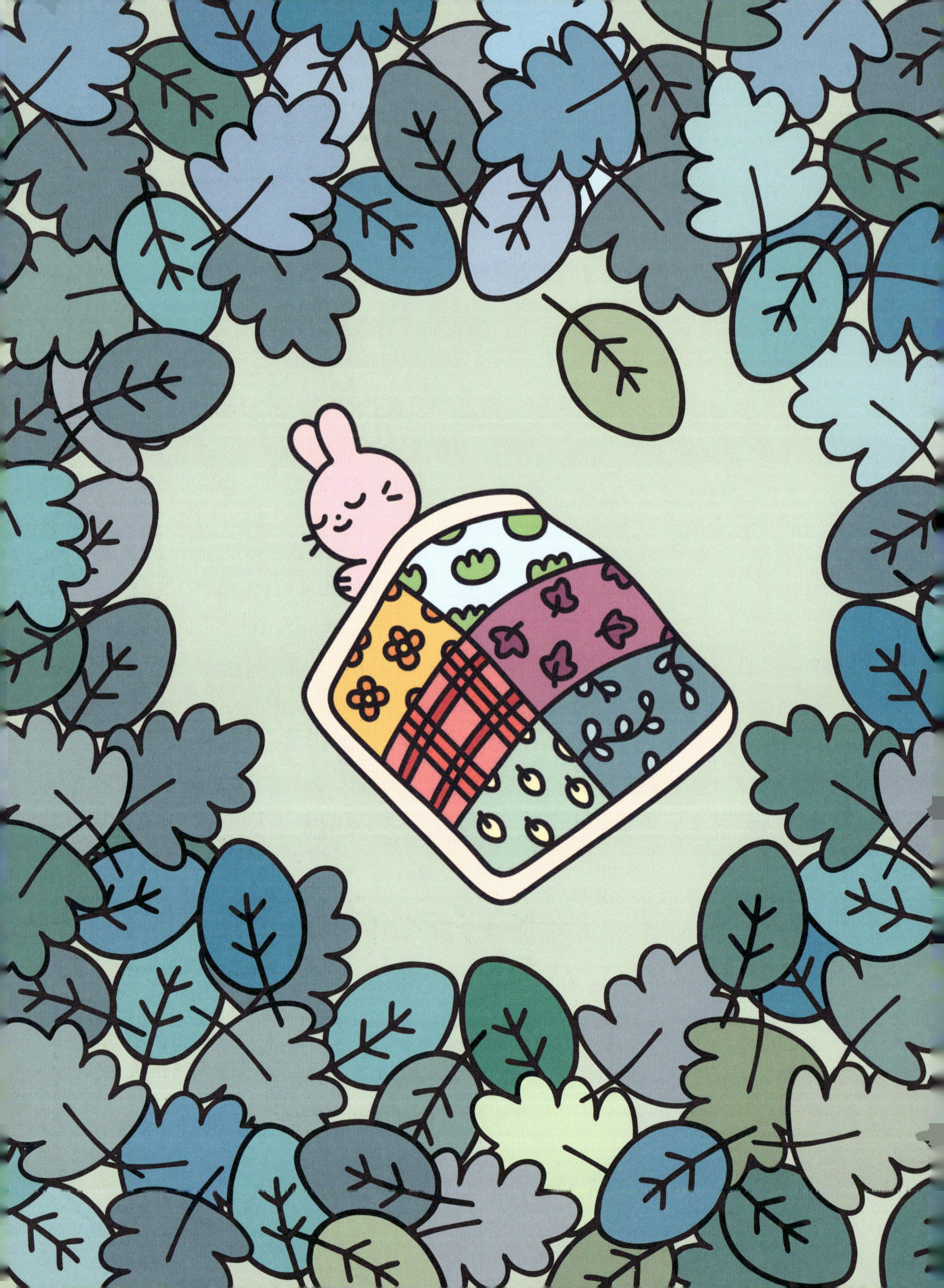

Chapter one

GETTING STARTED

You don't need special tools, materials or skills to draw your woodland world. Grab your pens and paper, then learn how to give your drawings some cute appeal! You can also have some fun creating the scenery for your woodland folk and creatures.

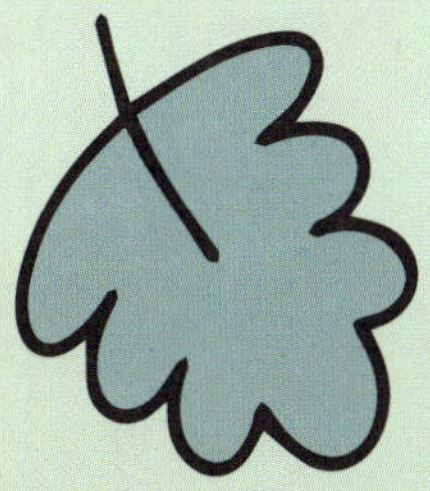

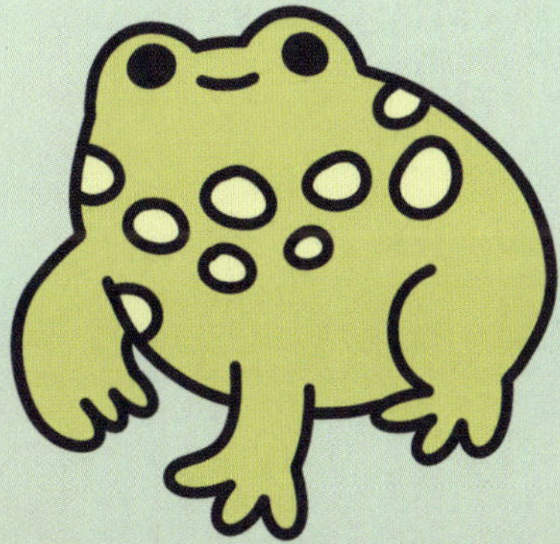

TOOLS AND SURFACES

There are many types of tools you can use to draw and colour cute woodland creatures. These are some of the tools that I love to use.

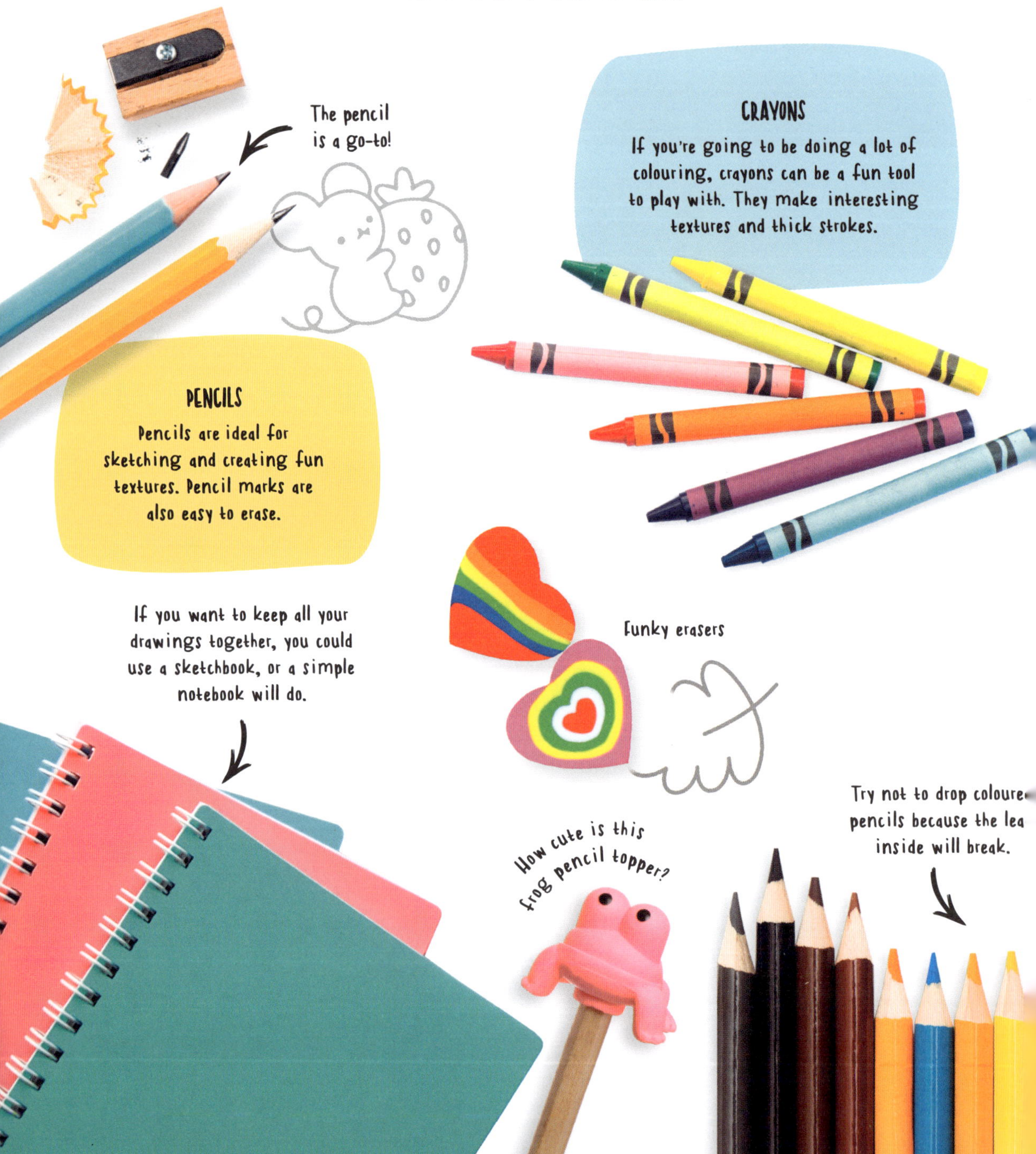

SURFACES

You don't need special paper; any kind of drawing surface is just fine.

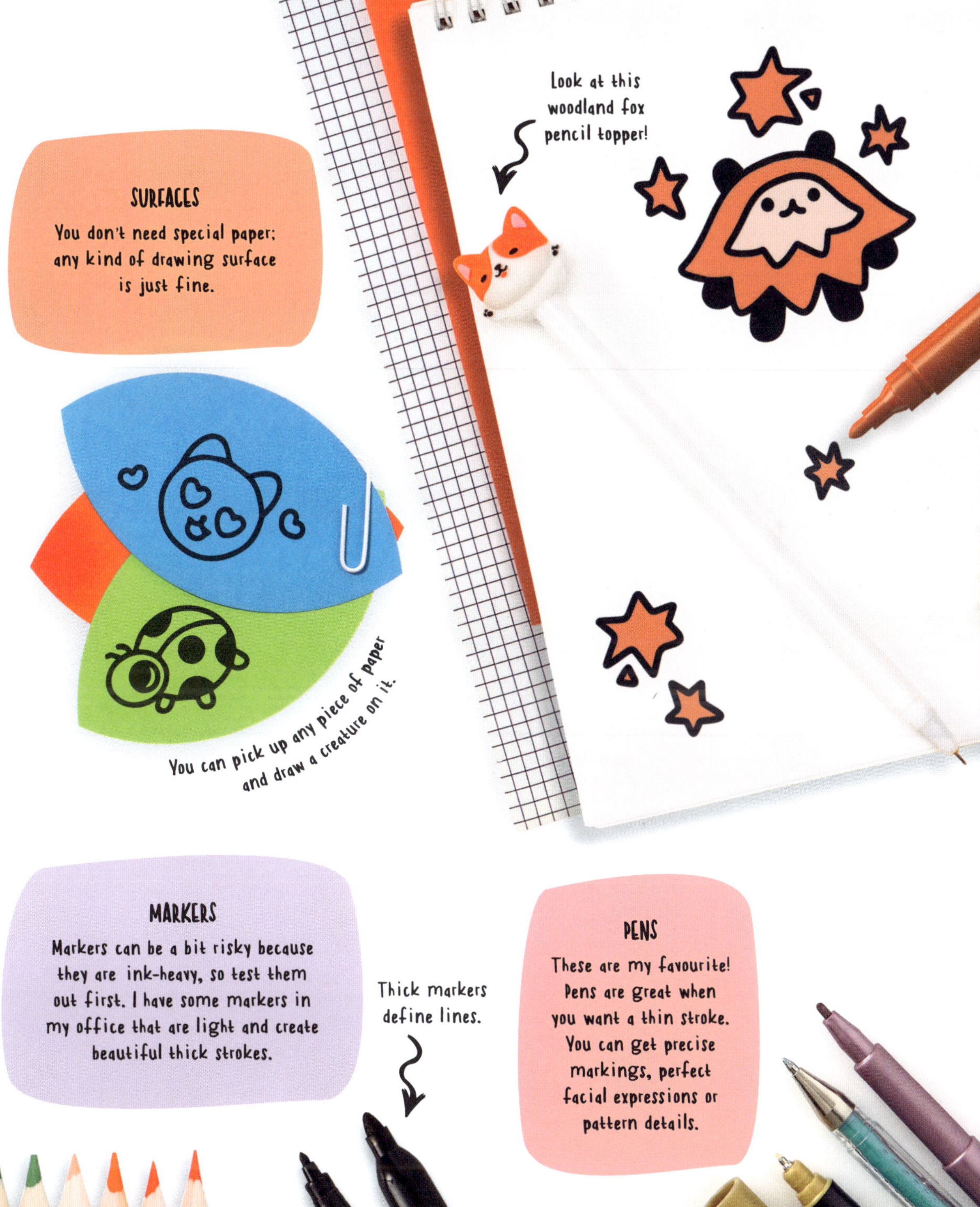

MARKERS

Markers can be a bit risky because they are ink-heavy, so test them out first. I have some markers in my office that are light and create beautiful thick strokes.

Thick markers define lines.

PENS

These are my favourite! Pens are great when you want a thin stroke. You can get precise markings, perfect facial expressions or pattern details.

SCENERY

The scenery you use in your drawings tells the story of where your character is from, how they live and what they are up to right now!

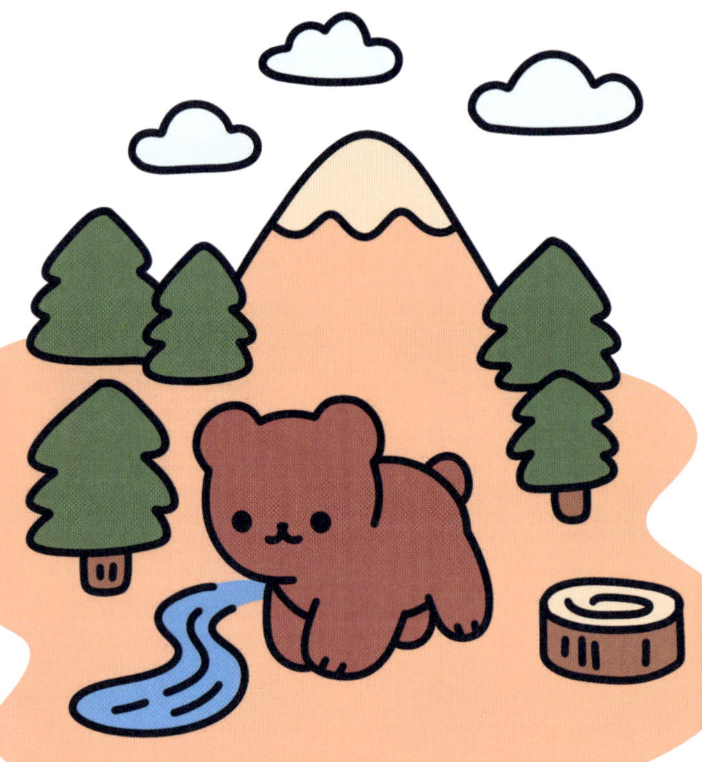

Mountain lands are high up, and so closer to the clouds. Forests of evergreens are usual on mountainsides, and there is often snow on the mountaintops. There's also lots of fresh water in mountain environments.

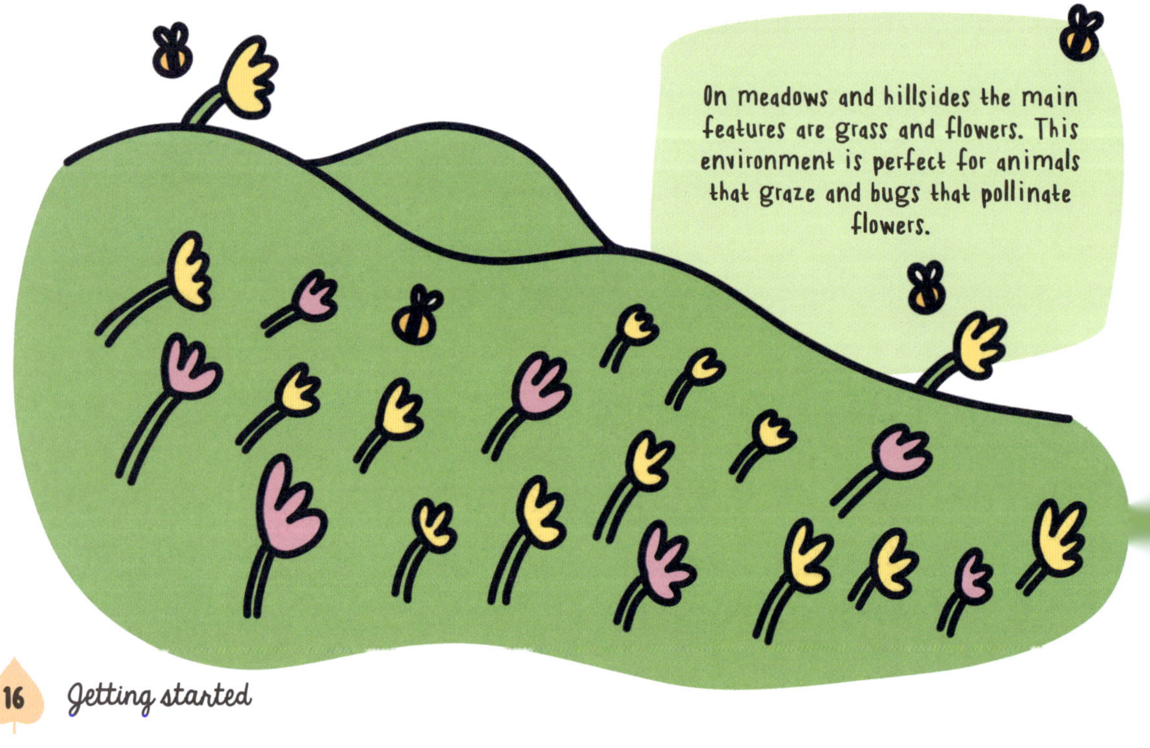

On meadows and hillsides the main features are grass and flowers. This environment is perfect for animals that graze and bugs that pollinate flowers.

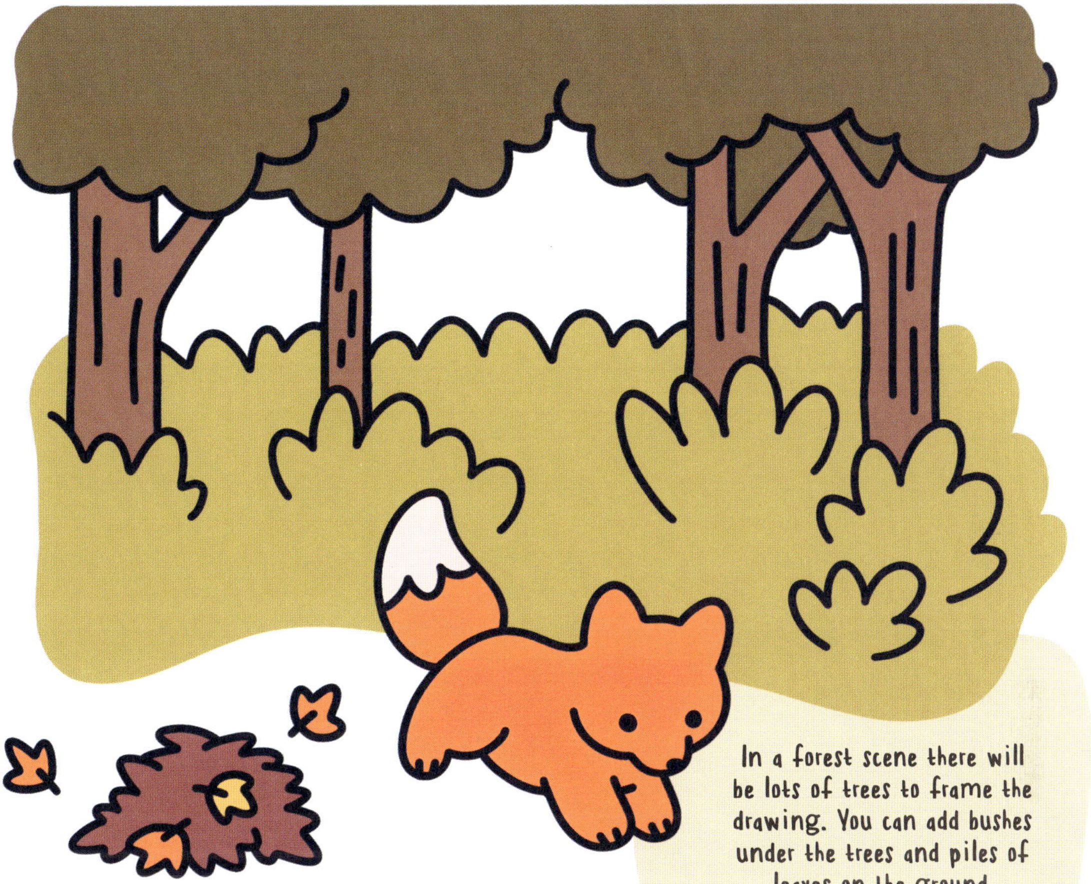

In a forest scene there will be lots of trees to frame the drawing. You can add bushes under the trees and piles of leaves on the ground.

Rivers and lakes are bodies of water surrounded by land. The land around the water is usually green and fertile.

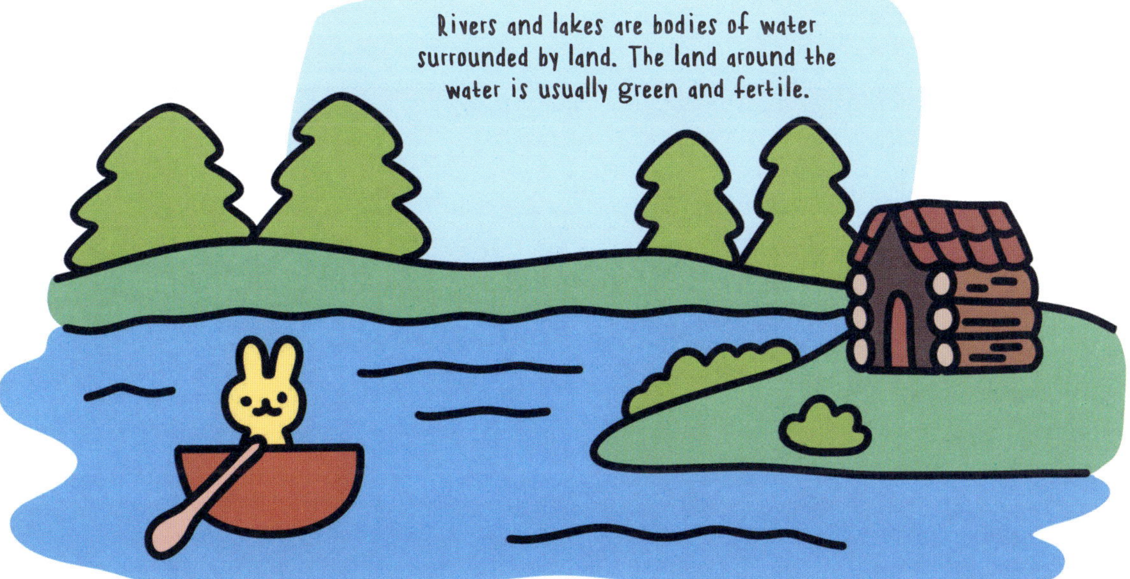

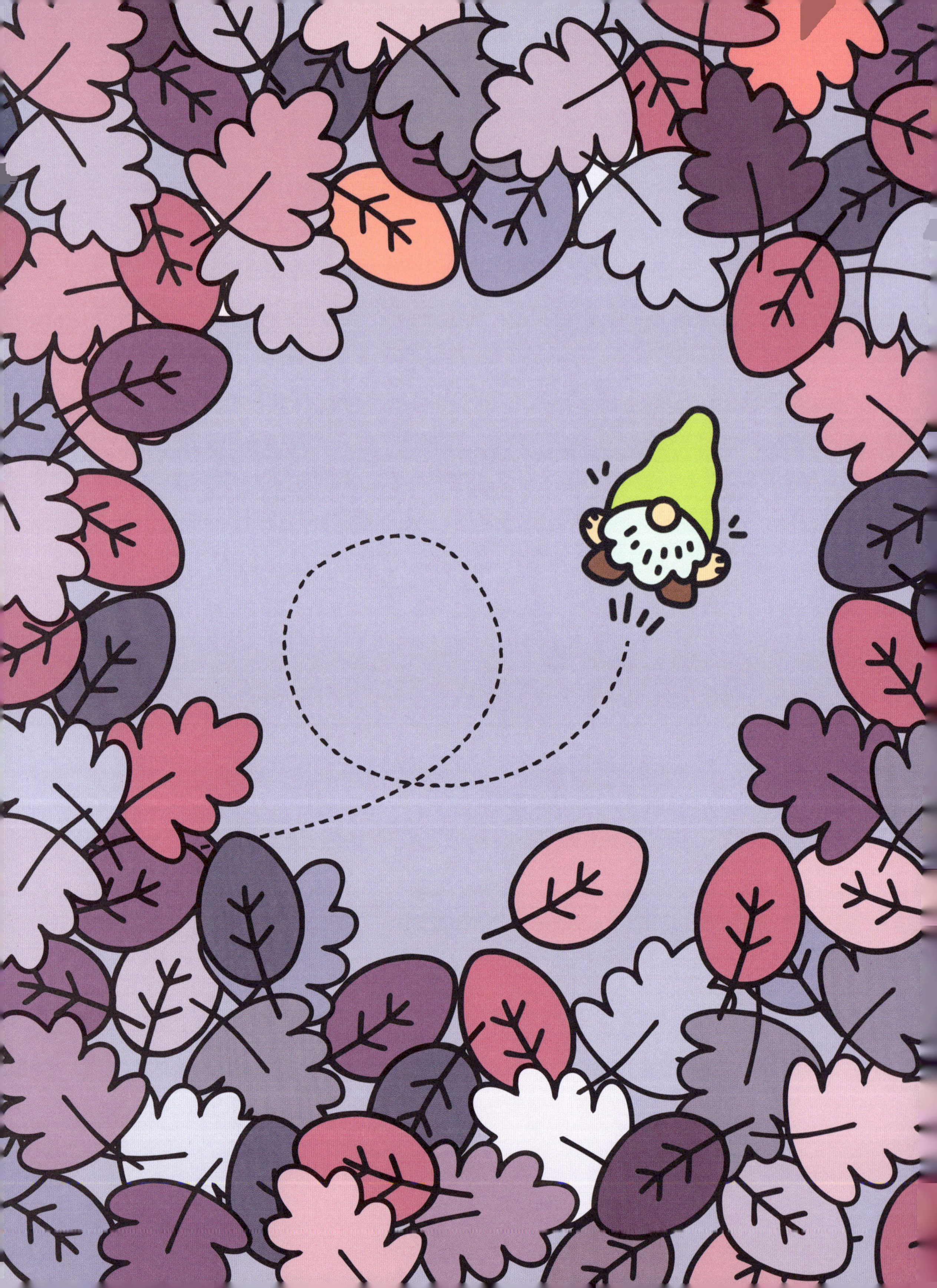

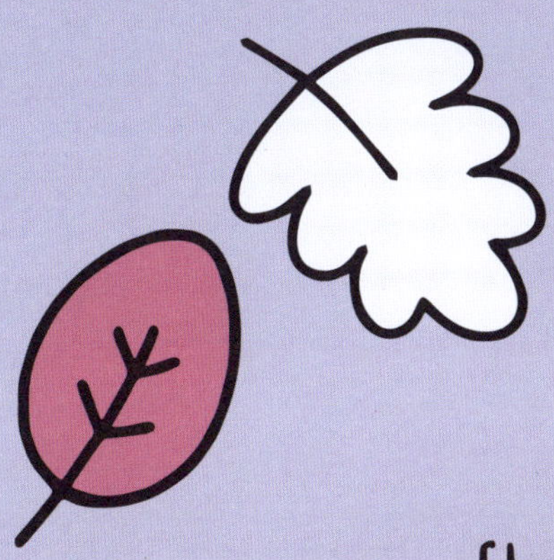

Chapter two

WOODLAND FOLK

Drawing cute people requires features to distinguish them, and accessories and clothes to decorate them. In this chapter, I'll show you how to bring all sorts of characters to life!

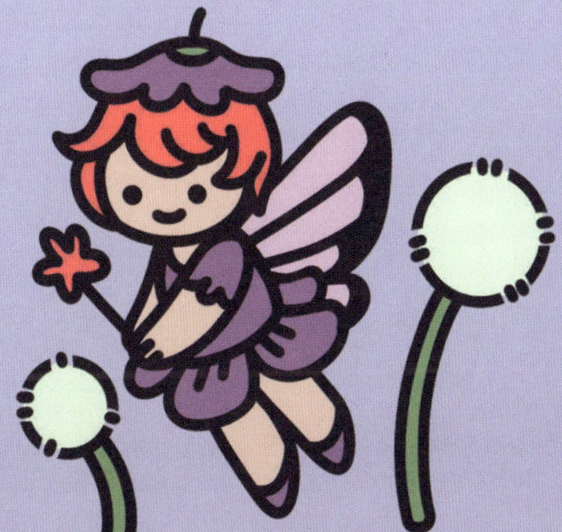

PEOPLE BASICS

PROPORTIONS

Two-and-a-half circles is the perfect proportion for cute characters. The top circle is the head. The body takes up roughly three-quarters of the middle circle, and the legs reach from the bottom of the body to the base line.

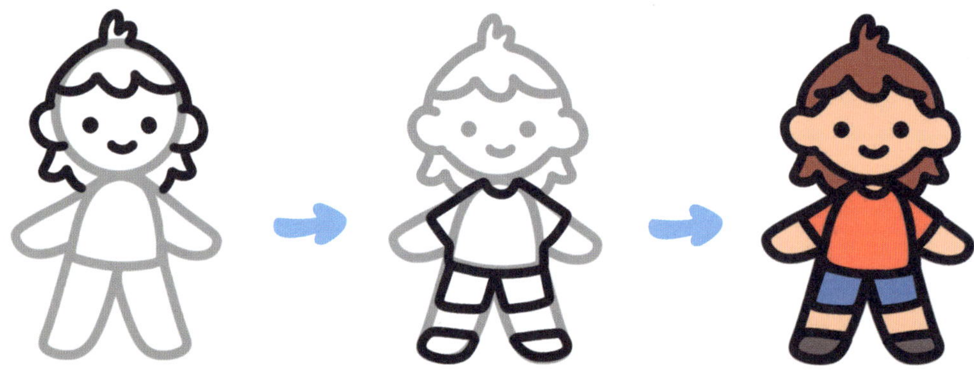

Add hair and facial features . . . . . . and clothes and finishing touches.

BODY SHAPES

Use the same proportion guidelines to draw different body shapes!

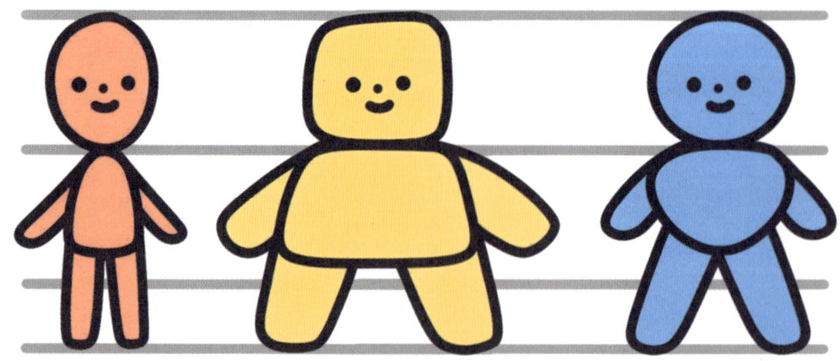

This character has an oval head with a narrow body and slim limbs.

Try square shapes with wide limbs.

You can even draw a triangular body.

DIRECTIONS

Draw a cross on your character's face. As you draw them turning in different directions, keep the eyes the same distance apart on the horizontal line, and the nose and mouth the same distance below on the vertical line.

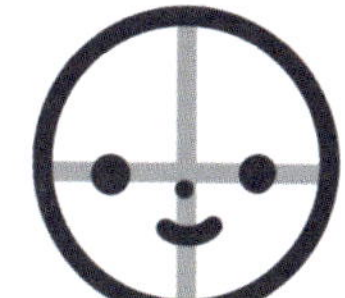

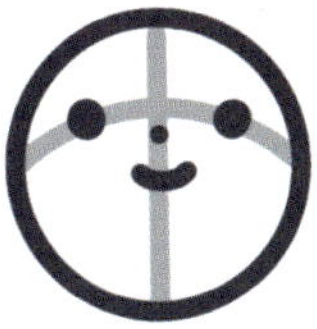

Draw the horizontal line higher when your character looks up . . .

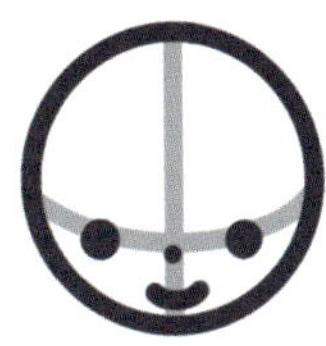

. . . and lower when they look down.

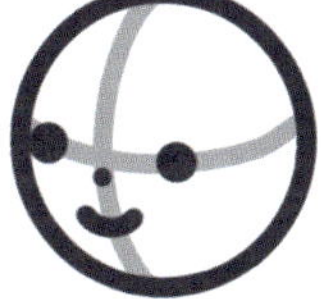

Move the vertical line when your character looks to the left . . .

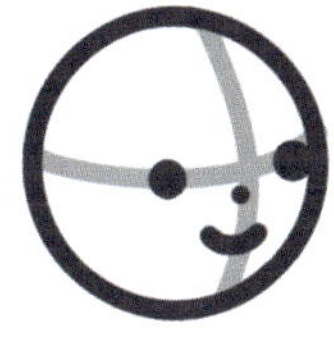

. . . or the right.

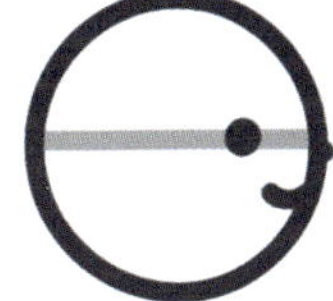

In profile we only need the horizontal line.

HAIRSTYLES

There are many hairstyles to choose from, so think about your character's personality and lifestyle to help you choose. These are just some examples you could try.

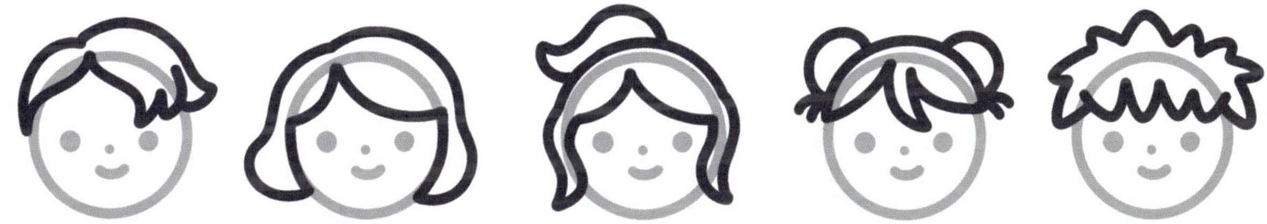

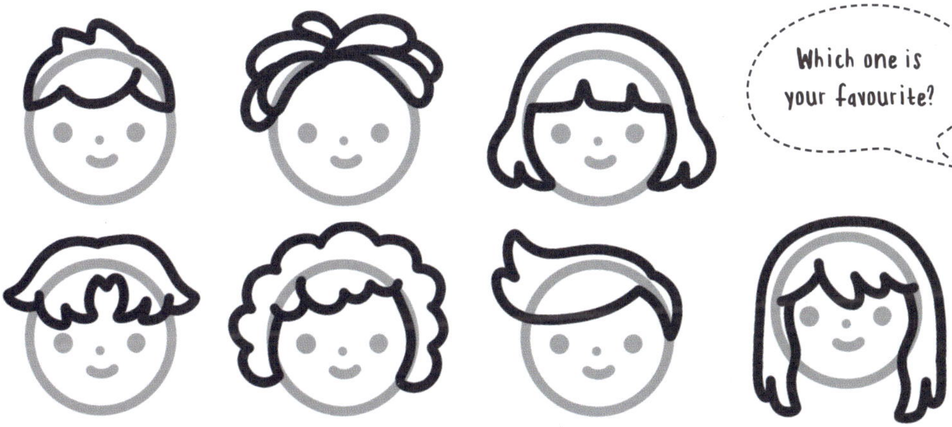

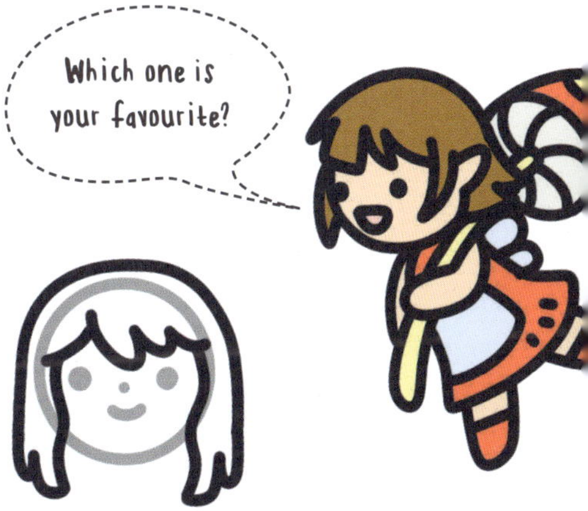

Which one is your favourite?

POSES

Once you've mastered the basic principles of body proportions, shapes and directions, you can start to explore poses for your characters.

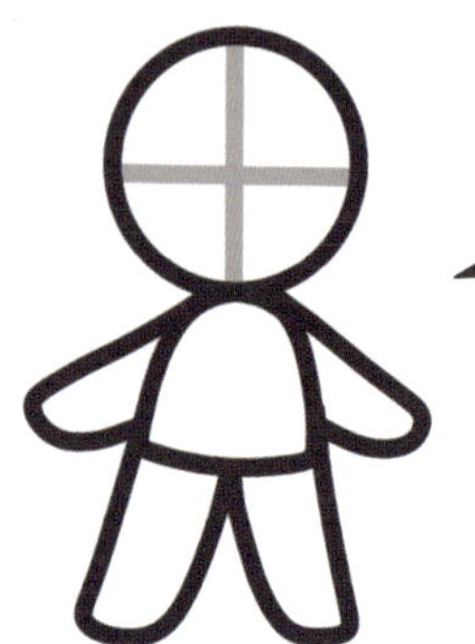

Here is a front-facing character with a gumdrop body shape.

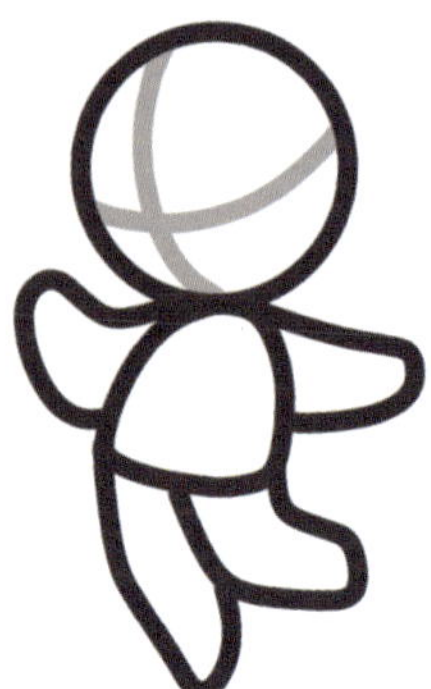

By changing the shapes of the body and limbs in small ways, you can create different poses.

Use the cross on the face to help you understand the direction your character is facing.

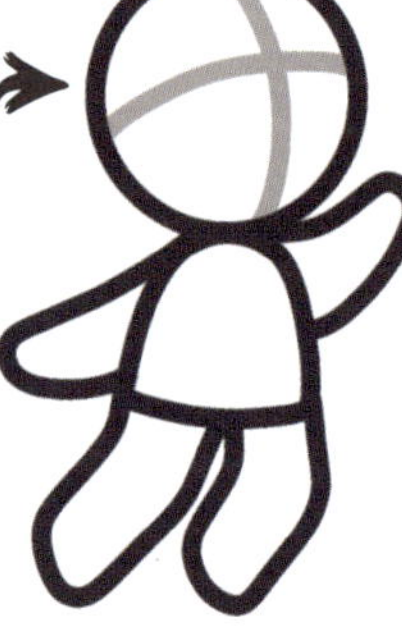

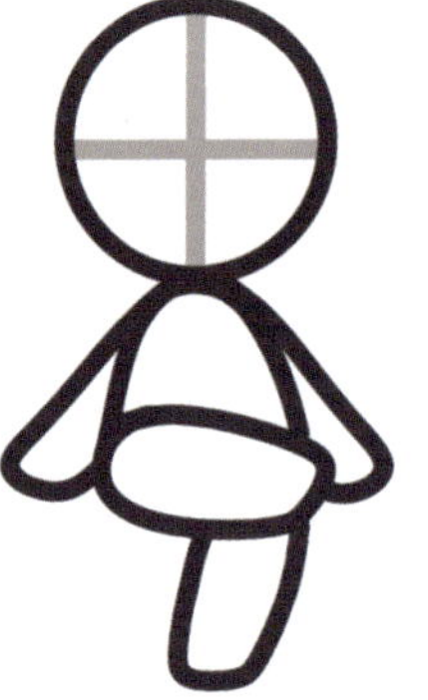

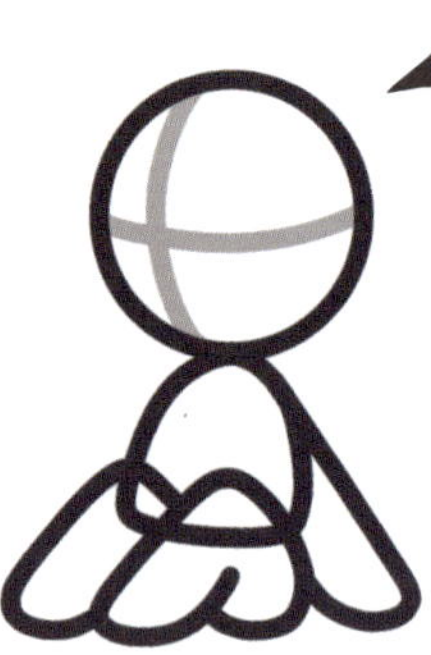

The head shape is a circle, even when it faces in different directions.

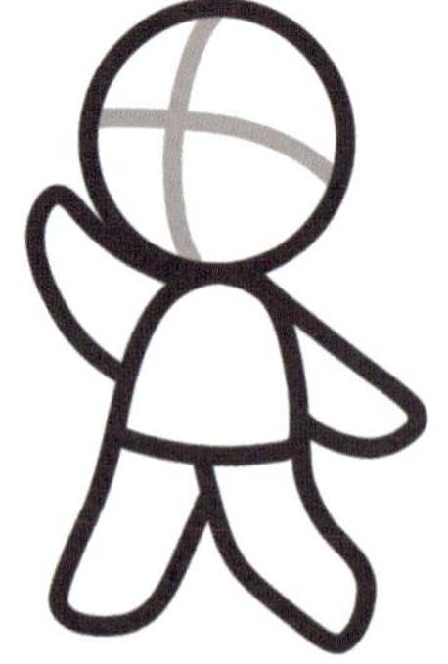

When the legs are lifted like this, it makes the person look like they are floating.

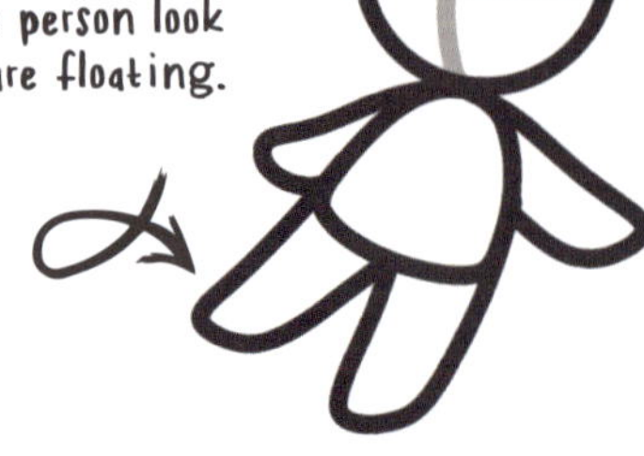

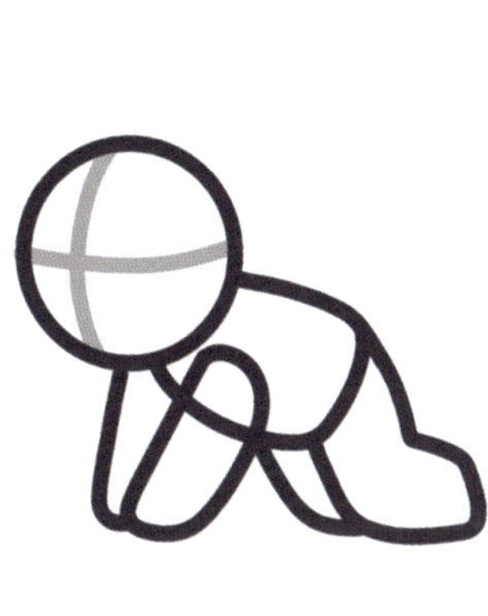

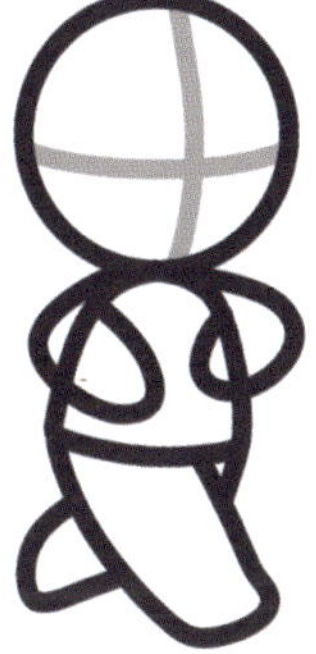

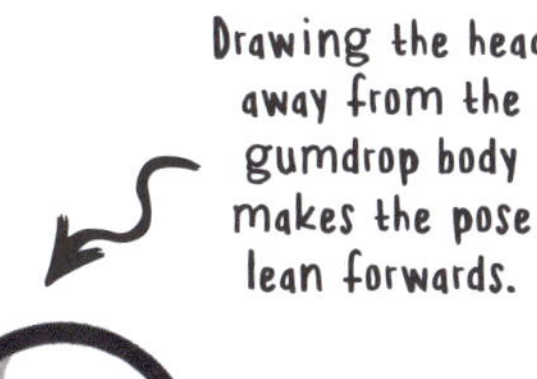

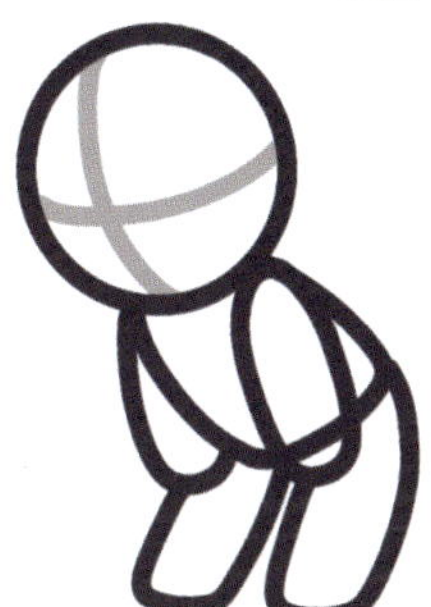

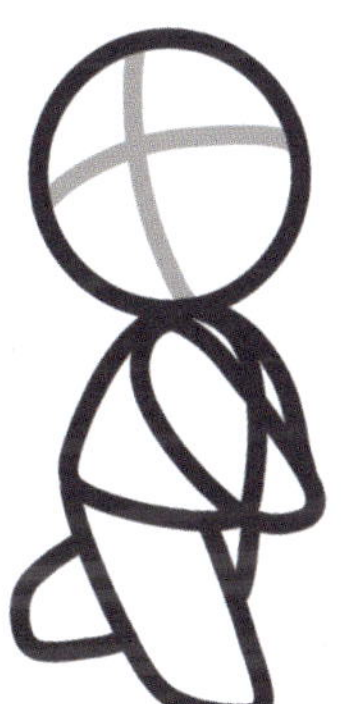

When the hands are together, you can add items for your character to hold.

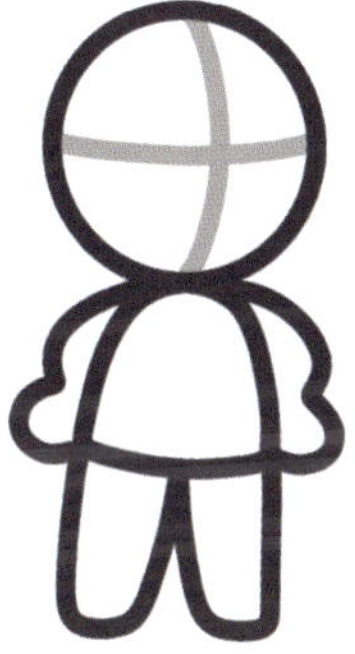

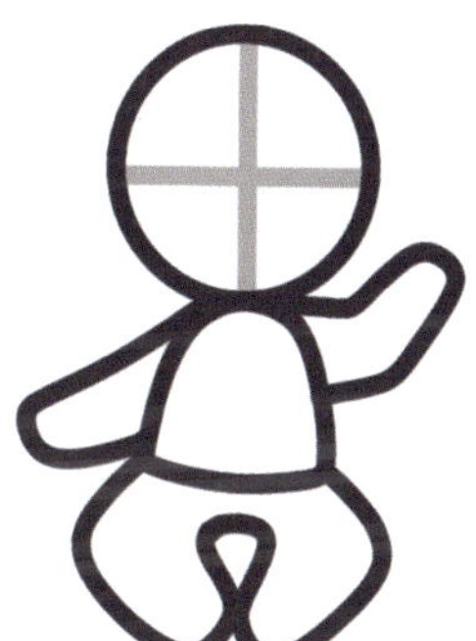

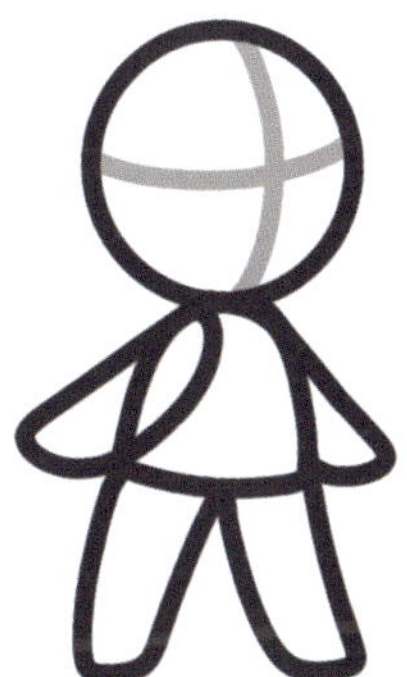

Try drawing people together and see how they can interact with one another, such as holding hands, taking a stroll or exploring woodlands together.

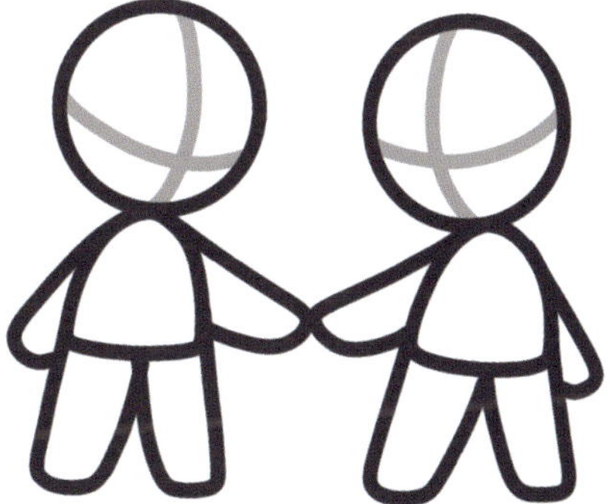

EXPRESSIONS

Use facial expressions to show how your character is feeling, and bring them to life. What kind of mood are your woodland friends in today?

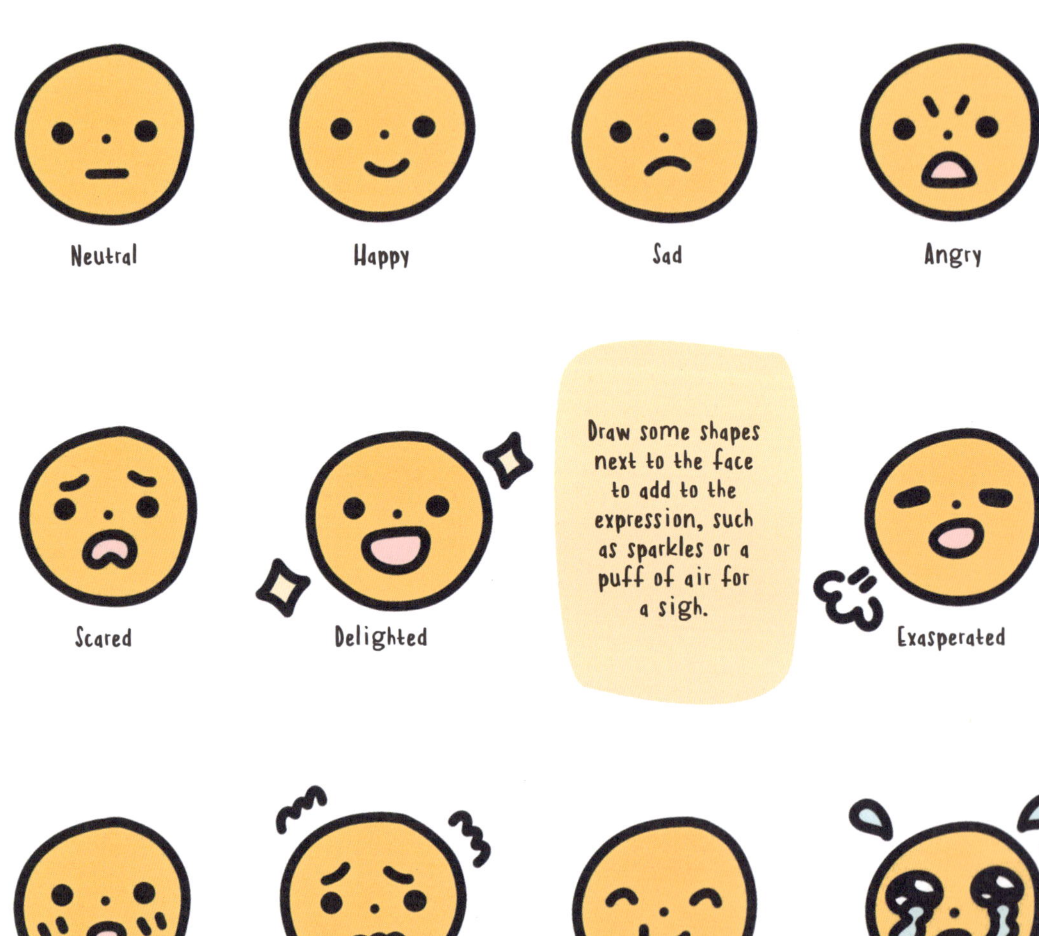

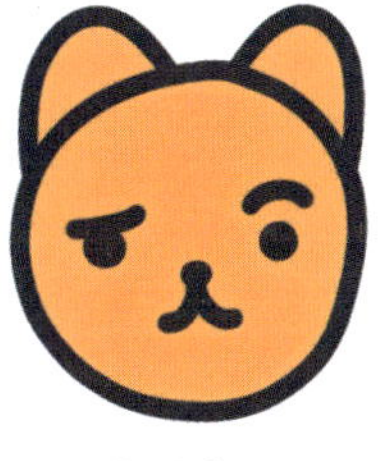

Smirky

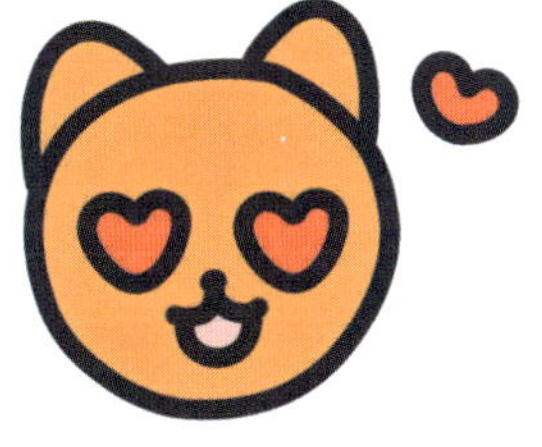

Loving

Even animal characters can have fun expressions! Try some of these.

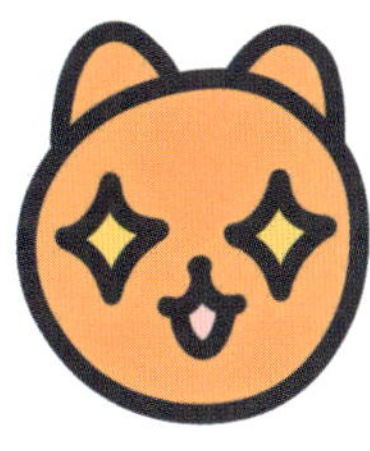

Excited

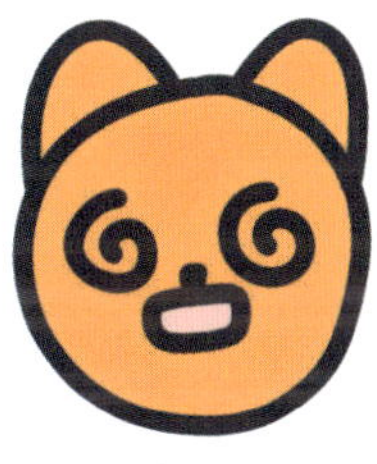

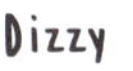

Dizzy

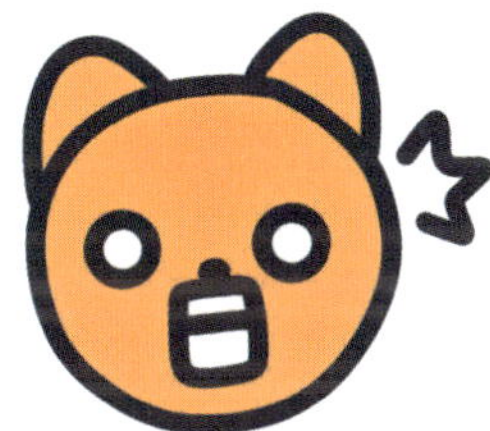

Shocked

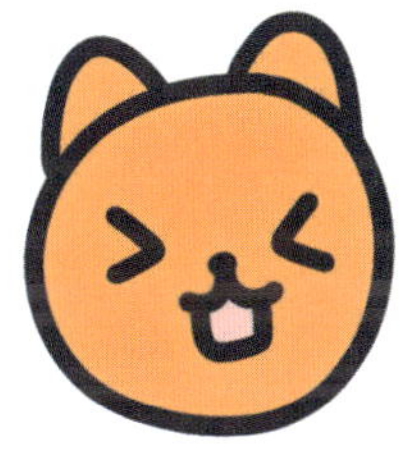

Laughing

Cheeky

Winking

One of my favourite expressions is the winking face. It's cute and simple!

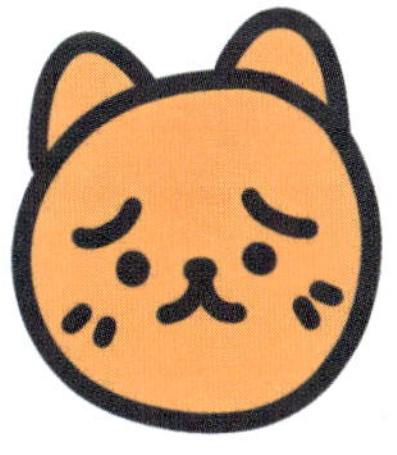

Worried

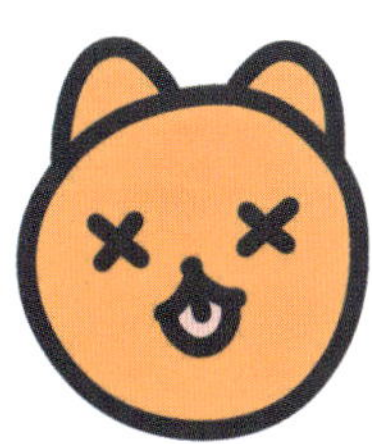

Tired

CLOTHES

When it comes to dressing your woodland folk, there are so many choices. Remember to think about accessories as well as the main outfit, to make sure your character looks the part.

Applying clothes

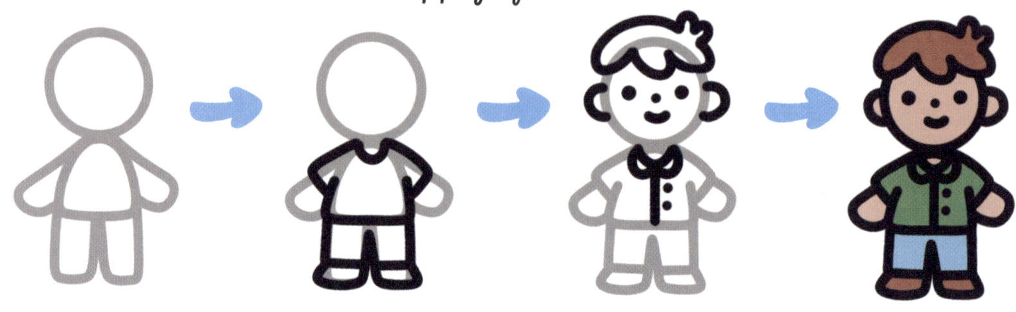

Start with your character's basic shape of head, body and limbs.

Add the main outfit, such as trousers or a skirt, and a top.

Don't forget the details, such as buttons, collars, pockets, zips, turnups, and so on.

Finish by choosing your character's colour scheme. This guy is very smart.

Tops

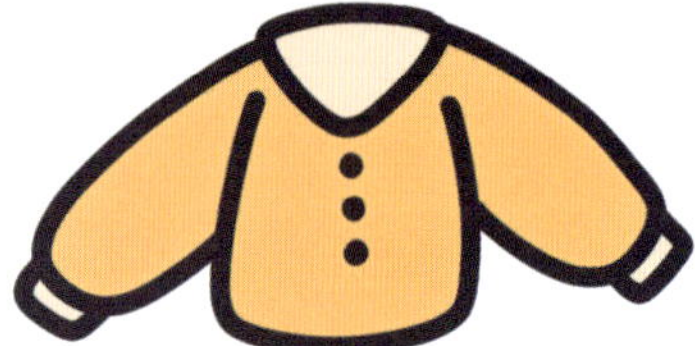

Long, puffy sleeves have a cuff at the wrist.

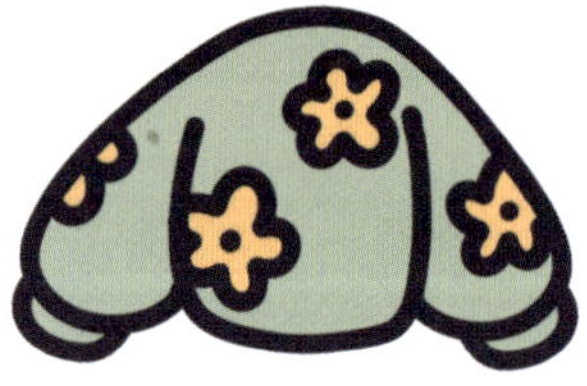

Add patterns to your clothes.

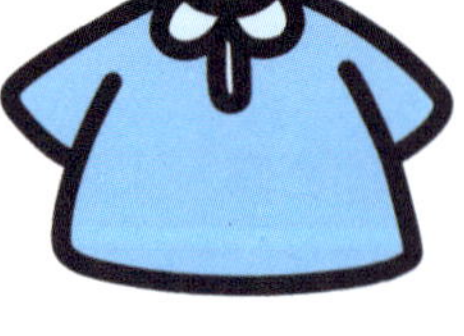

This short-sleeved top has a wide body and a collar detail.

Overalls are practical for woodland folk.

Use wavy lines to give a dress some frilly details.

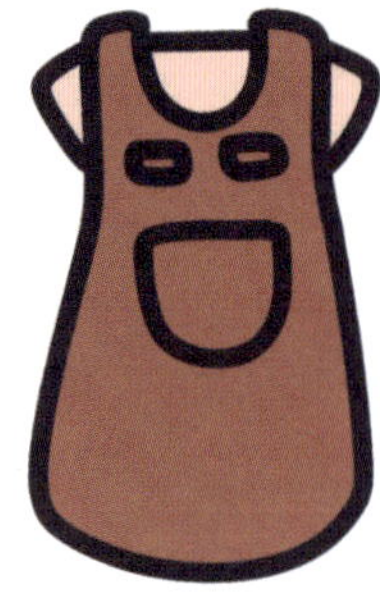

An apron could be a useful piece of clothing for an artist.

Bottoms

These shorts are really puffy, with frilly cuffs.

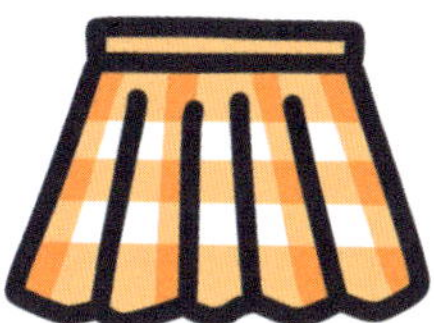

A plaid pattern works well on a skirt.

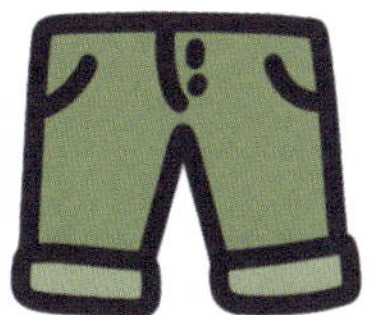

These shorts have turnups, pockets and a zip.

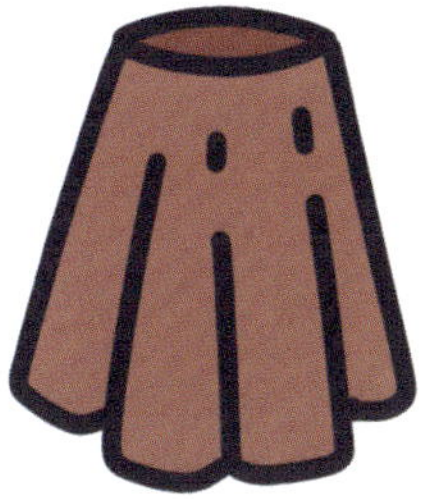

Pleat lines look good on a long skirt.

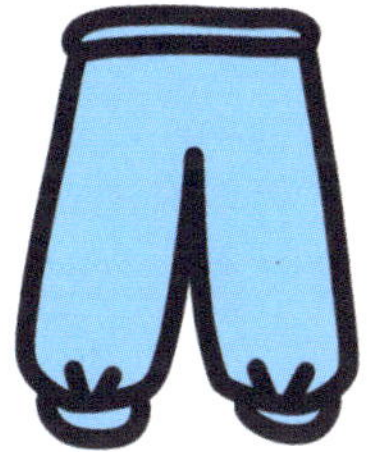

You might want to add a waistband feature to your trousers, shorts or skirts.

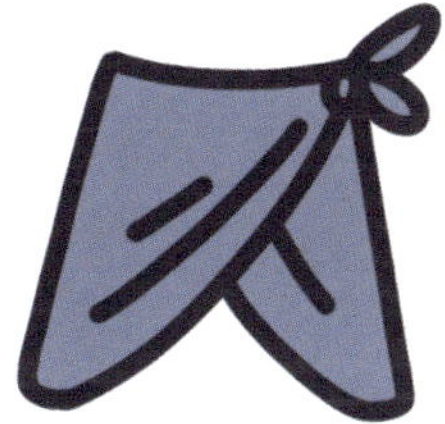

Explore your own fashion ideas. This cool skirt is tied at the waist.

Accessories

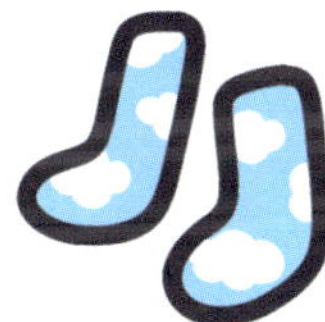

Why wear boring socks? Add playful patterns to your accessories.

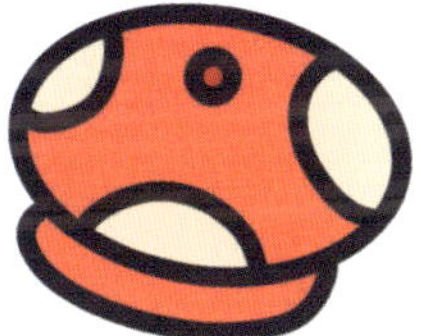

This hat is perfectly forest themed, with its mushroom shape and pattern.

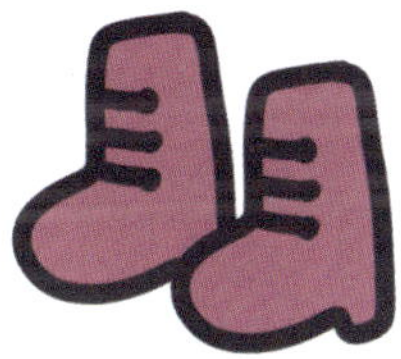

Some woodland folk will need shoes, or even sturdy boots like these.

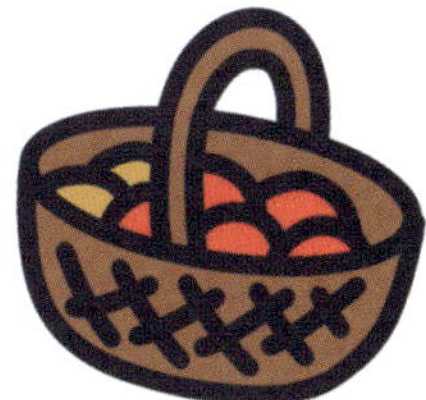

If your character is picking fruit, they'll need a basket.

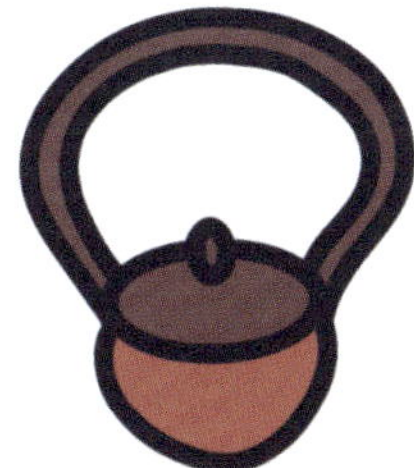

If your character is collecting nuts, then an acorn bag may be just the thing to hold them in.

Hats are fun accessories, as are other types of headdress, like this flower crown.

WOODLAND CREATORS

Creators like artists, florists, musicians, bakers, and more, are inspired by the world around them, and forest life is a never-ending source of inspiration.

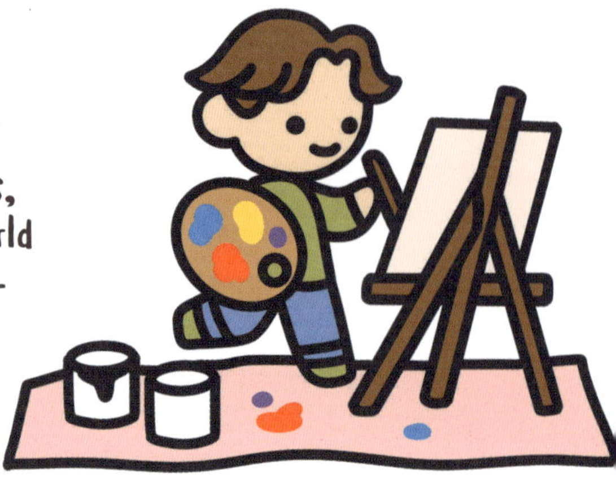

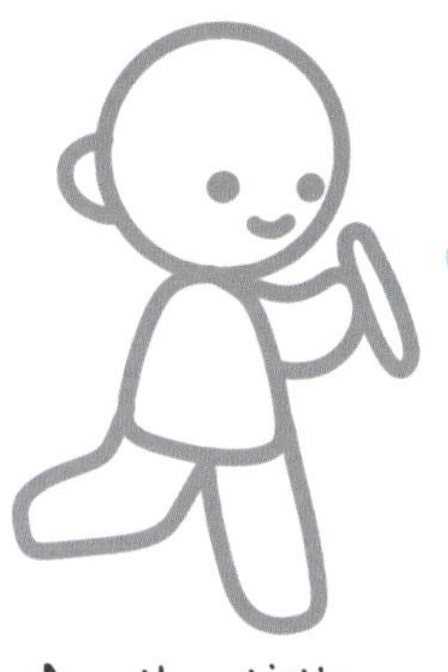

Draw the artist's painting pose, with brush in hand.

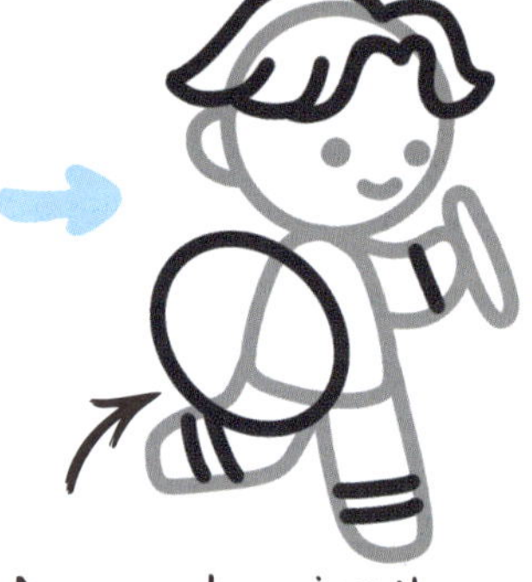

Draw an oval covering the front arm for the paint palette. Add a hairstyle and clothes.

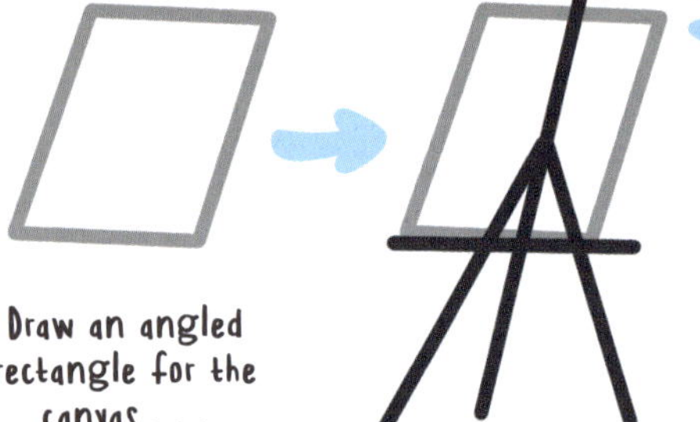

Draw an angled rectangle for the canvas . . .

. . . and add the outline of the easel.

Florist

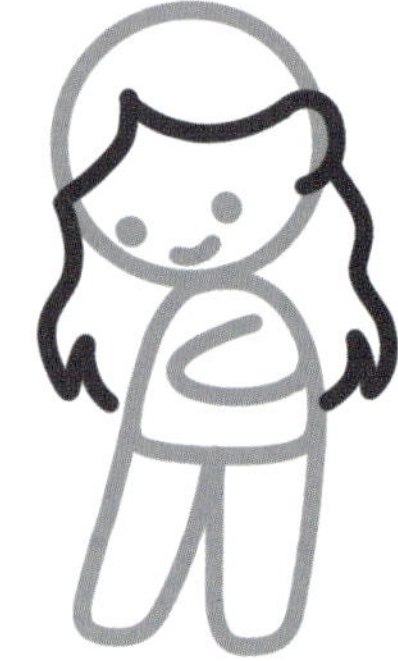

Draw the pose and add long, wavy hair.

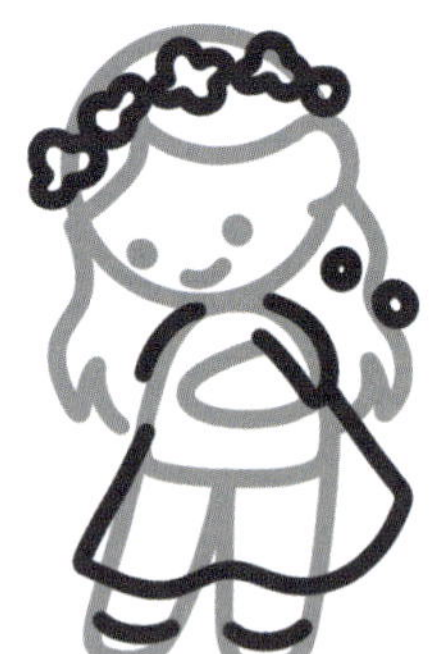

Add a floaty dress, lines for shoes, a flower crown and flowers in her hair.

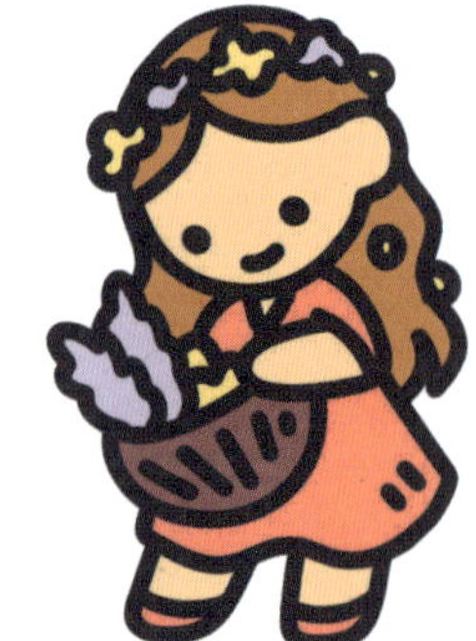

Give the florist a basket and fill it with blooms.

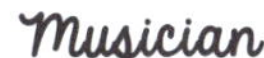

Musician

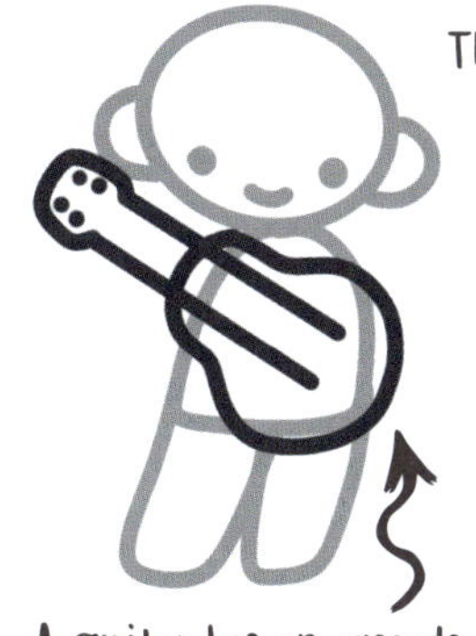

This character has an oval head.

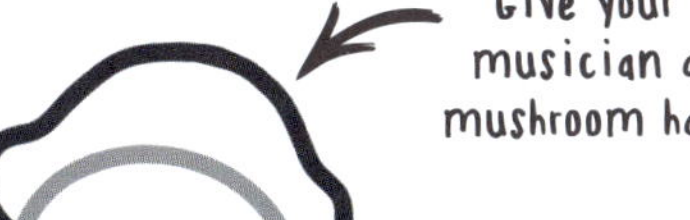

Give your musician a mushroom hat!

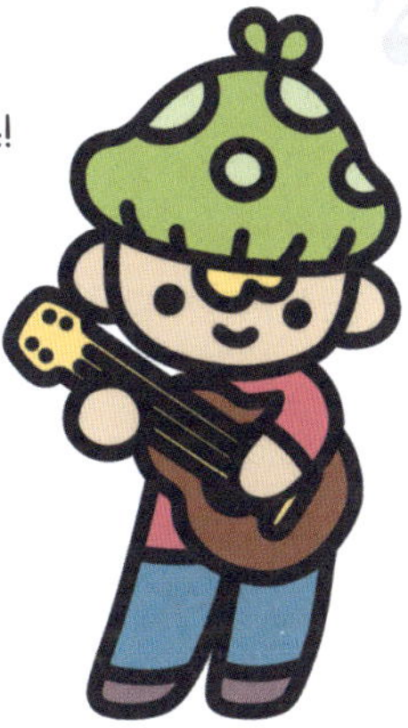

A guitar has an avocado shape, with straight lines coming out at the thin end.

Draw hands on top of the guitar.

Baker

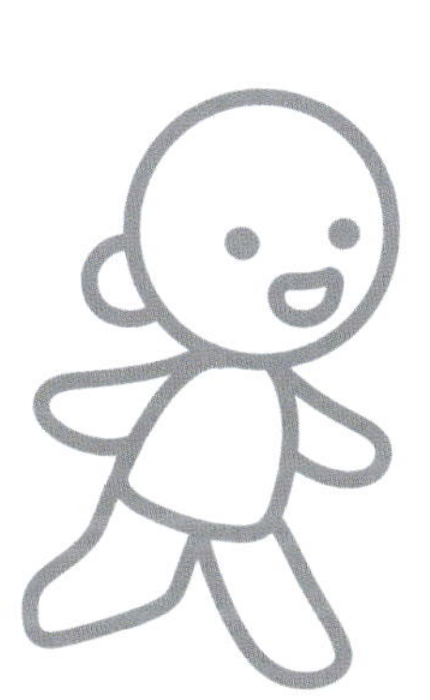

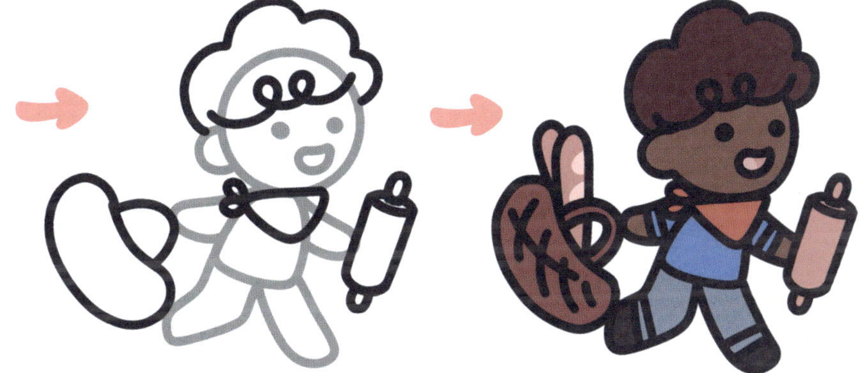

This baker is in a rush! Draw them in a running pose.

Add the hair, a neckerchief, a basket to fill with bread and a rolling pin.

Reader

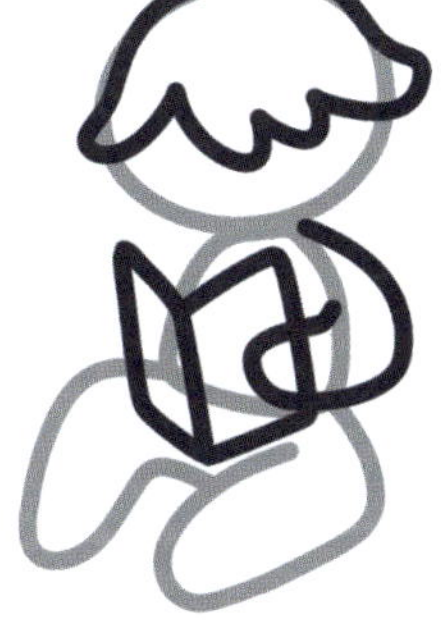

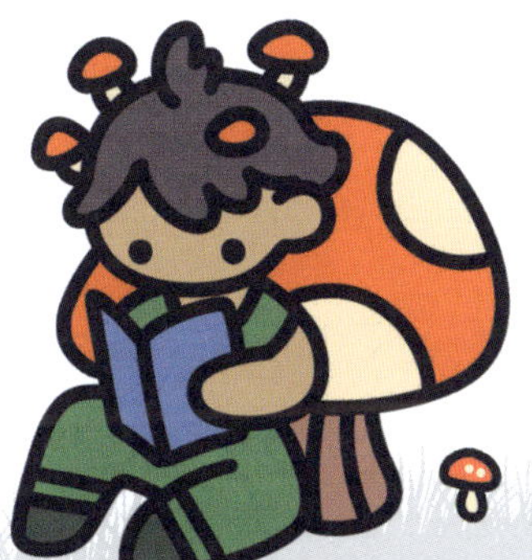

A reader is also a type of creator! They use their imagination and can get inspired by the stories they read.

WITCHES

Witches are powerful beings that can perform magic. They love animals and studying new spells, and have cool accessories like crystal balls, wands and broomsticks.

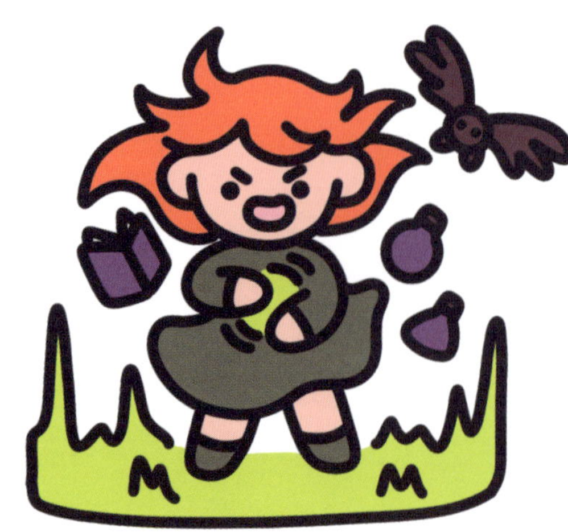

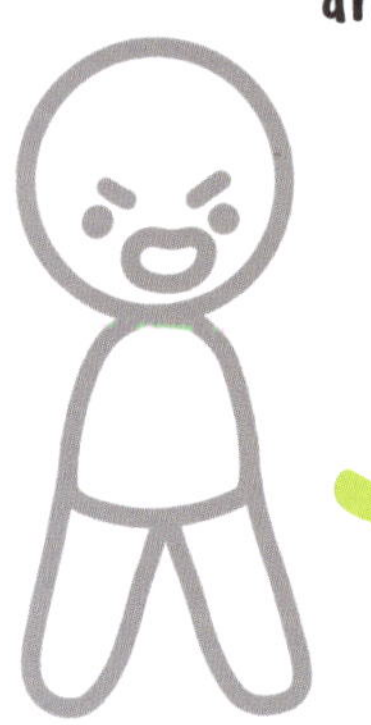

Start with the base of the body and a powerful facial expression.

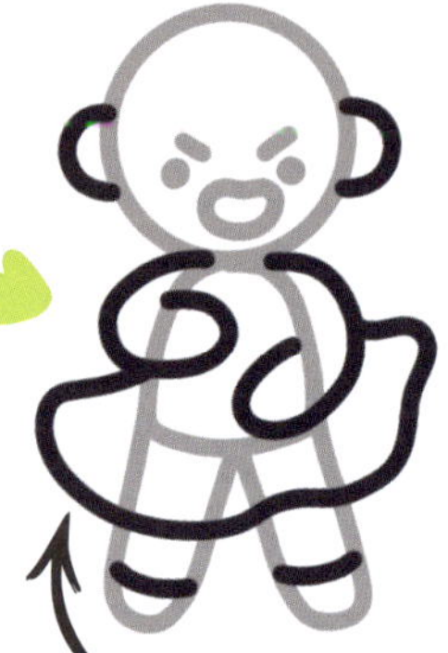

Make the dress flare out and the arms wrap in front of the body.

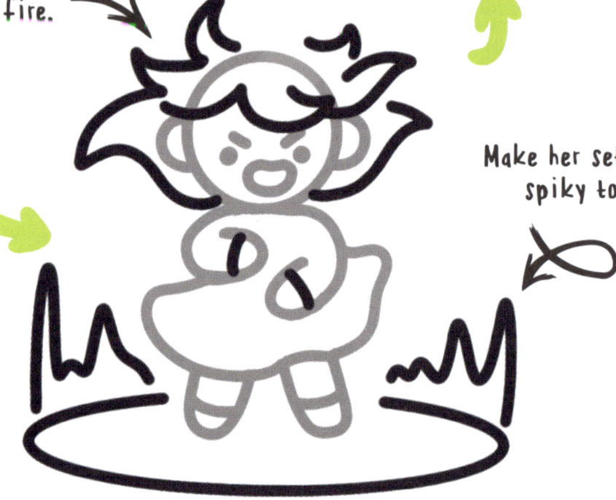

Make the hair spiky like fire.

Make her setting spiky too.

Casting a spell

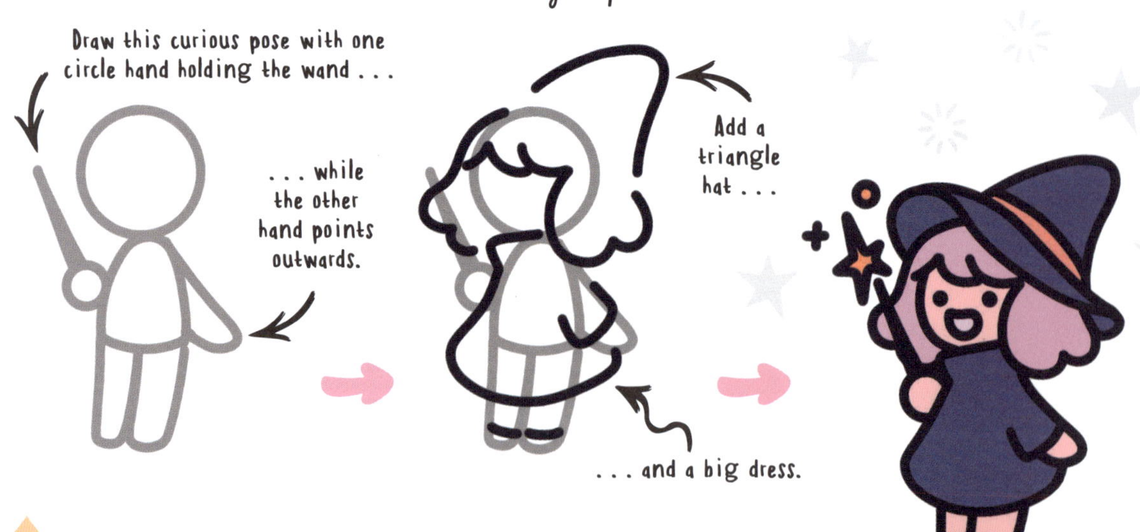

Draw this curious pose with one circle hand holding the wand . . .

. . . while the other hand points outwards.

Add a triangle hat . . .

. . . and a big dress.

Animal pals

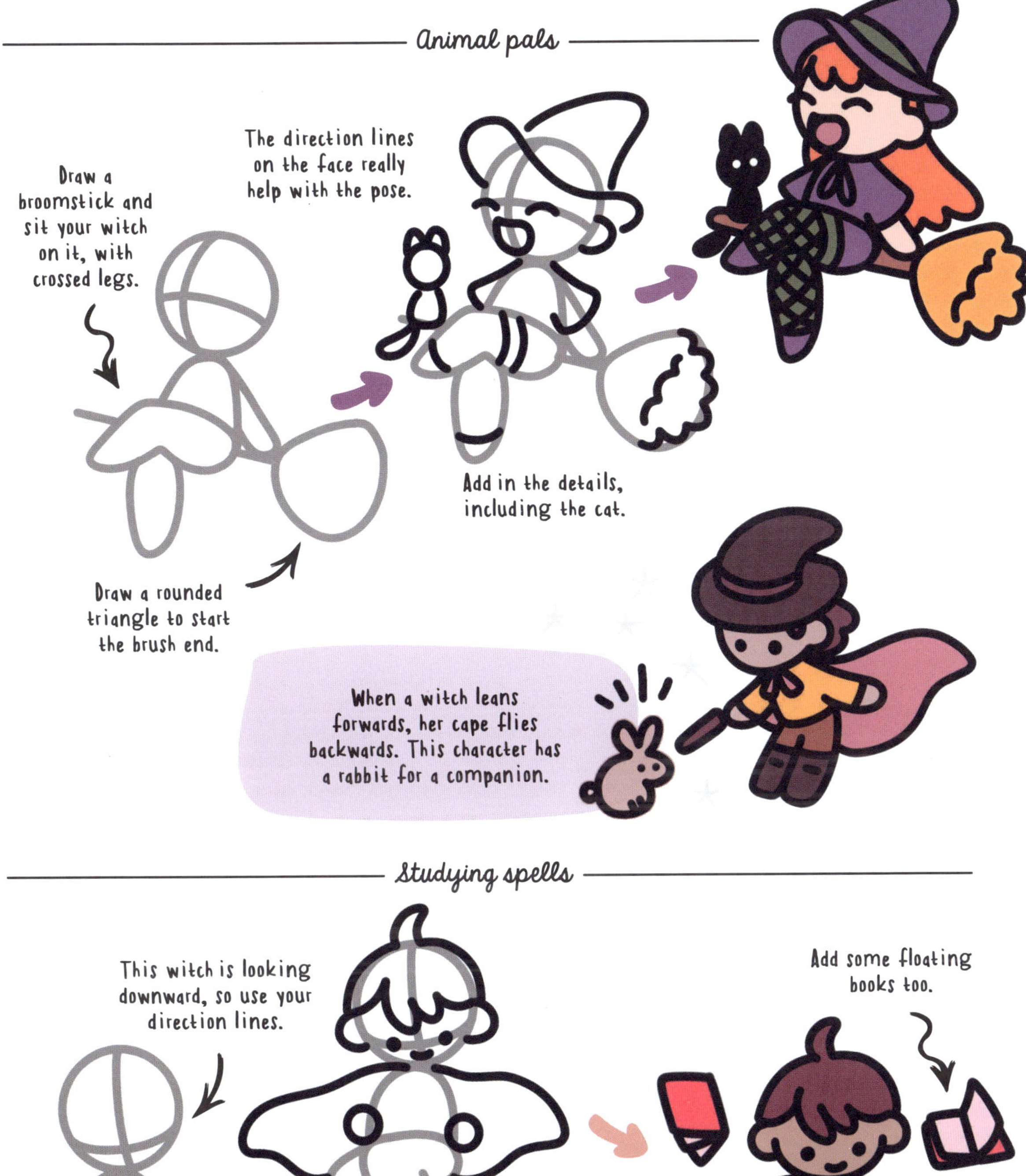

Draw the cape flared outwards on both sides of the body. The hands are circles, ready to hold a book.

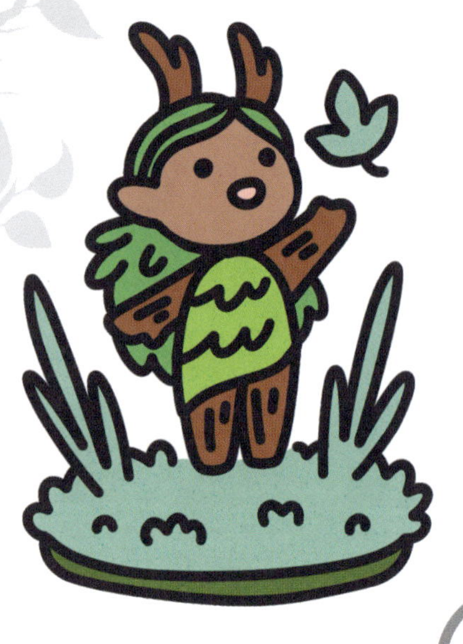

DRYADS

Dryads are mythical forest-dwelling beings. They are infused into the forest itself, which is why they have tree-like bodies.

Draw one arm up and the other down.

Add lines to show that the body is made of wood.

Give your dryad long hair and branches on top of their head, like antlers.

Branch arms

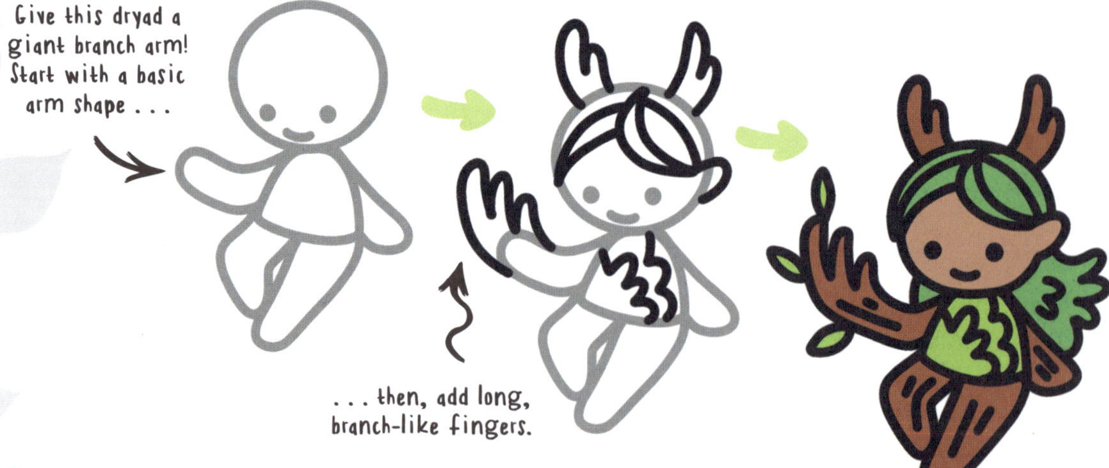

Trunk legs

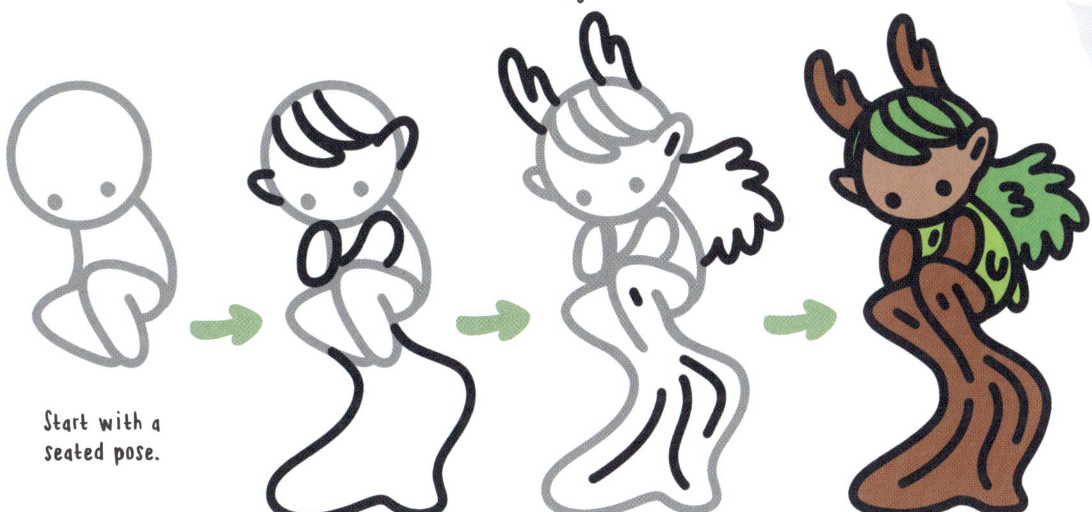

Add a tree trunk coming out from the legs.

Add bark lines to the trunk.

Make the hair bushy with leaves.

Root arms

Draw the long arms like rectangular wings to start.

Draw the roots inside and around the rectangle bases.

Notice the cute leafy pigtails.

Another fun way to draw dryad limbs is as roots. Roots can intertwine with one another and make fun shapes.

GNOMES

These small woodland creatures bring good luck if you spot one. Because they are tiny and good at hiding, it is particularly difficult to find them! Try checking under a leaf.

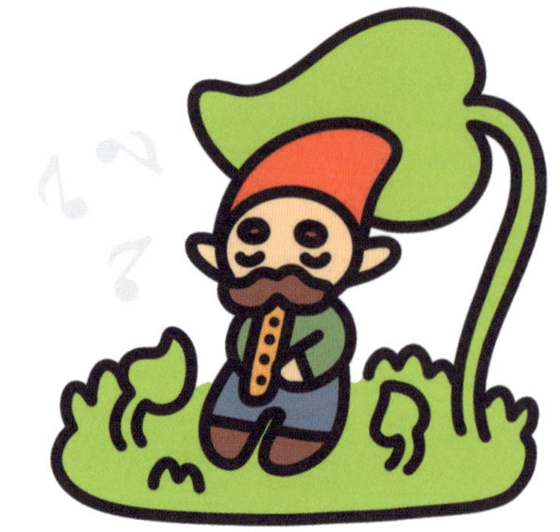

Start with a relaxed pose. Give your gnome pointy ears.

Add a triangle hat and a bushy moustache.

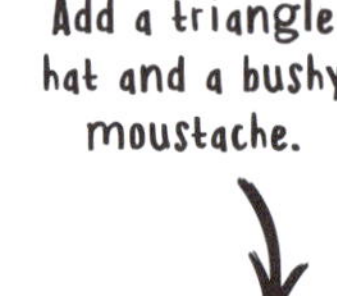

Draw hands close to the body so the gnome can hold a flute.

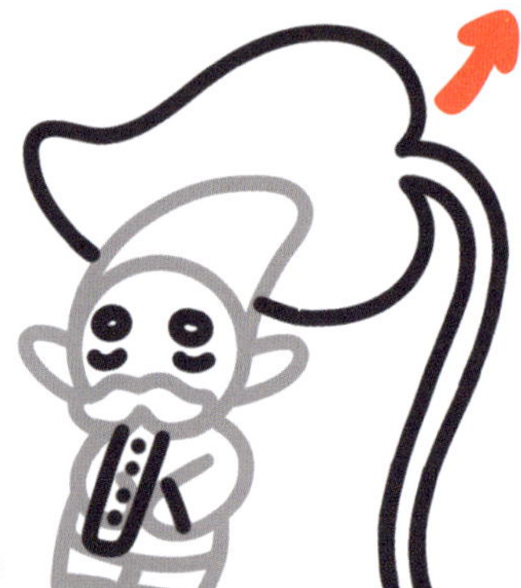

Draw a big leaf behind the gnome to show how small it really is.

Tall and short

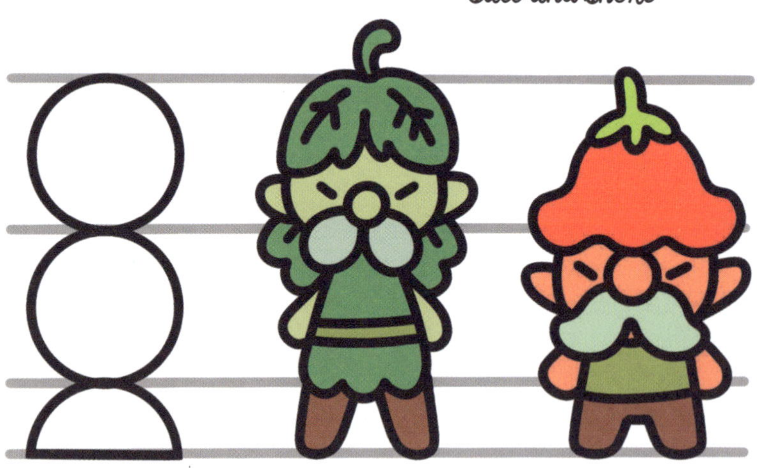

You can use the people size guide (see page 20) to proportion your gnomes, or you can make smaller gnomes by using one less circle.

Stubby gnome

The base of this gnome is simply a wide oval with small, stubby limbs.

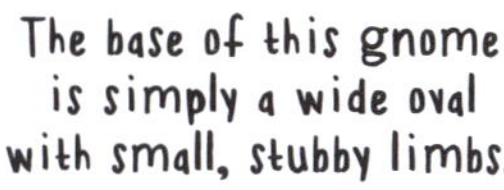

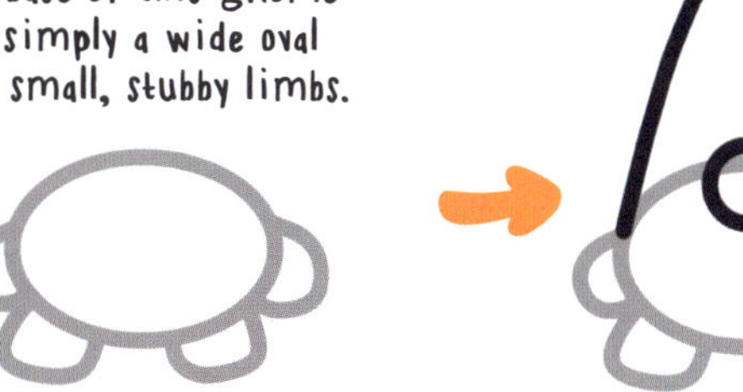

Add a circle nose near the top of the oval and a big triangular hat.

Draw a beard around the bottom of the oval.

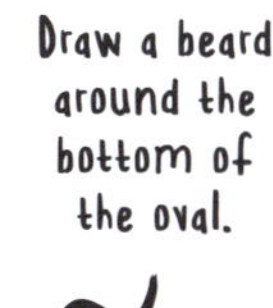

Give your gnome a cute flower to hold.

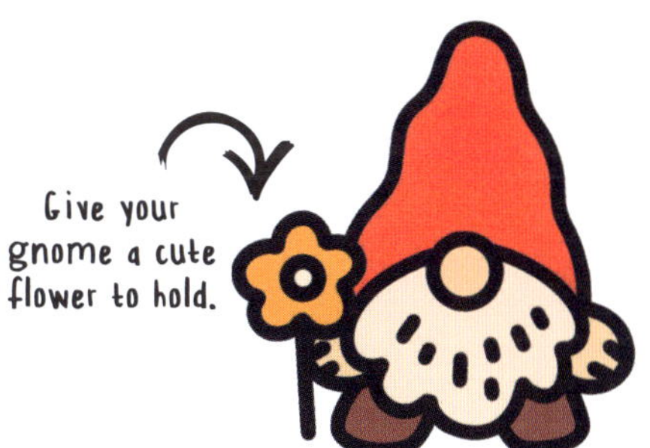

Change the position of the hands and add lines around your character to change its expression without a face! This gnome is jumping for joy!

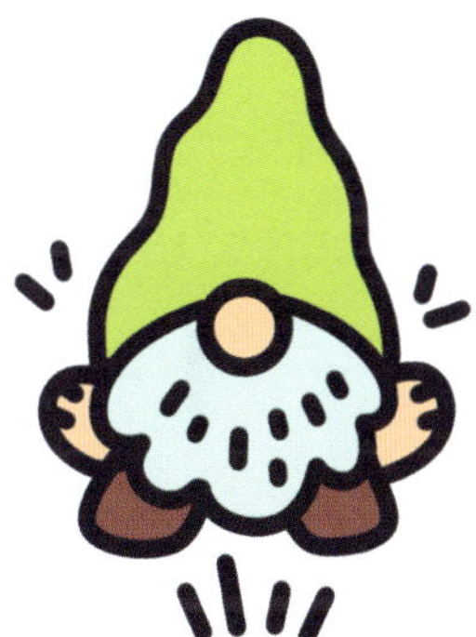

Snail ride

Draw a sitting gnome with the classic triangle hat.

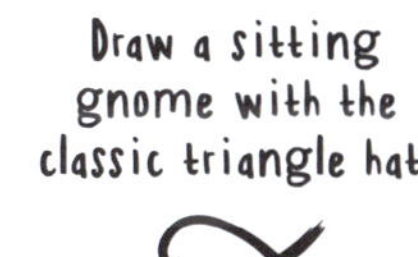

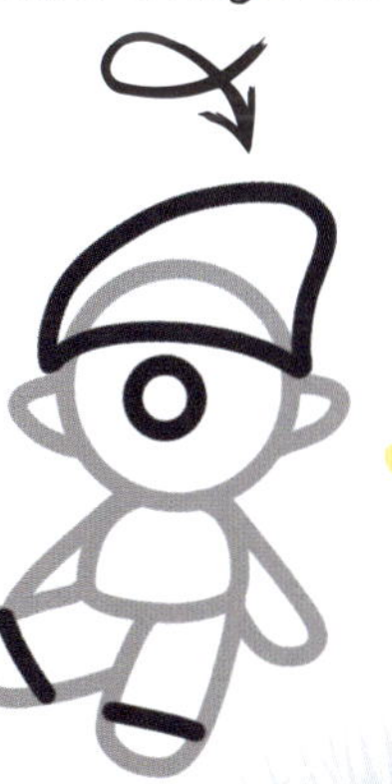

Add a beard and eyes.

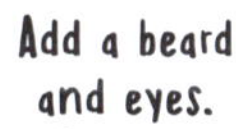

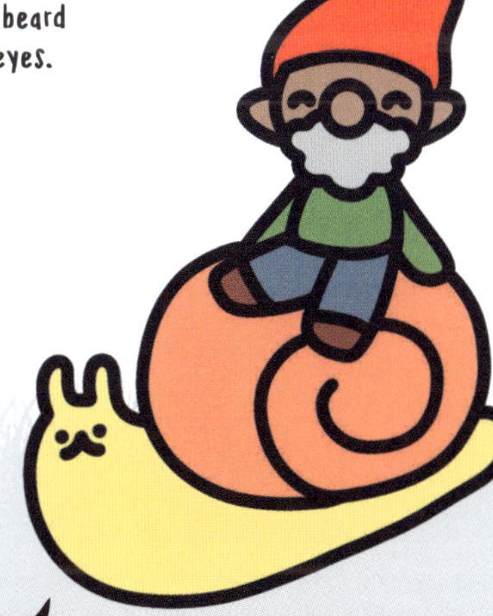

Draw a snail (see pages 68–69) for your gnome to ride on.

TROLLS

Trolls are incredibly strong, and like to roam from forest to mountain exploring caves and rocky areas.

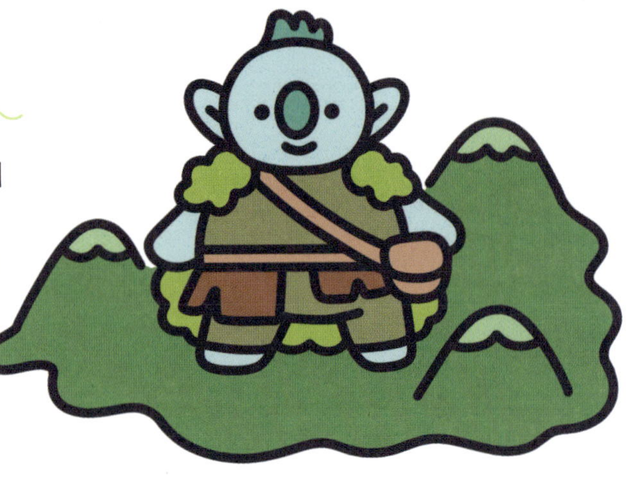

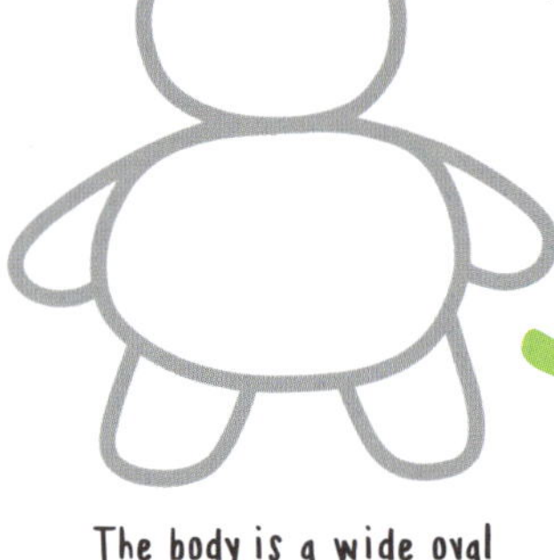

The body is a wide oval with a small circular head and chubby limbs.

The ears and nose are also oval-shaped.

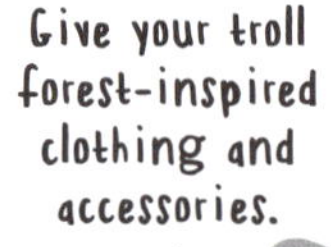

Give your troll forest-inspired clothing and accessories.

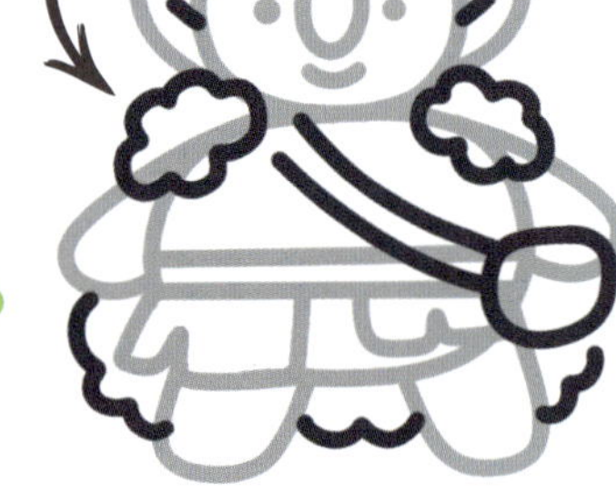

Scruffy troll

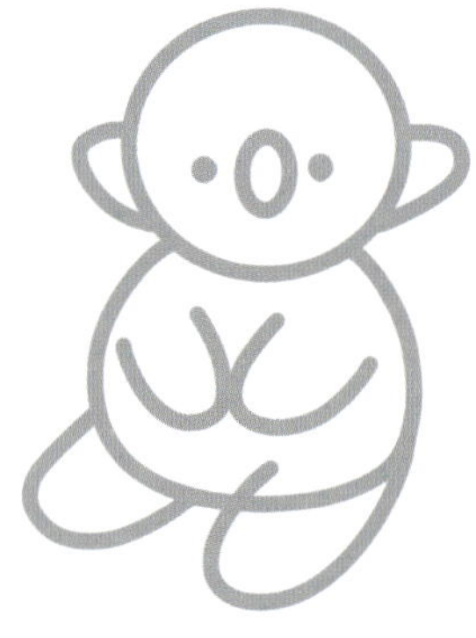

Draw a seated base with the legs close to the body.

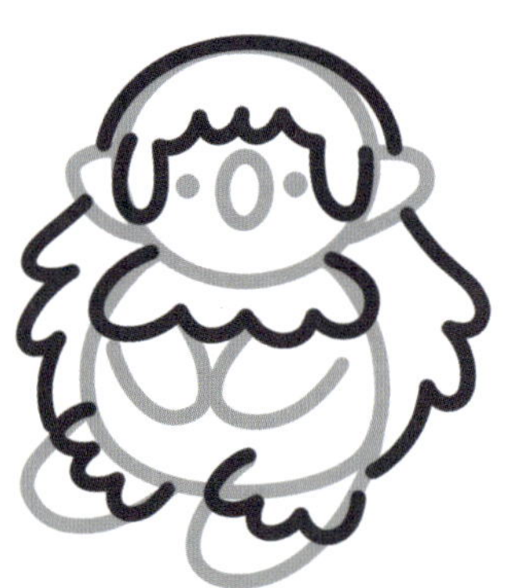

Use wavy lines to give your troll lots of foliage hair and detailing.

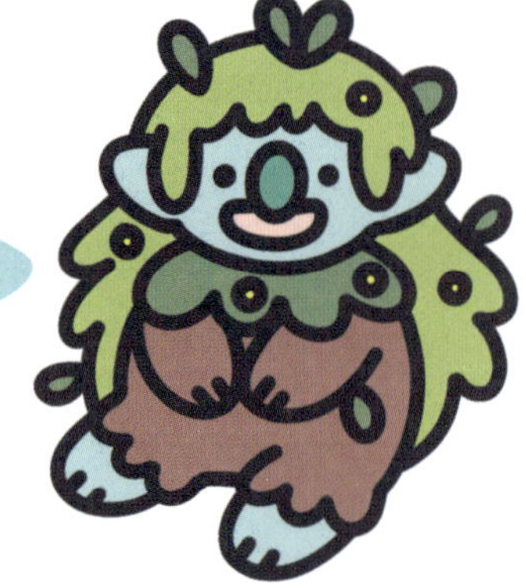

Add leaves sticking out all over the troll.

Animal lover

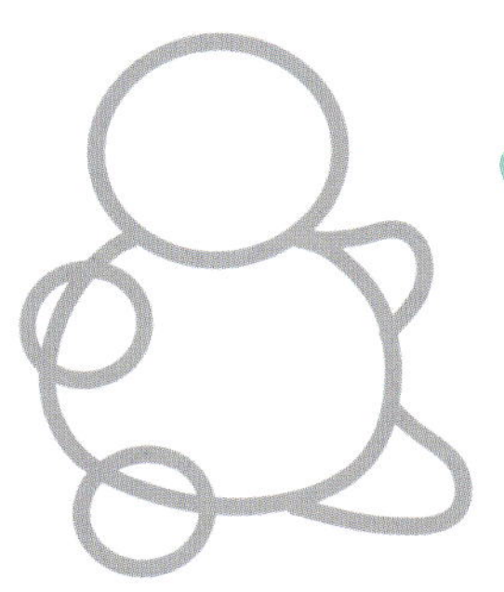

To make limbs point towards you, draw them as circles.

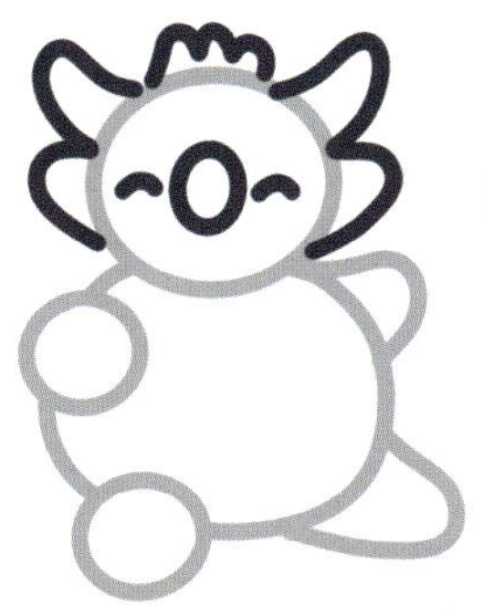

The horns and ears are rounded triangles.

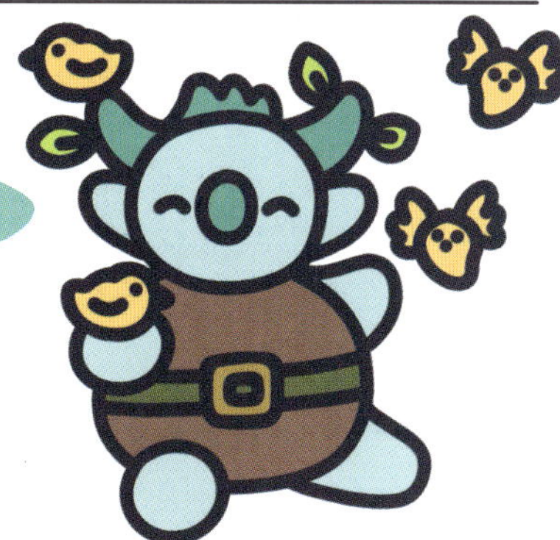

Draw little birds around your animal-loving troll!

Sad troll

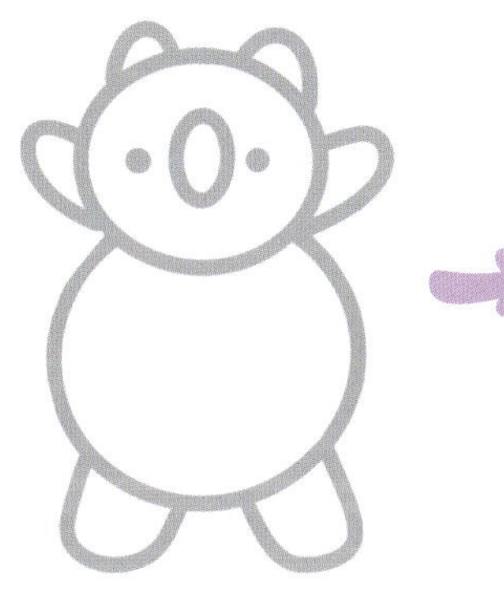

This troll's body is a circle rather than an oval.

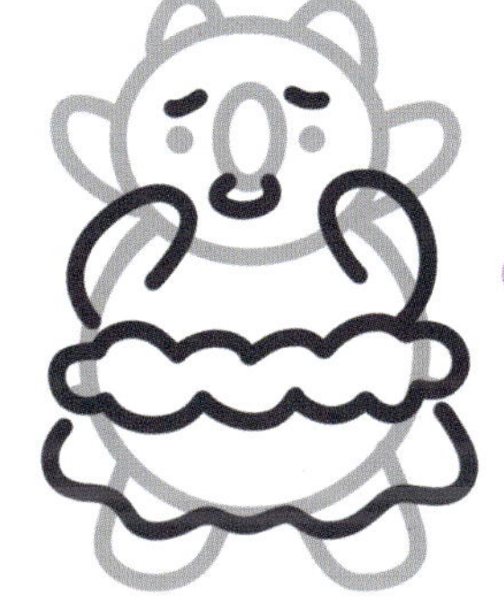

Continue with a worried face and a frilly outfit.

Draw fallen tears on the outfit too.

Draw tears on the face and coming out at the sides.

Travelling stick

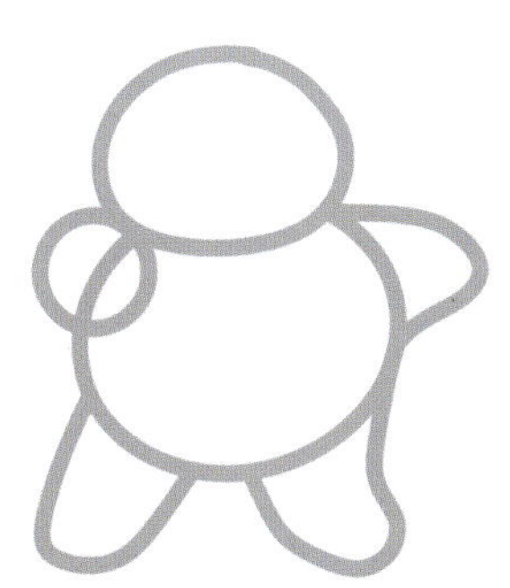

Draw one arm as a circle while the other arm points out and back.

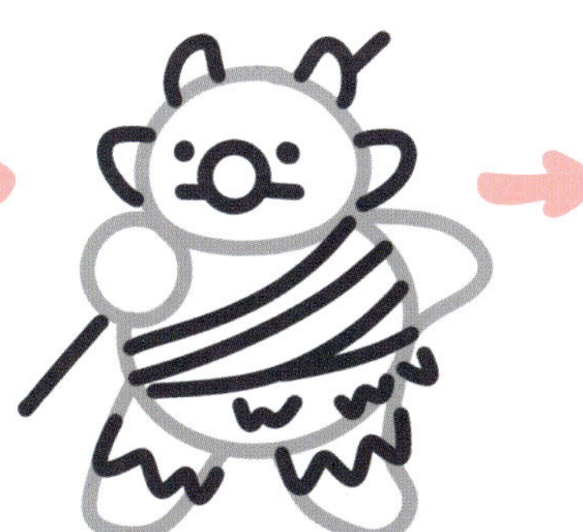

Draw wrapped clothes and rugged trousers using triangles.

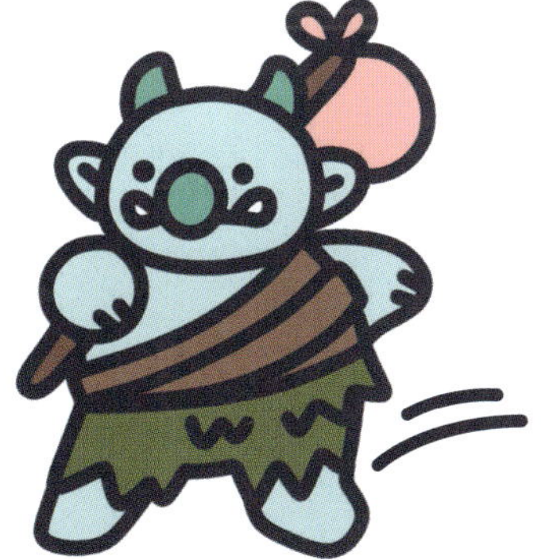

Give the troll a travelling stick with a bundle of their possessions tied at the end.

FAIRIES

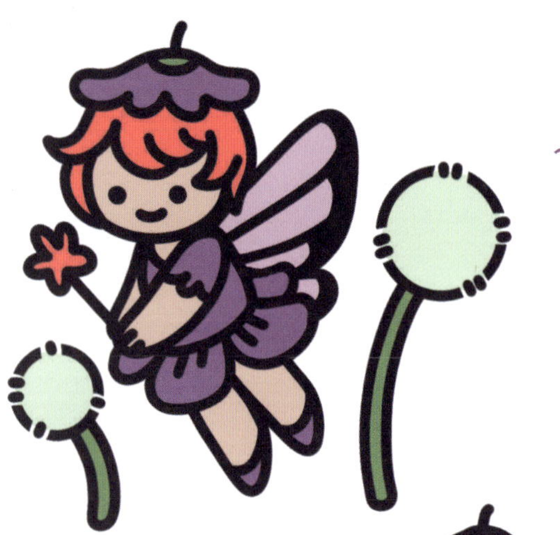

Fairies are tiny and love their natural habitats. To show how small they are, make sure you draw big flowers or foliage around them.

For a flying pose, draw the legs lifted and slightly behind the body.

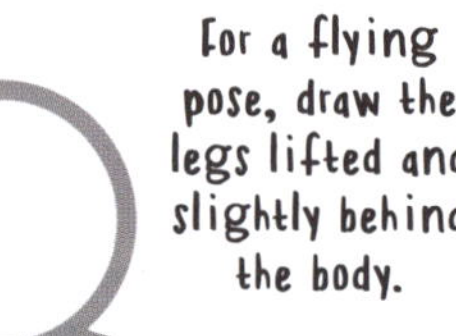

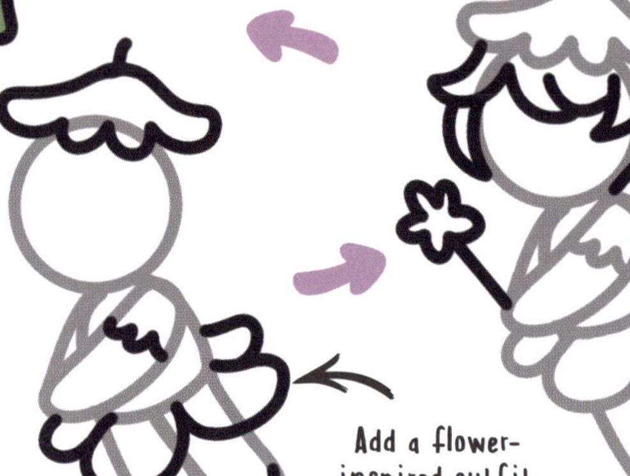

Add a flower-inspired outfit.

Don't forget the wings and wand!

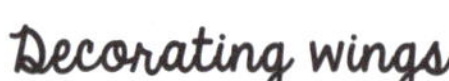

Start with the outline.

Draw wavy and curved lines down the length of the wings.

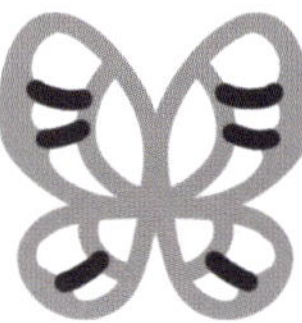

Add curved lines between the previous lines.

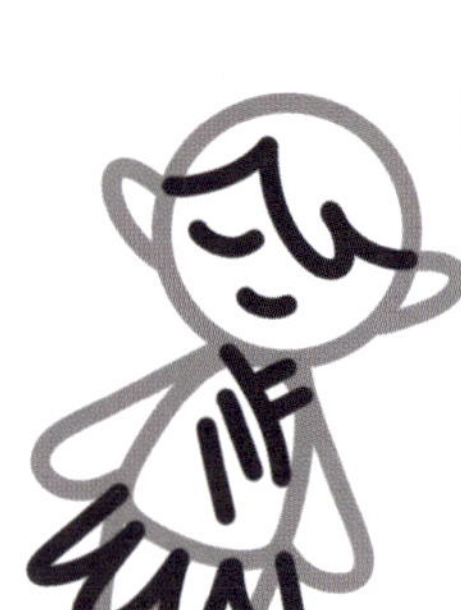

Start with the fairy's figure and character, then add the wings.

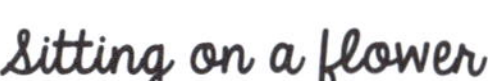

Sitting on a flower

Position your fairy sitting on a curved line. Draw a large circle at the end of the line.

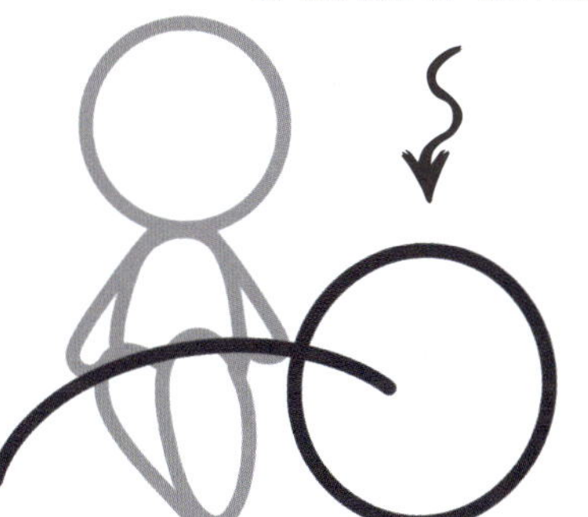

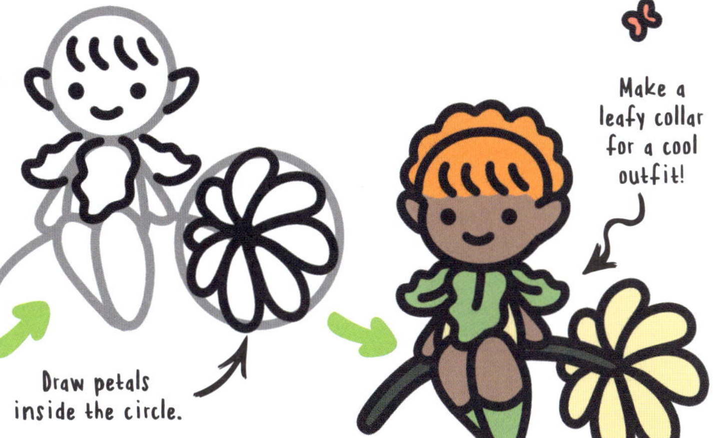

Draw petals inside the circle.

Make a leafy collar for a cool outfit!

Holding a mushroom

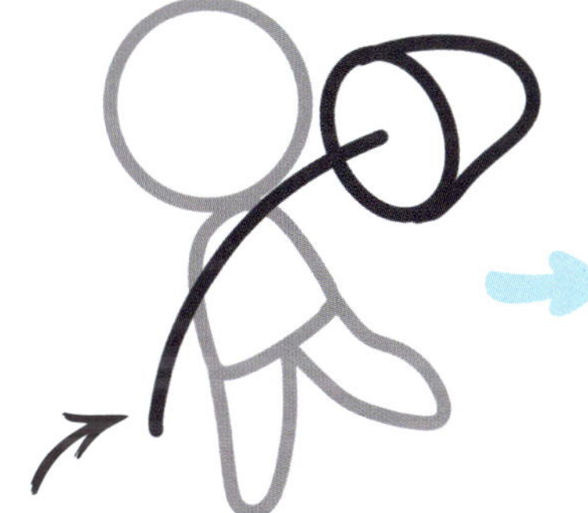

Draw a line across the body, then a circle and a curved triangle at the end of the line.

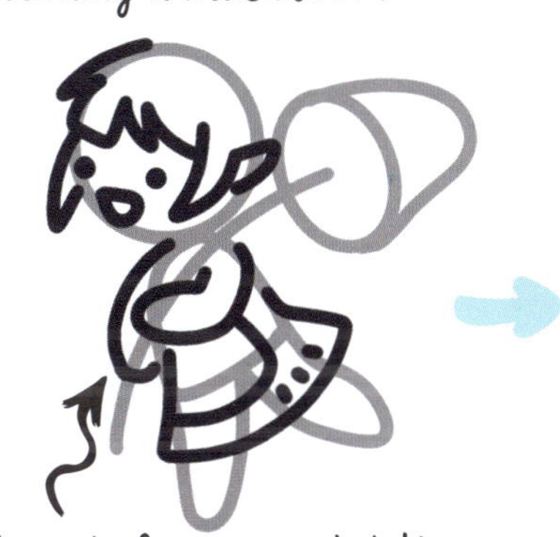

Curve the front arm so it holds the mushroom.

Flower hat

Add petal shapes on top of the head.

Add on wings to the back. They are similar in shape to the petals!

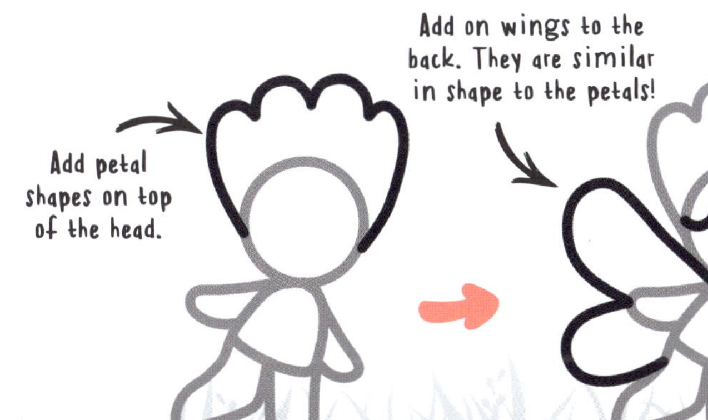

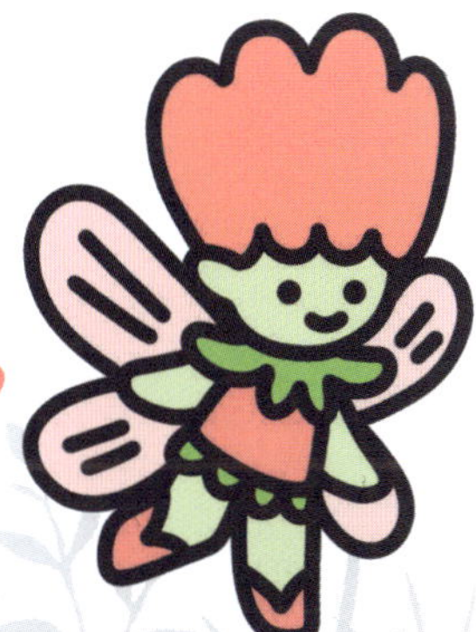

PLANT PEOPLE

Plant people are infused with the shapes, colours and patterns of plants. Check out these examples and have a go at inventing your own plant people!

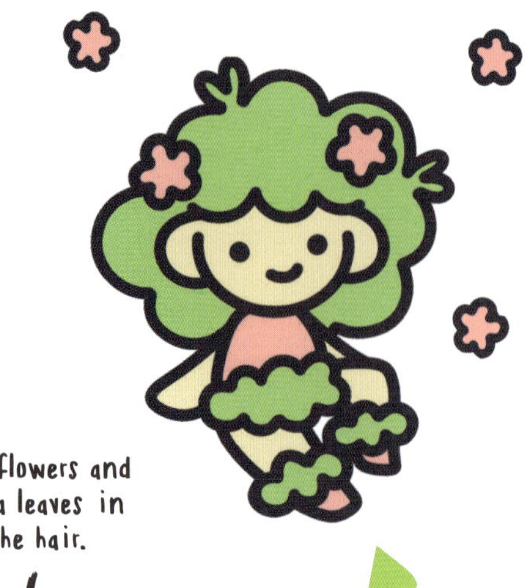

Start with a seated pose.

Give this character big bushy hair and bush-shaped clothing.

Add flowers and extra leaves in the hair.

Sapling person

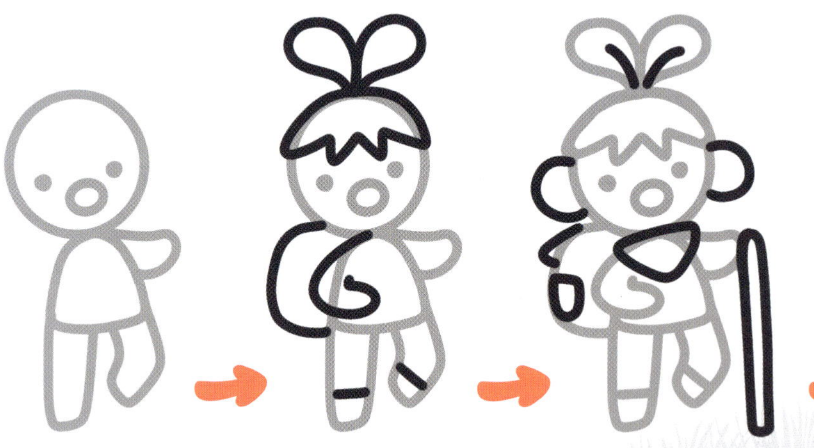

Draw a person with a surprised look!

For the hair, draw spiky triangles. Add teardrop shapes for the leaves on top.

Give this character a backpack, scarf and a walking stick.

Acorn person

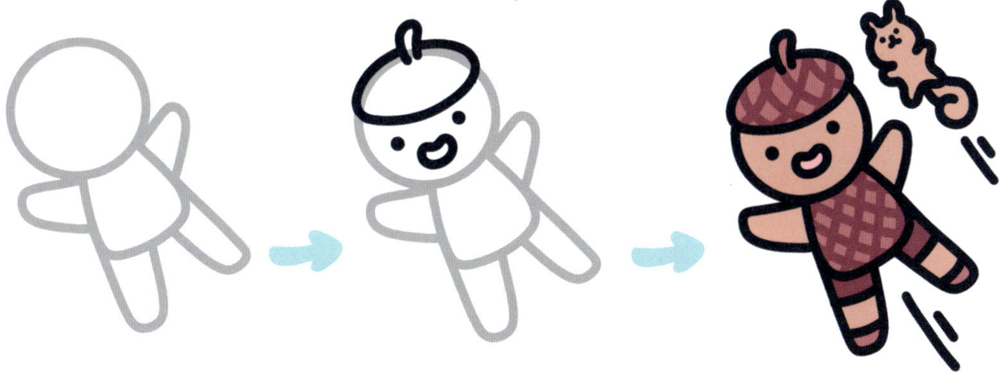

This acorn person is leaping from tree to tree, like a squirrel.

Add an acorn hat and acorn patterns on the clothes.

Draw in jumping lines and a squirrel friend too!

Leaf hair

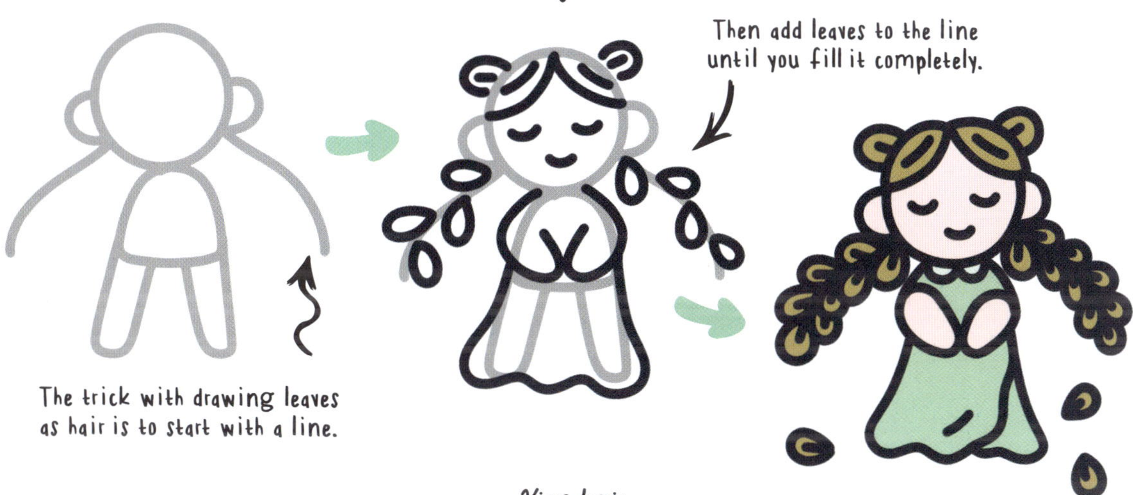

The trick with drawing leaves as hair is to start with a line.

Vine hair

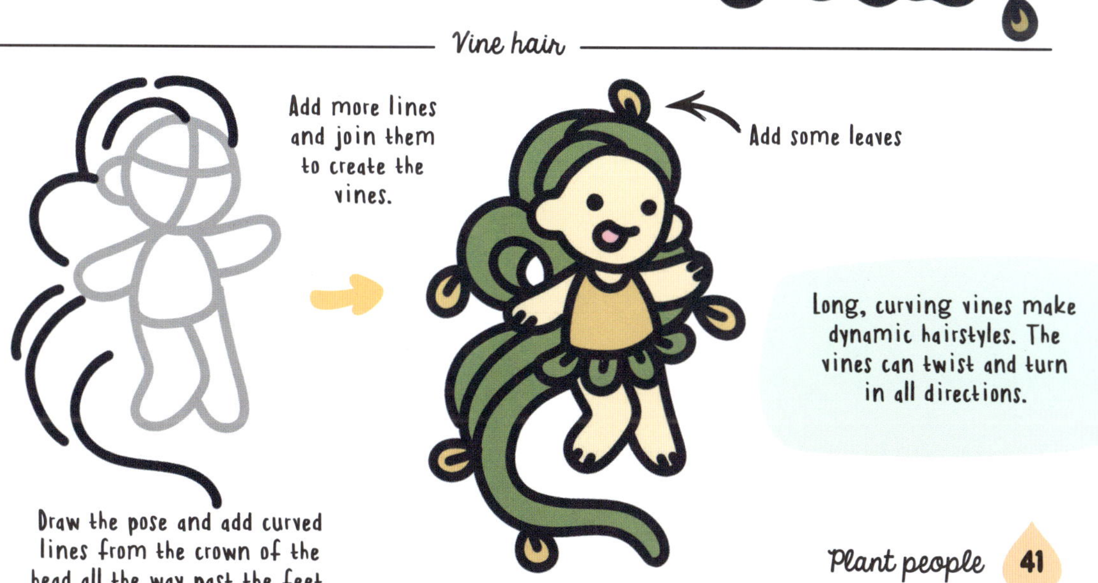

Draw the pose and add curved lines from the crown of the head all the way past the feet.

Long, curving vines make dynamic hairstyles. The vines can twist and turn in all directions.

FLOWER PEOPLE

There are so many flowers out there, so there are infinite possibilities for creating flower characters! You can make the face, outfit or pose flower-inspired!

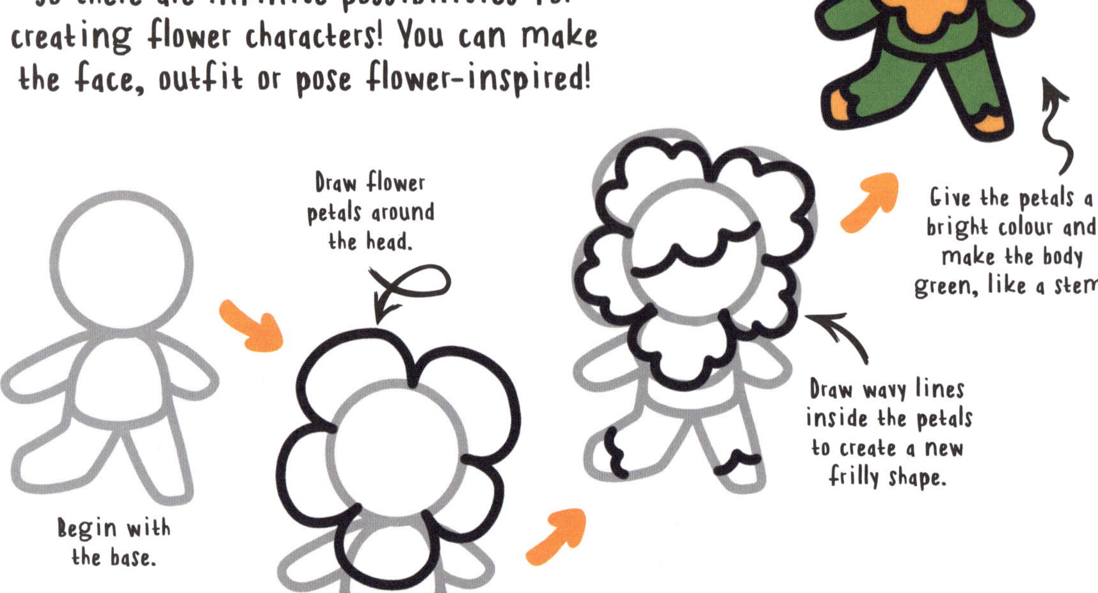

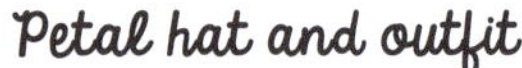

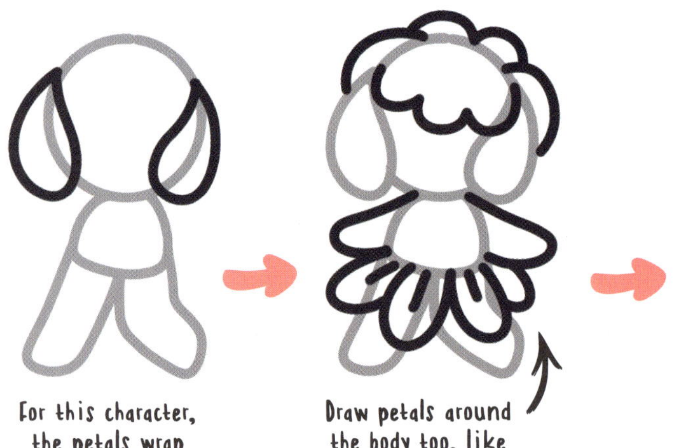

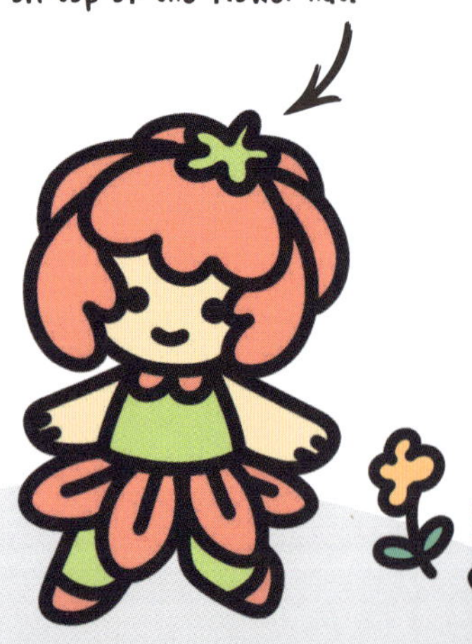

Flower bud

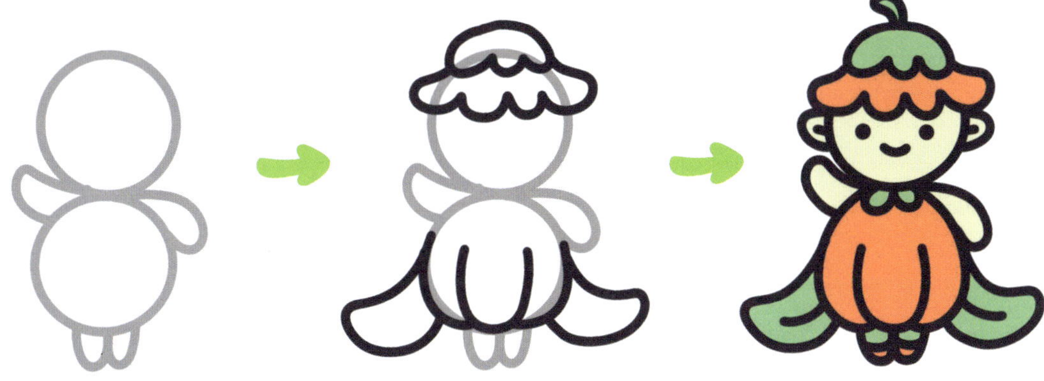

The base of this pose is a circle instead of a gumdrop.

Draw lines on the circle body to turn it into a flower bud. Draw leaves to the side of the bud and a stem hat.

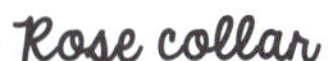

Rose collar

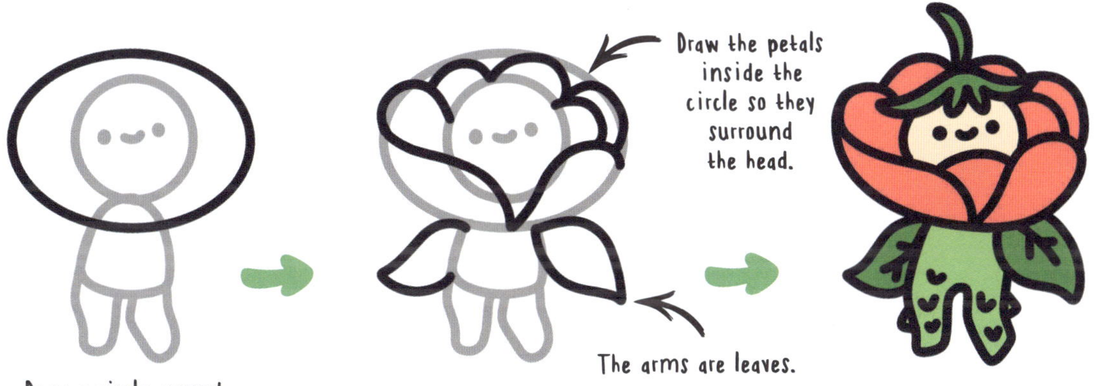

Draw the petals inside the circle so they surround the head.

The arms are leaves.

Draw a circle around the head.

Fuzzy pollen

After making the base, draw petals around the neck.

Make the head fuzzy and draw a cute face!

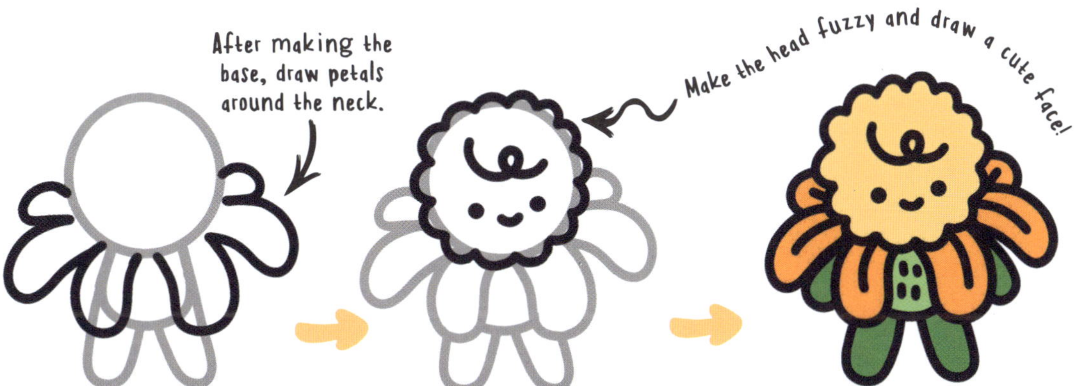

CAT PEOPLE

Cat people have the characteristics and personality traits of cats. They like to meet new people and jump up and down in joy when they can hang out with friends.

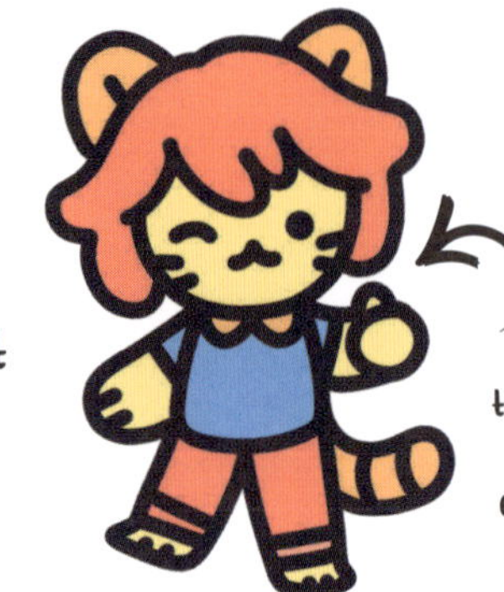

To make a thumbs-up pose, draw a small circle on top of the paw circle.

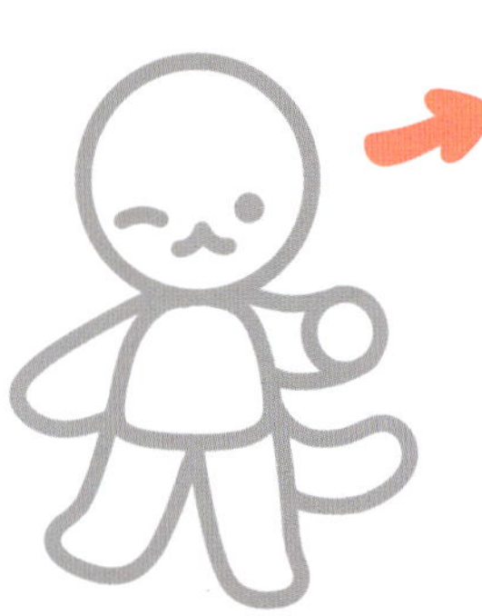

Draw the base of a person with a winky face. The front paw is a circle.

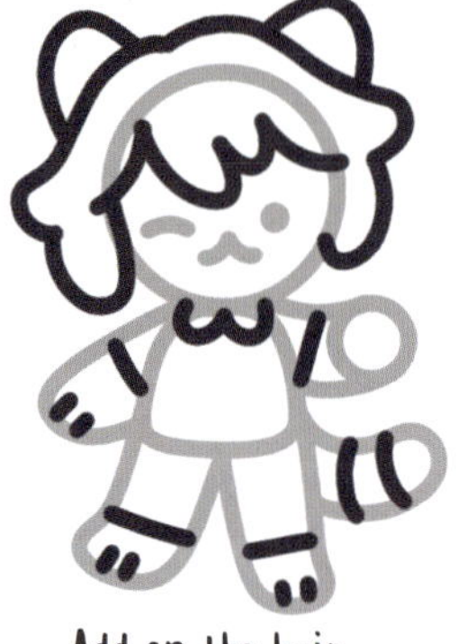

Add on the hair and triangular ears. The clothes are simple lines.

Draw me with arms up and a happy face, jumping for joy!

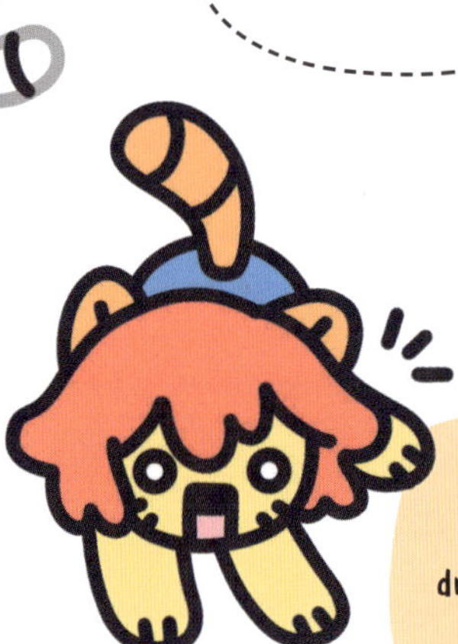

I drew inspiration from a surprised cat's pose for this drawing. The arms point down and the tail points up.

Sleepy kitty

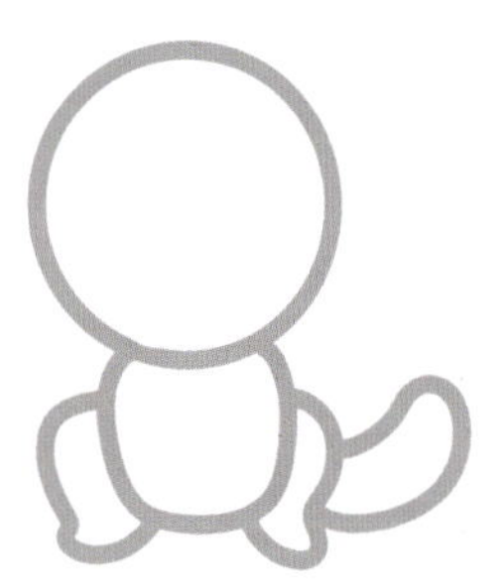

For this pose, draw the back legs close to the body.

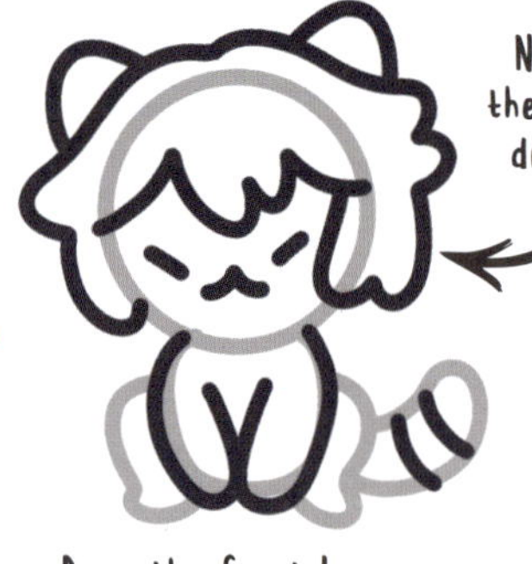

Draw the front legs closer to the body too.

Notice how the eyes slant downwards.

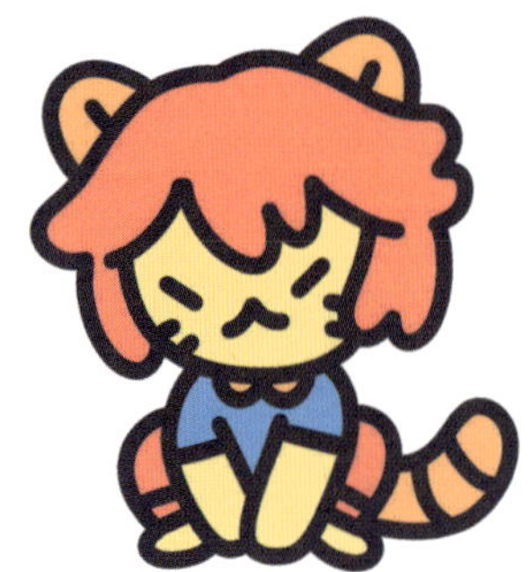

WATER SPRITES

Water sprites live near freshwater lakes because they enjoy swimming every day. Use cool pastel colours so they look watery.

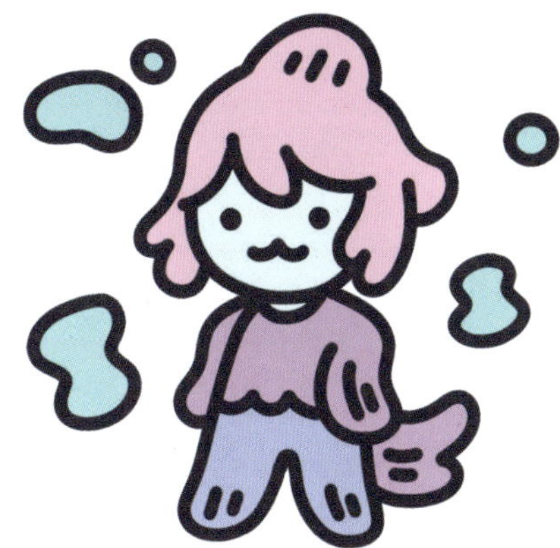

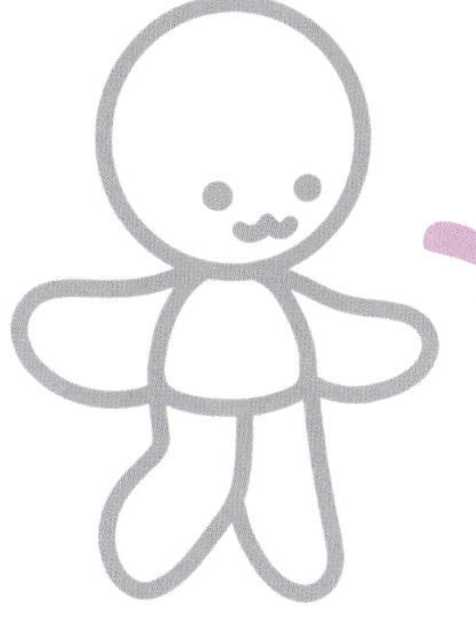

Notice that the shapes of the body and limbs are rounded.

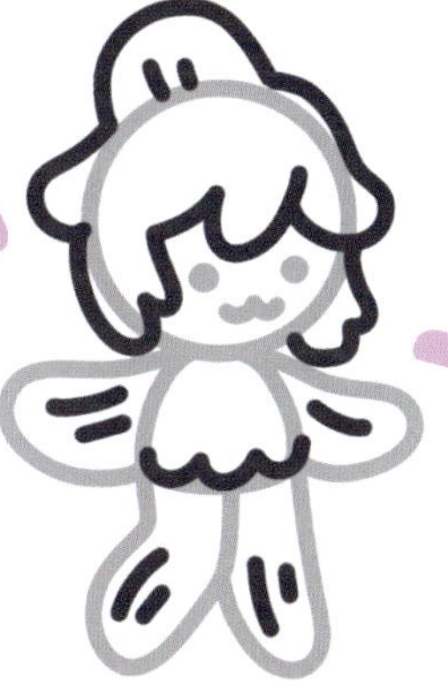

Even the hair and top fin are rounded. Add lines on the limbs to make fin patterns.

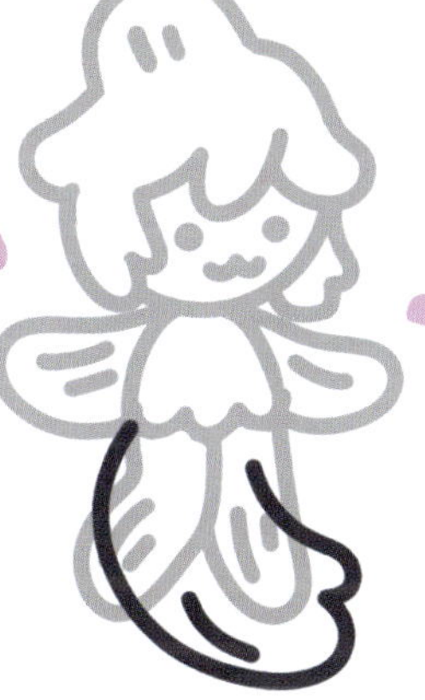

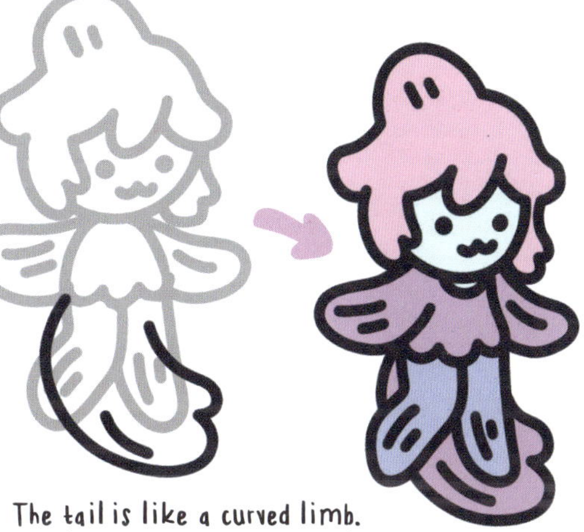

The tail is like a curved limb. Don't forget to add the same fin patterns there too!

Floating away

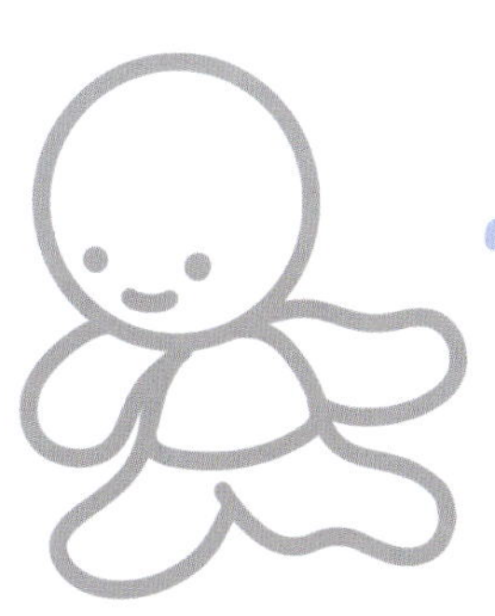

In this pose, the limbs are wavy, like water.

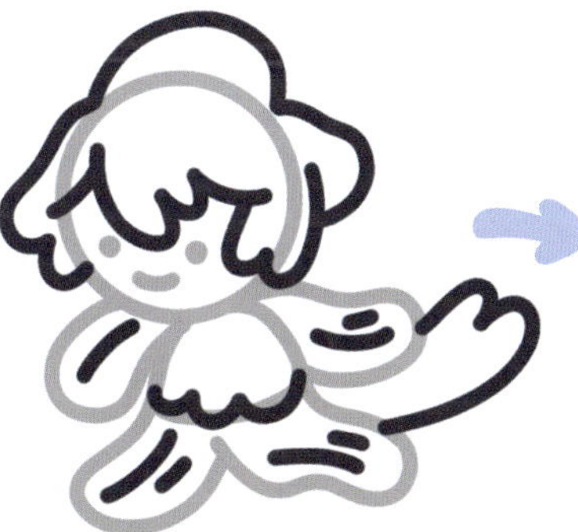

Draw the fin lines in the same wavy direction as the limbs.

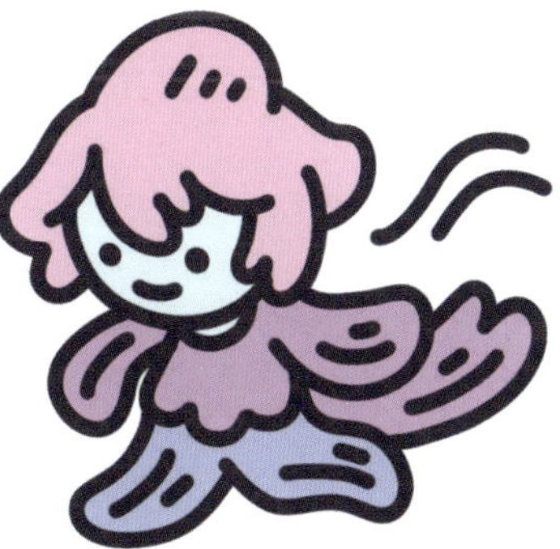

Finish with wavy lines behind the character to show that they are swimming or walking.

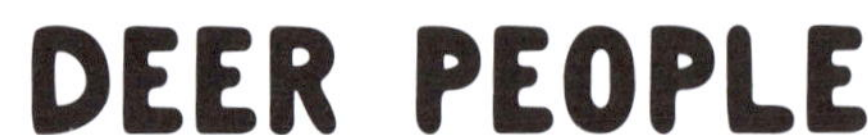

DEER PEOPLE

Notable qualities of deer people are their long antlers and big ears. The antlers point upwards while the ears point outwards!

Start with the base of a person. Then add arms and antlers.

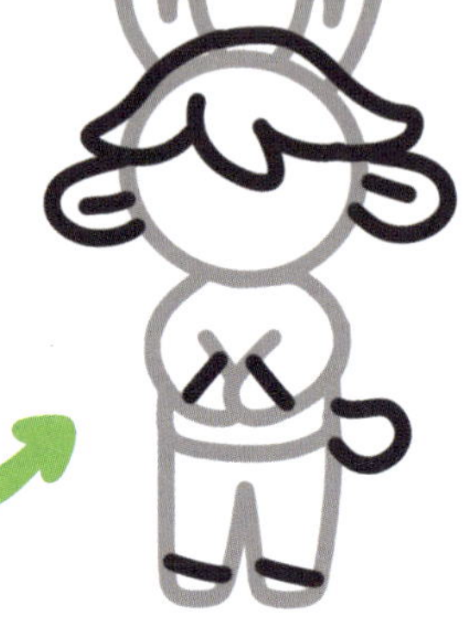

Draw in the hair, ears, tail and details for the clothes.

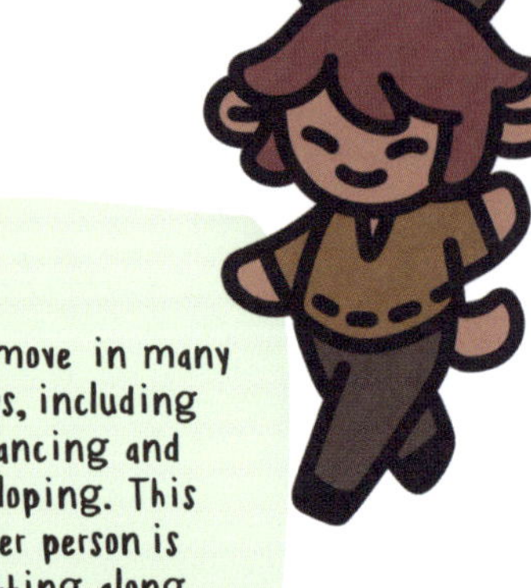

Deer move in many ways, including prancing and galloping. This deer person is trotting along.

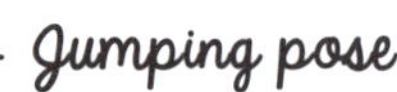

Jumping pose

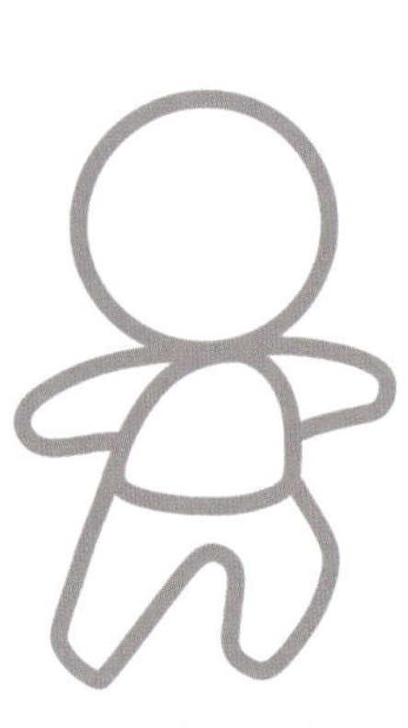

Try drawing this jumping pose!

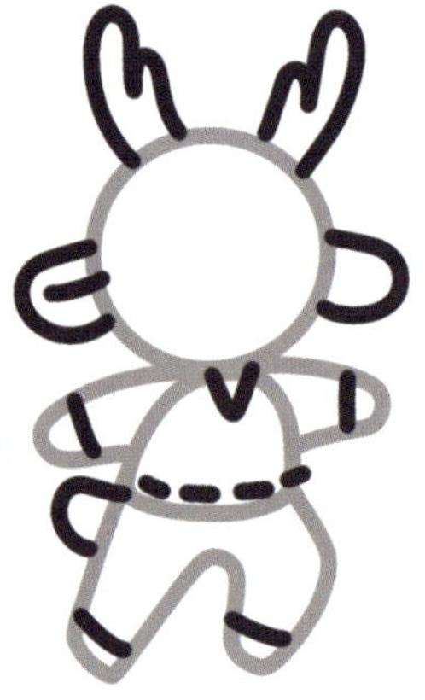

Add antlers, ears and clothes.

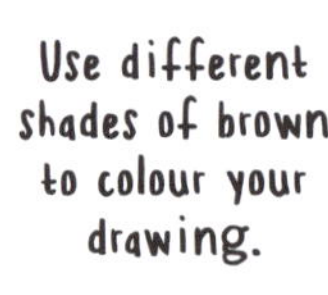

Use different shades of brown to colour your drawing.

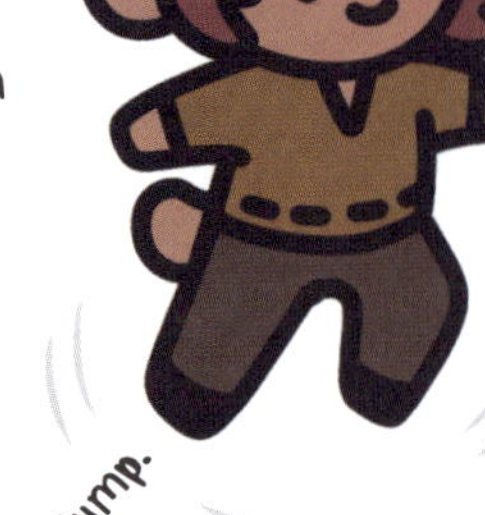

Add direction lines to emphasise the jump.

BIRD PEOPLE

Bird people are fun to draw because of their giant wings! The wings can be used to express the character's feelings and make dynamic poses.

With the wings open or upward, your bird person will look friendly and welcoming. Draw the wings covering the body if your bird person is worried or afraid.

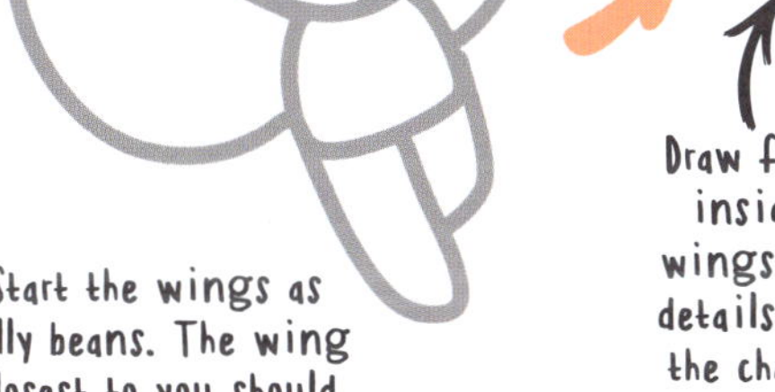

Start the wings as jelly beans. The wing closest to you should look bigger than the one behind.

Draw feathers inside the wings and as details around the character.

Cheeky bird

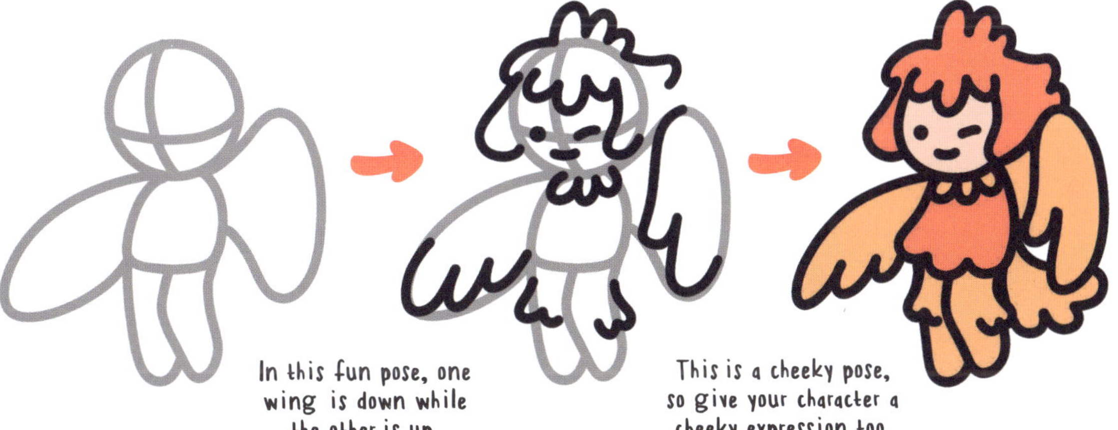

In this fun pose, one wing is down while the other is up.

This is a cheeky pose, so give your character a cheeky expression too.

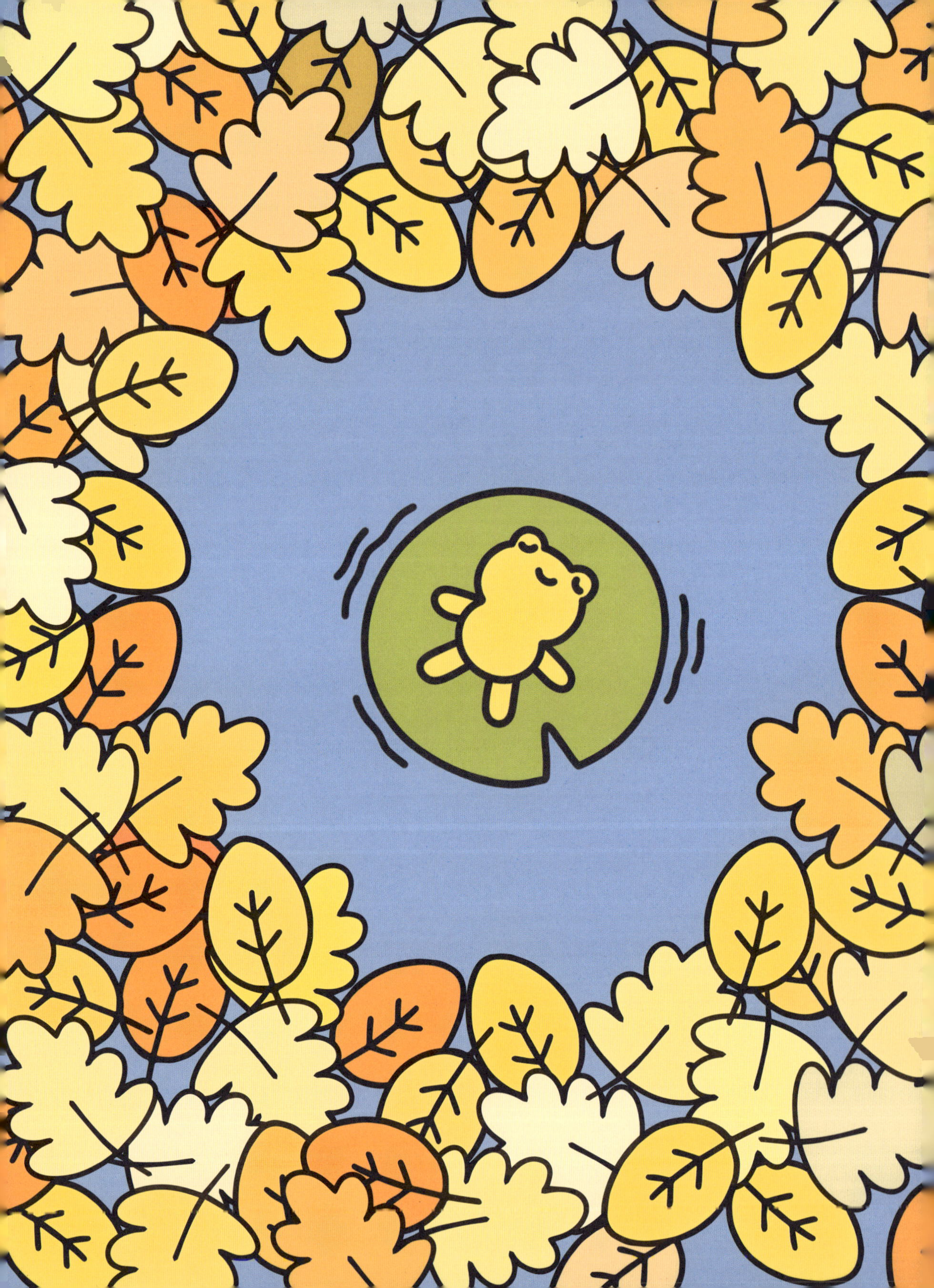

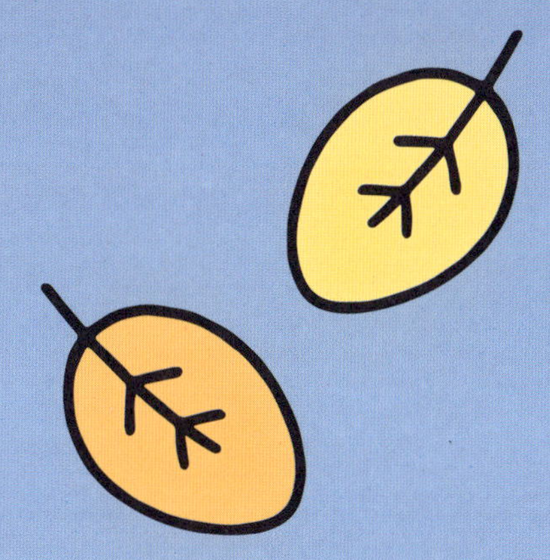

Chapter three

FOREST CREATURES

A whole host of woodland creatures awaits: birds, bears, bugs, and more, as well as new creatures that have popped straight out of my imagination!

FOXES

Foxes are playful creatures with triangle ears and bushy tails. They like to pounce when they are playing and curl up into cosy balls when they're napping.

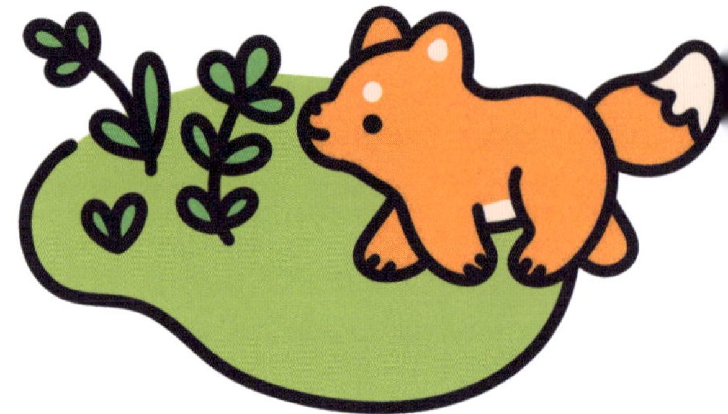

Start with a circle and a jelly bean body. Add the tail pointing upwards.

Draw the rounded snout, ears and limbs. Add a zigzag line to the tail.

Add the face, and paws, and colour it in.

Fox face

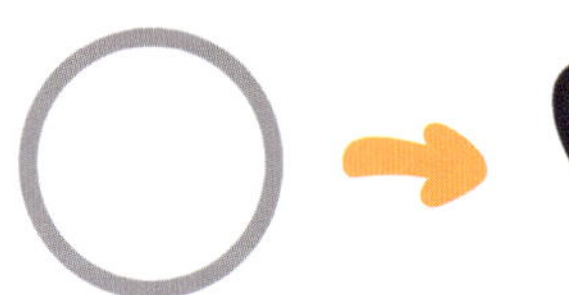

Begin with a circle.

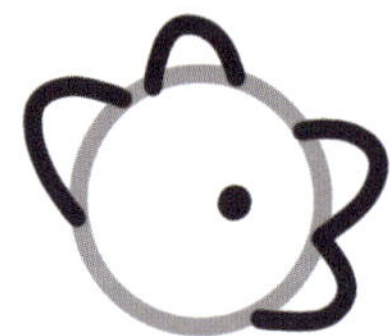

Add four soft triangles to create the ears and mouth.

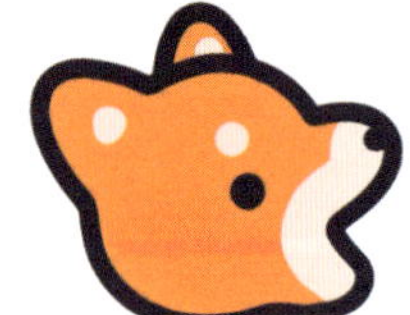

Colour the fox orange and add white fur details.

Foxes have triangular faces and ears so keep that in mind when you draw them from different angles.

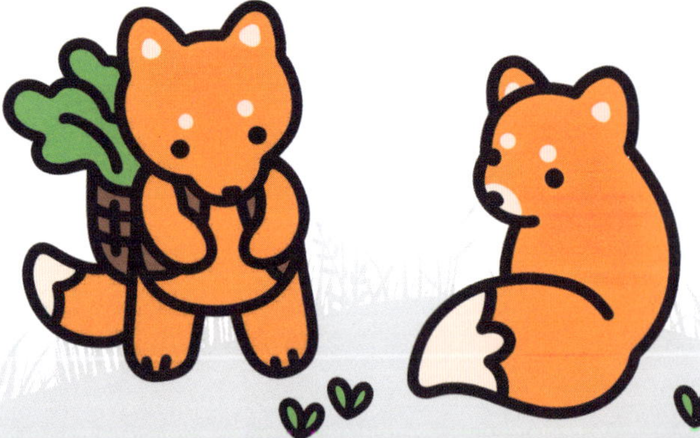

A foxy bouquet

Start with an oval and add circle paws and triangle ears.

Add the flowers.

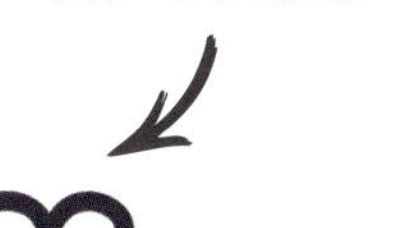

Create the bouquet with an upside-down triangle.

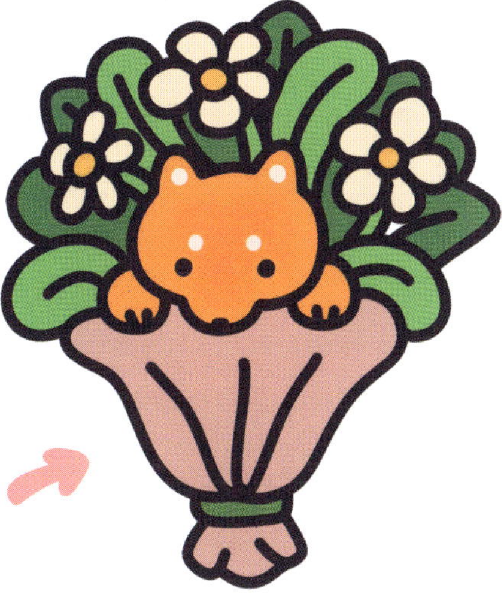

Add the foliage, face and paw details, and colour it in!

Jumping fox

Start with a circle, oval and a jelly bean tail.

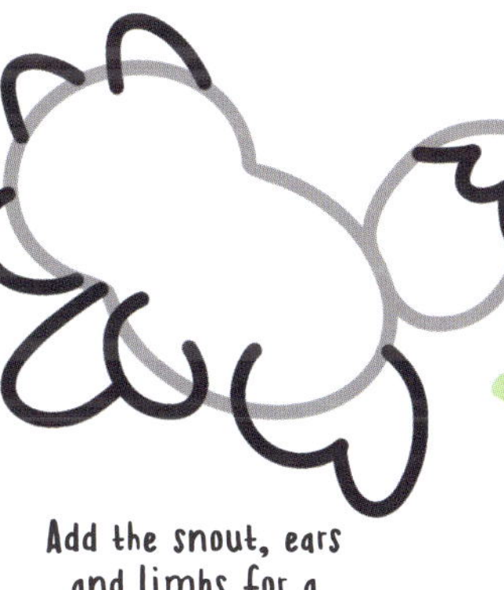

Add zigzag lines to show the white-tipped tail (the brush).

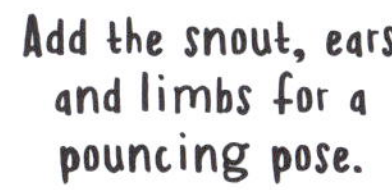

Add the snout, ears and limbs for a pouncing pose.

Add the details, including white dots for the eyebrows and ears.

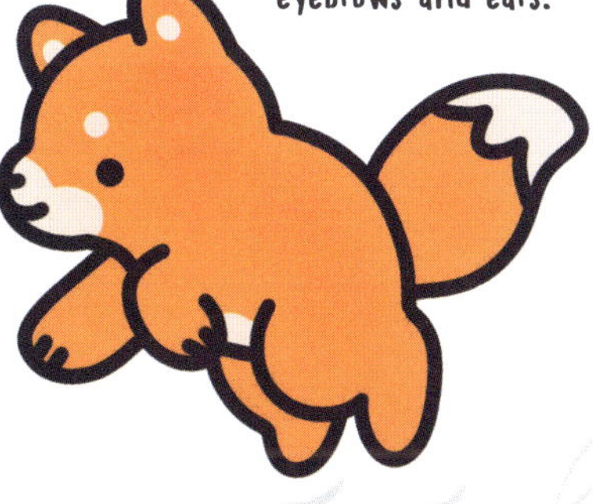

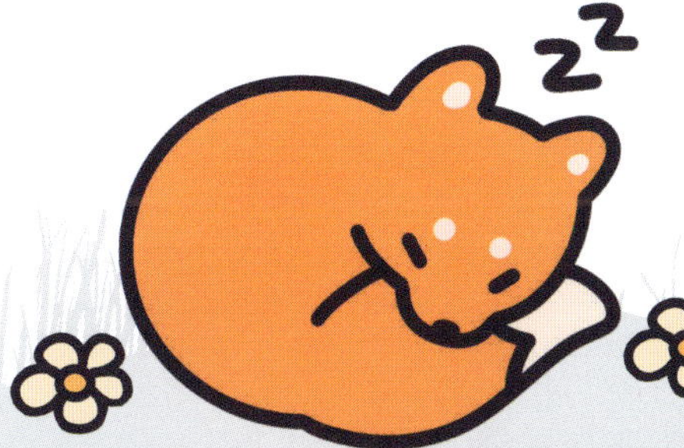

RABBITS

Woodland rabbits are adorable creatures that love to play together. They sometimes even leave the forest to steal carrots from nearby fields.

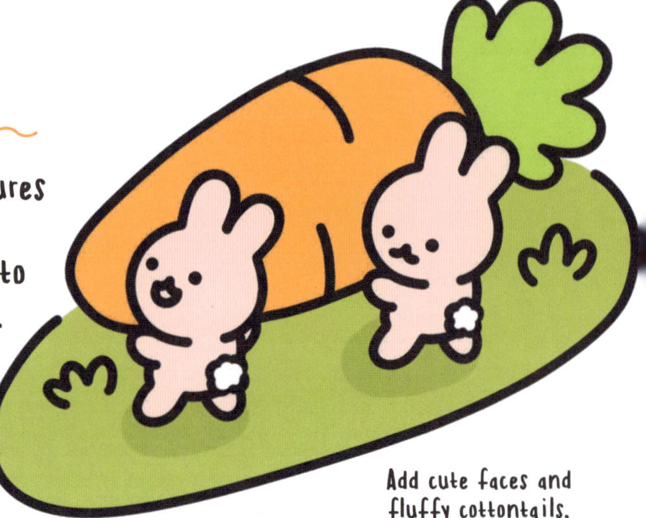

Add cute faces and fluffy cottontails.

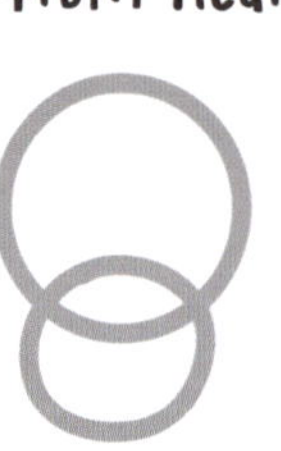

For each rabbit, draw a circle for the body and a larger circle for the head.

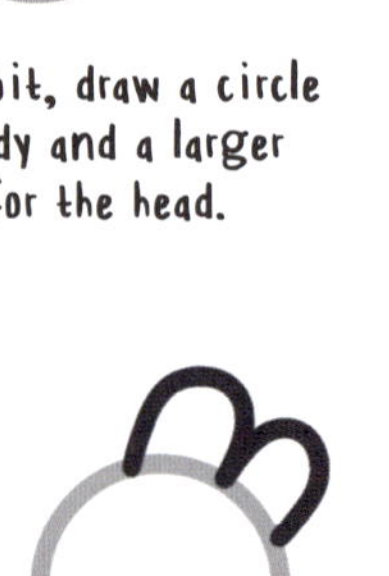

Add on short limbs and longer ears, keeping your lines rounded.

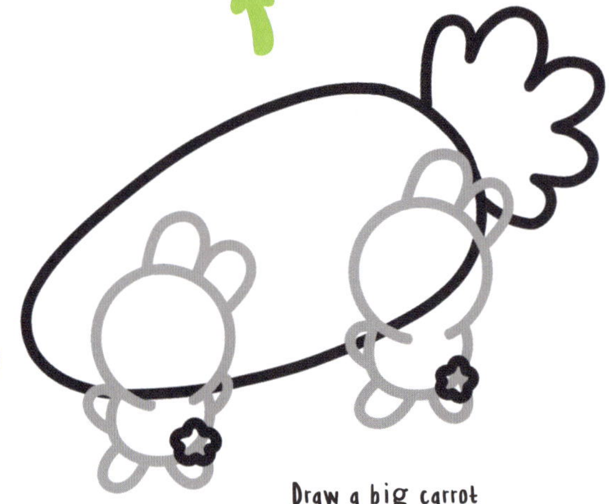

Draw a big carrot between the two rabbits.

Little carrots

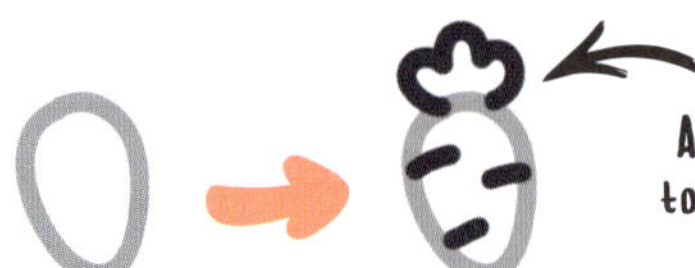

Add a leafy top and line details.

Whether you draw a giant or a small carrot, start with a rounded triangle.

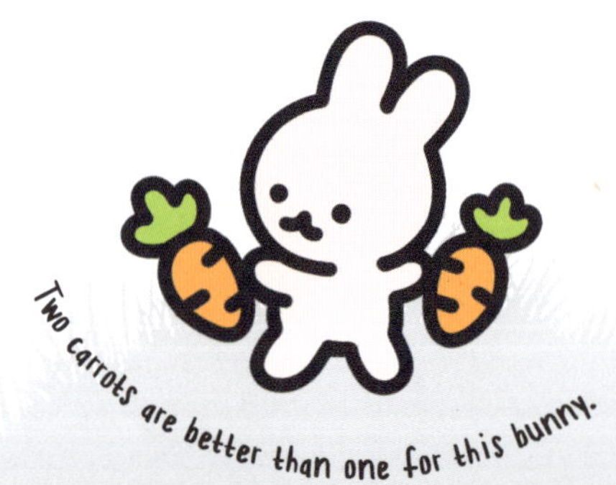

Two carrots are better than one for this bunny.

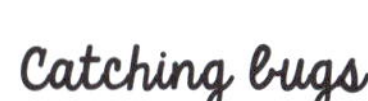

Catching bugs

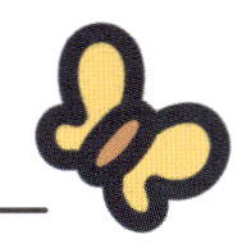

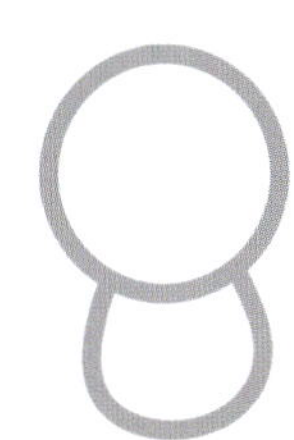

Draw a circle head and gumdrop body.

Then add on the limbs and ears.

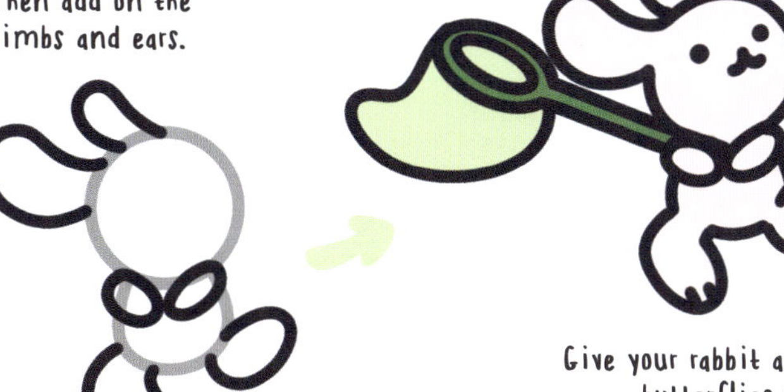

Give your rabbit a net and some butterflies to chase.

Flower bunny

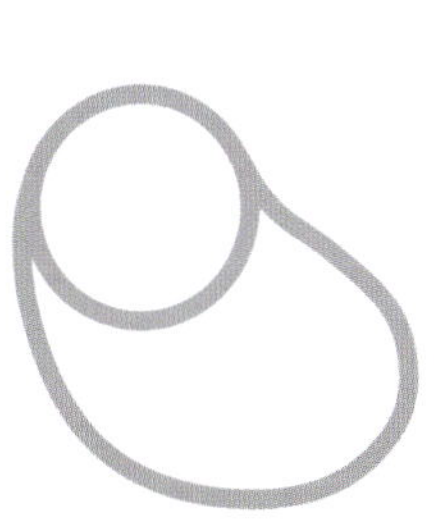

Draw a circle head and jelly bean body.

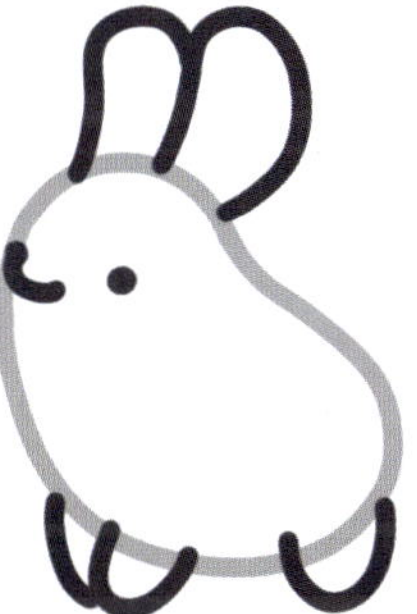

Add on the round legs, long ears and a face.

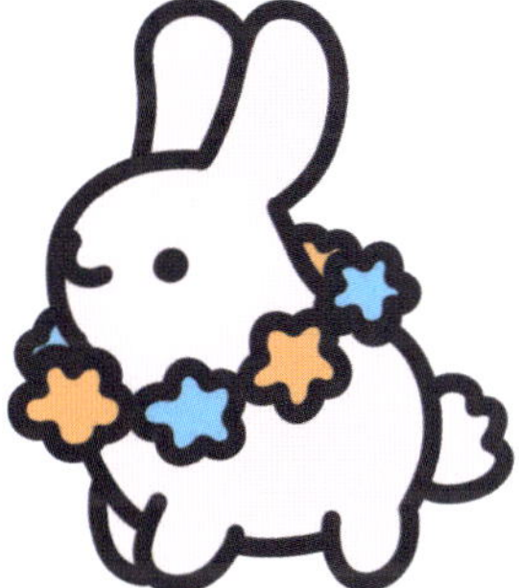

Add the fluffy cottontail and finish with a flower necklace.

Snoozing bunny

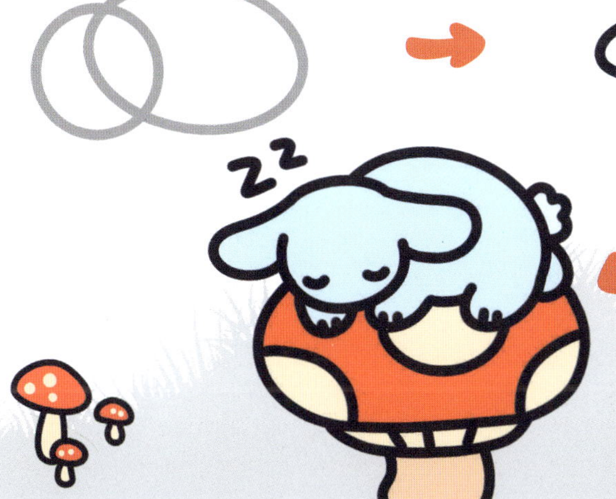

Similar to the body, the mushroom is also an oval shape.

Give the mushroom a stem and a fun pattern.

BIRDS

Lots of birds live in forests, some in the trees and others in bushes or on woodland lakes.

Duck

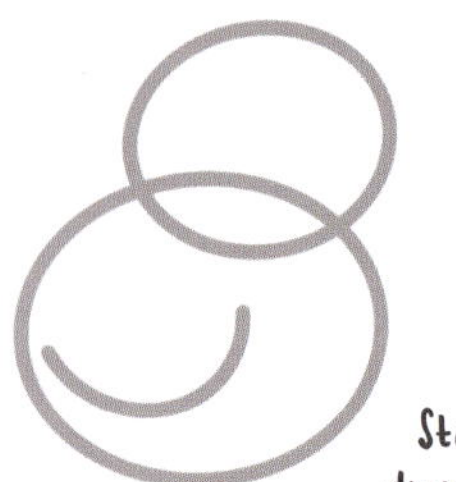

Start a duck by drawing two ovals and a curved line for the wing.

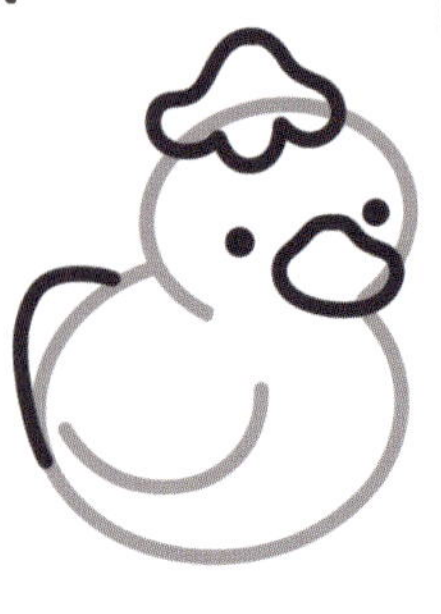

Add the tail, beak and eyes, and give your duck a dainty flower hat.

Draw a pond around your duck, and include some floating flowers and petals.

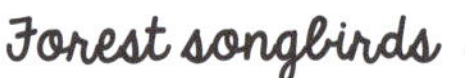

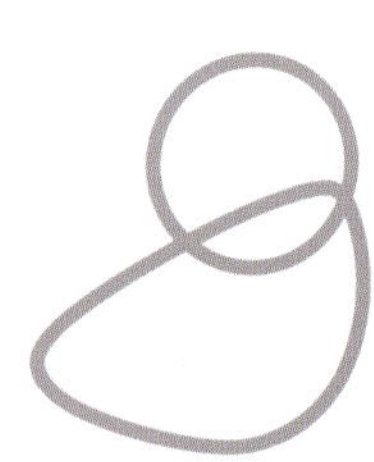

The cardinal has a circle head and semi-circle body.

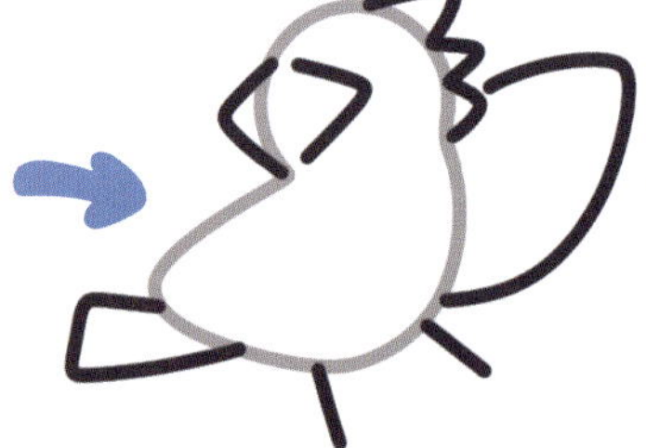

Draw a rectangle tail and add triangle features on the head.

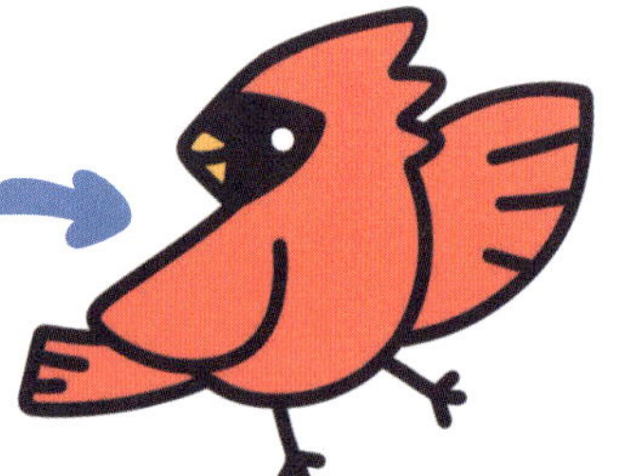

A blue jay has a triangle-shaped crest on its head.

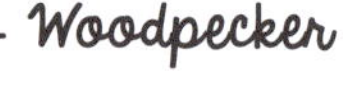

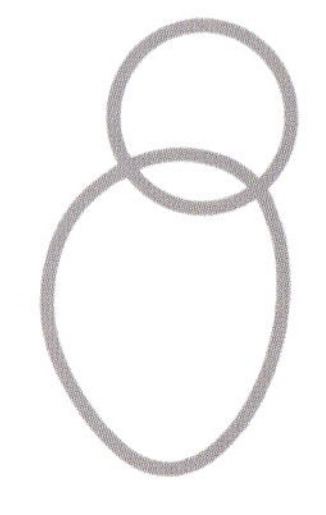

Start with a circle head and egg-shaped body.

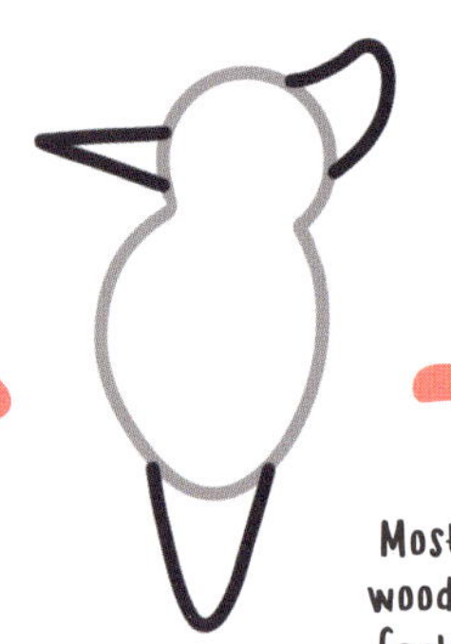

Most of the woodpecker's features are triangles.

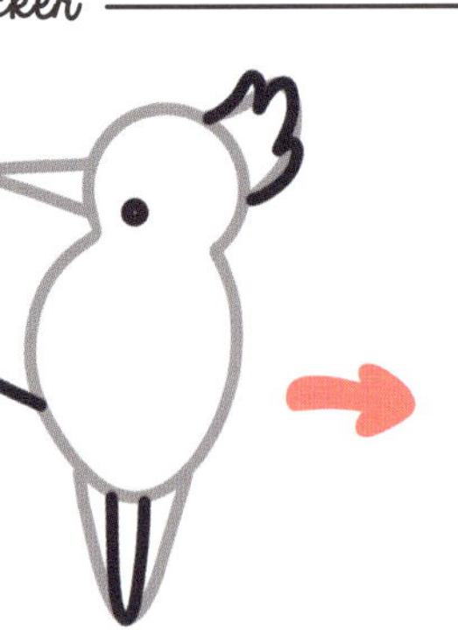

Give the woodpecker a tree trunk and action markings to show it is pecking for food.

Owl

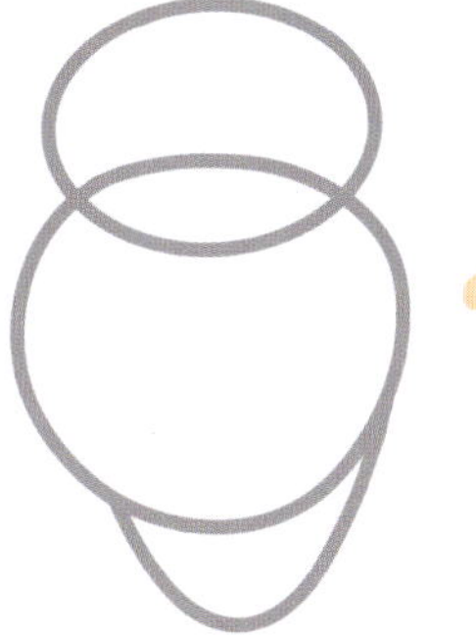

The base of an owl consists of two ovals and a triangle tail.

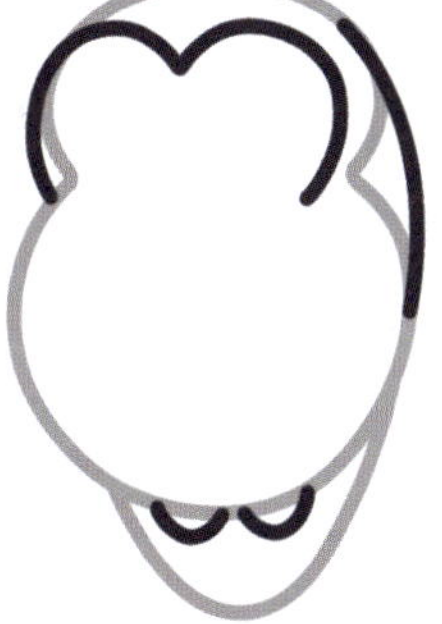

Use curved lines to smooth the body out and add facial shaping.

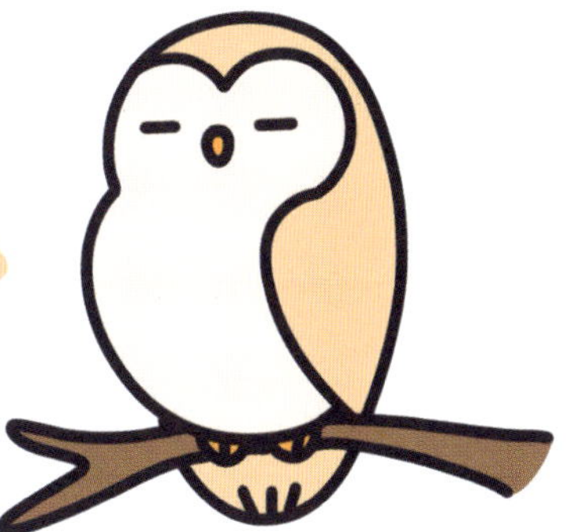

Give your owl a branch to perch on.

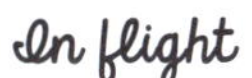

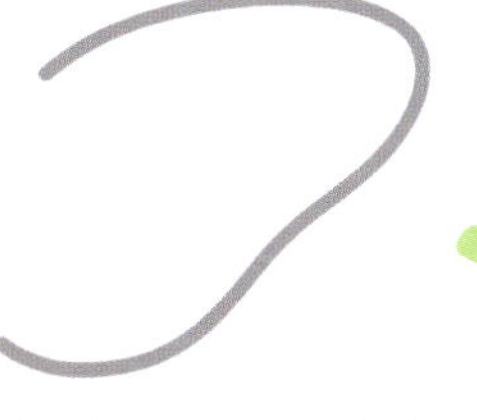

To draw outstretched wings, start with a jelly bean . . .

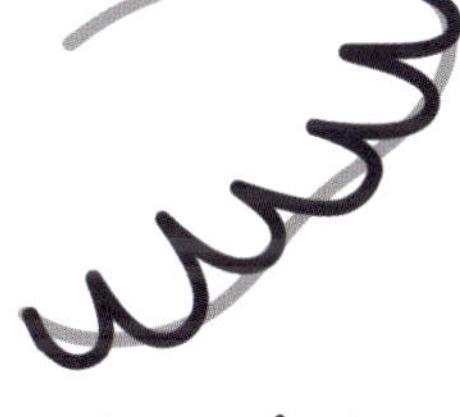

. . . then add feathers along the outline.

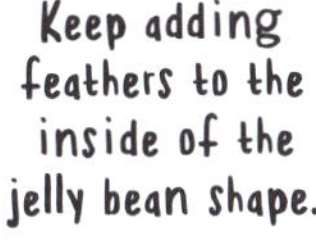

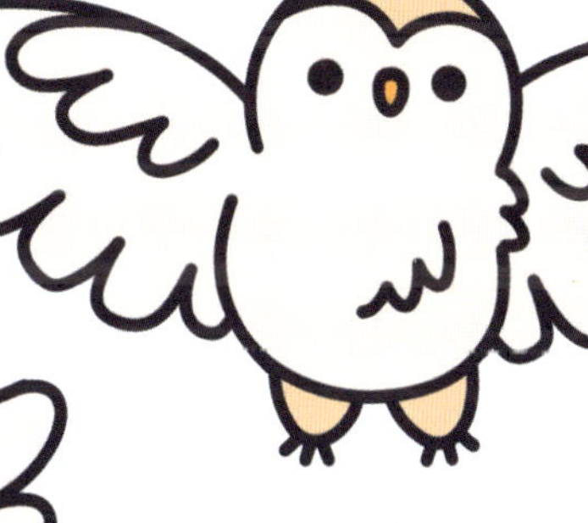

Use the same technique to draw the wings flapping back.

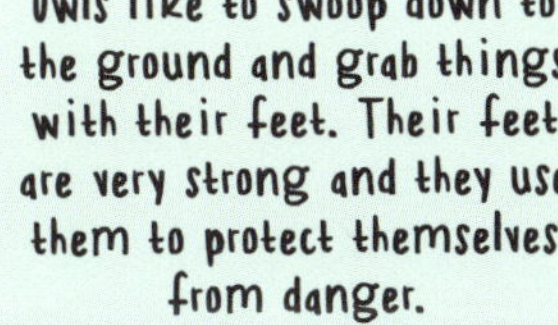

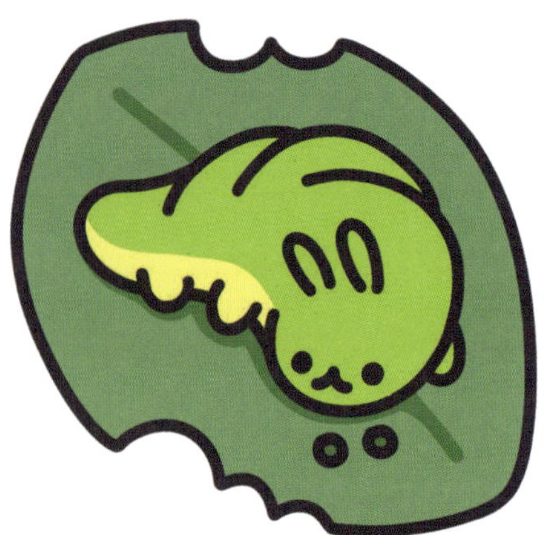

CATERPILLARS

Before they turn into butterflies or moths, caterpillars spend much of their time munching on leaves. So why not draw your caterpillar on a leaf, so it has a tasty snack?

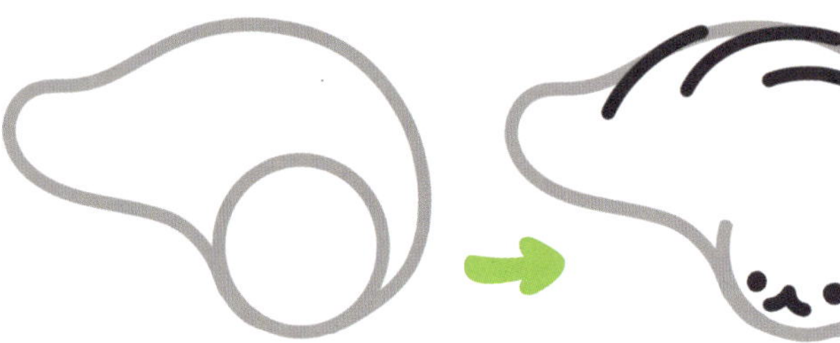

First, draw a circle. Then, draw the body coming out from the circle.

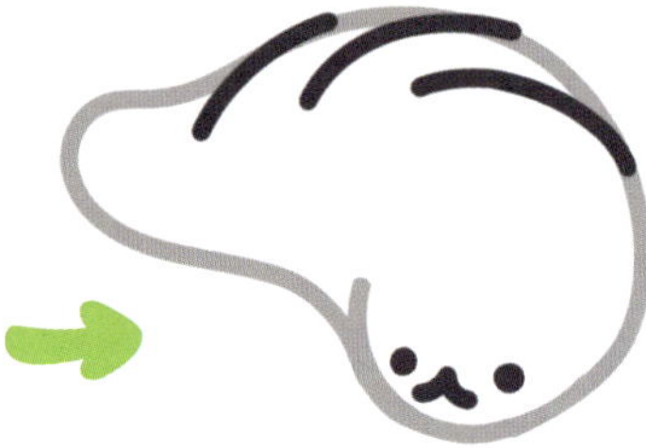

Draw the face and add lines for the details.

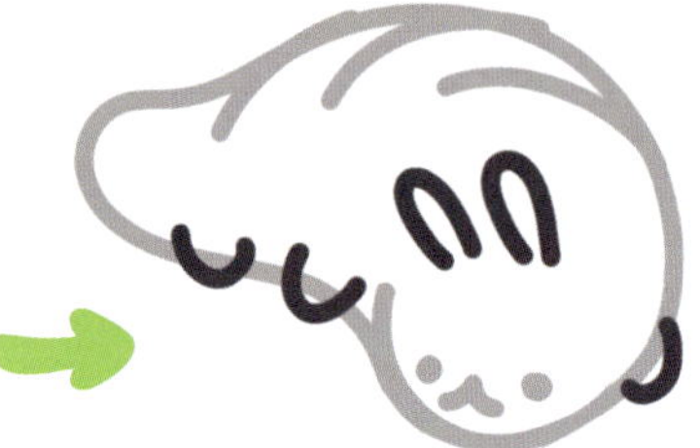

Finish with the antennae and little legs.

Other ideas

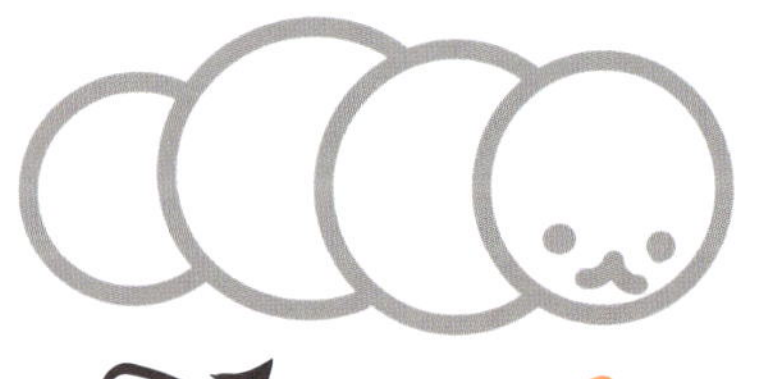

This caterpillar is made up of circles.

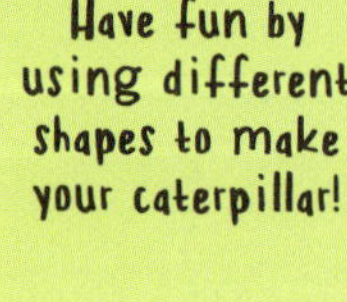

This one is created with a jelly bean shape.

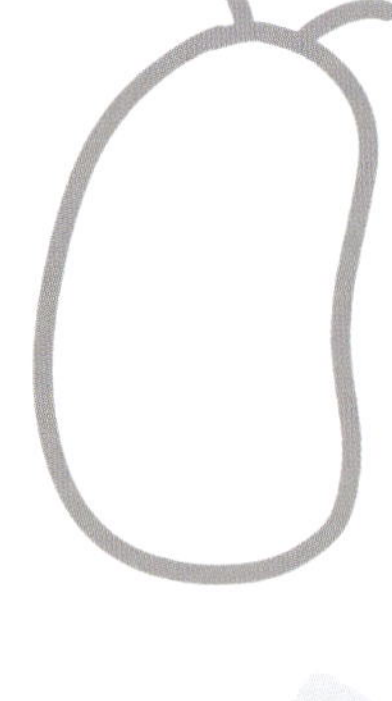

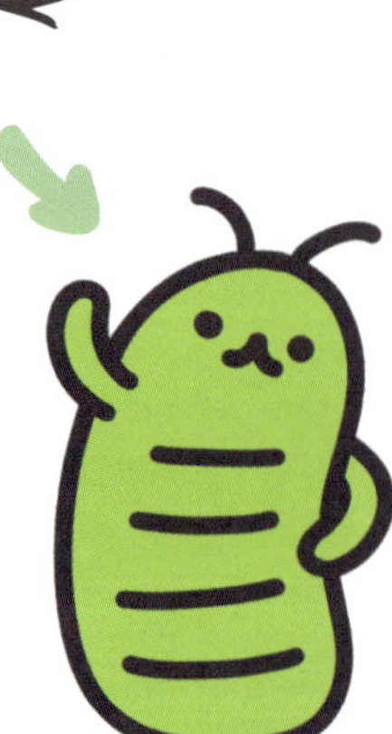

BUTTERFLIES AND MOTHS

Butterflies and moths are very similar, but one of the differences is that butterflies hold their wings up, while moths hold their wings closer to their bodies.

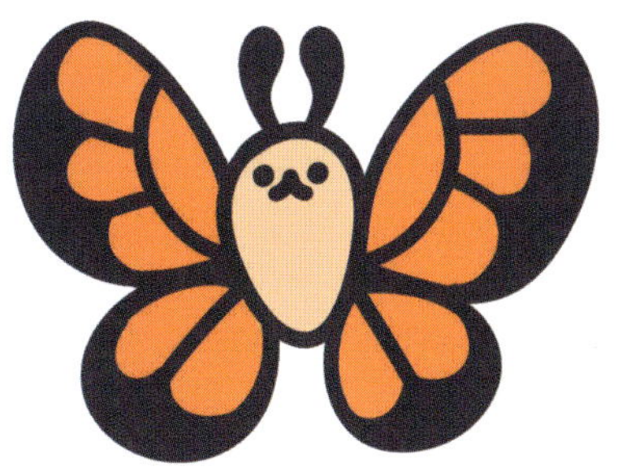

Give your butterfly a face and fill out its antennae.

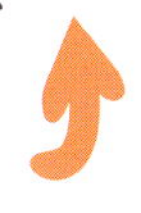

For a butterfly, draw an egg shape for the body, and a double-wing on each side that reaches above and below the body.

Use curved lines to start drawing the wing pattern.

Complete the wing pattern with a few straight lines, and start the antennae.

Moth wings

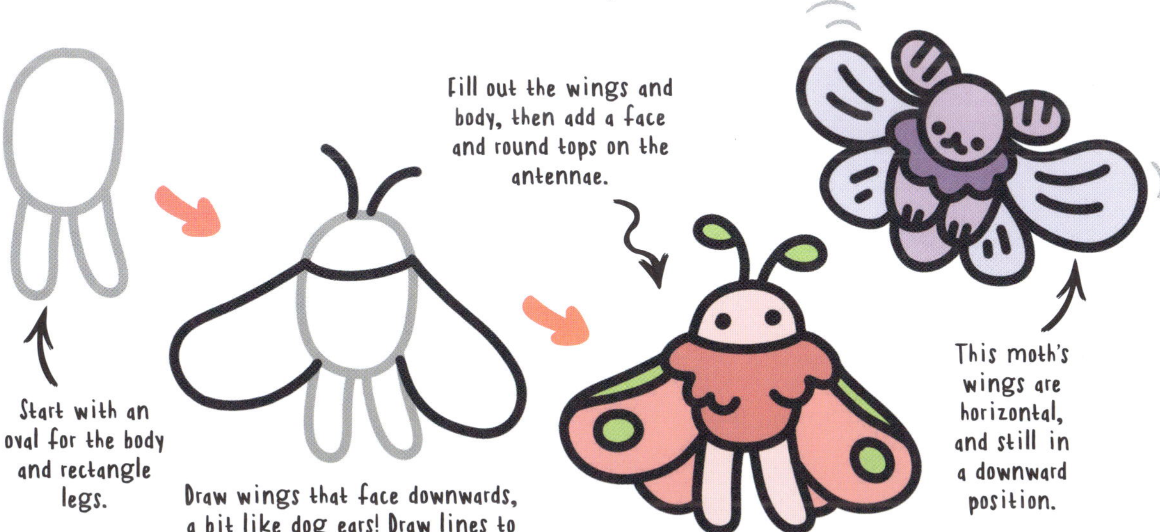

Start with an oval for the body and rectangle legs.

Draw wings that face downwards, a bit like dog ears! Draw lines to start the antennae.

Fill out the wings and body, then add a face and round tops on the antennae.

This moth's wings are horizontal, and still in a downward position.

SMALL CRITTERS

Some of the small critters you might find in the forest include cute mice, skunks and hedgehogs.

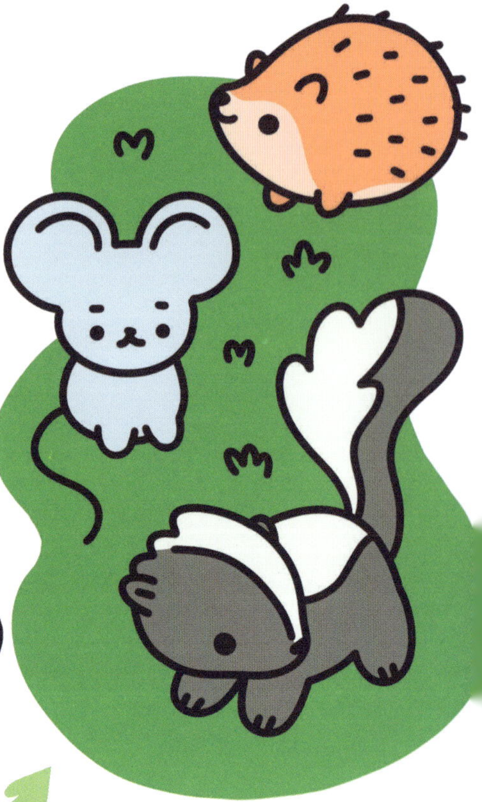

When colouring a skunk, make the centre of the face and tail white. The rest can be coloured gray.

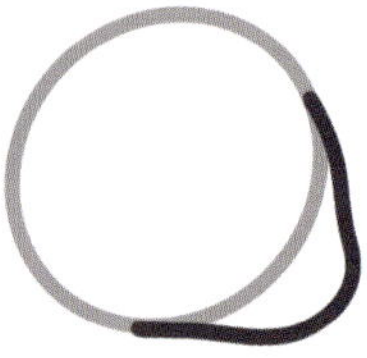

Draw a circle for the head and add a curved triangle for the snout.

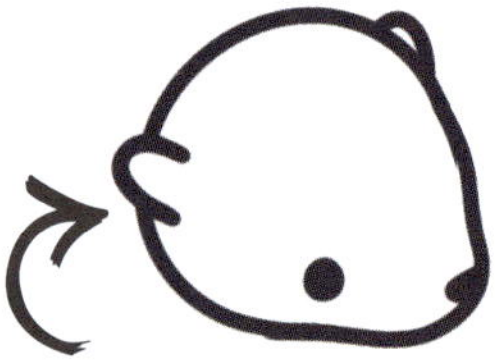

Add little ears and facial features.

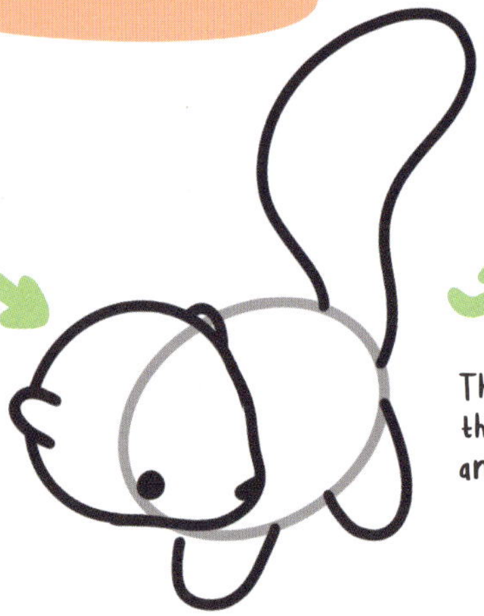

The body is an oval, the legs are round, and the tail is big and wavy.

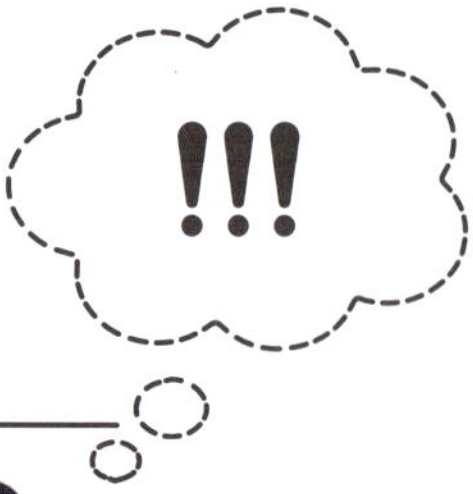

!!!

Sitting skunk

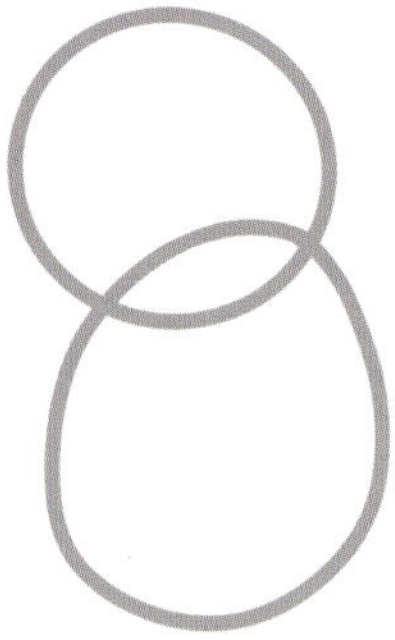

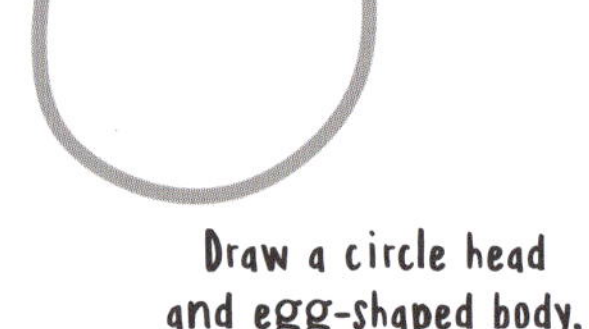

Draw a circle head and egg-shaped body.

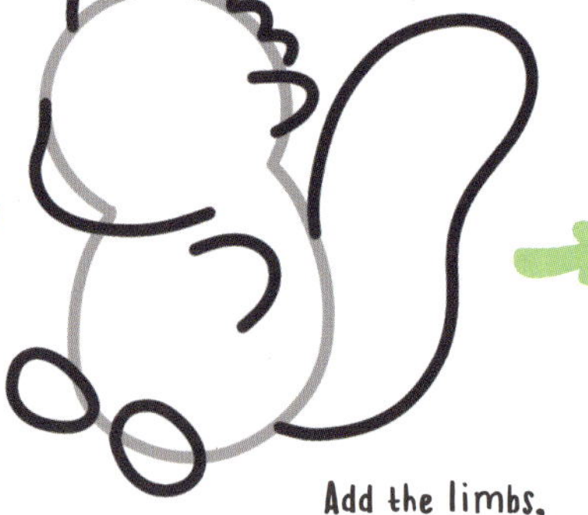

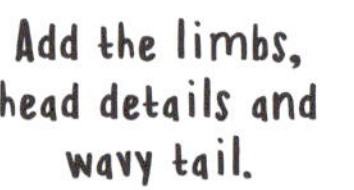

Add the limbs, head details and wavy tail.

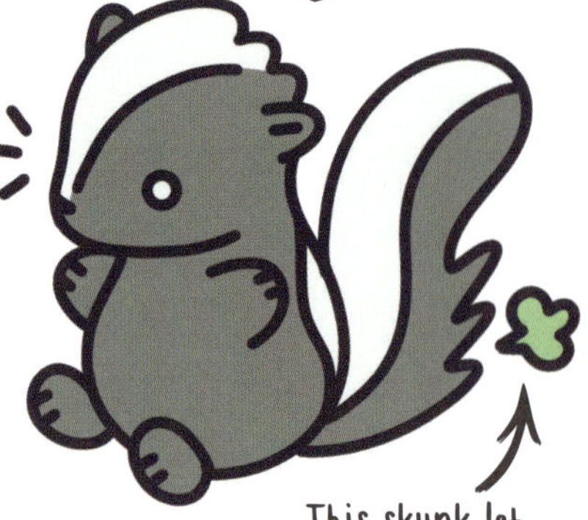

This skunk let out a scent!

Hedgehog

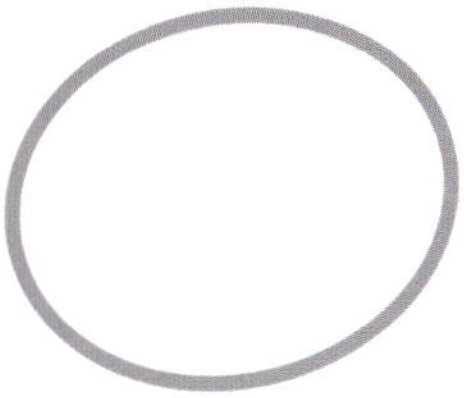

The hedgehog is simple to draw: start with an oval.

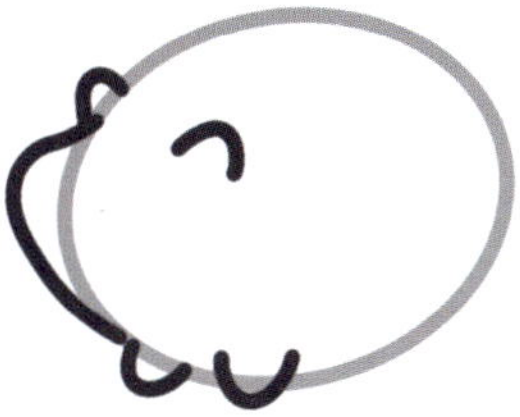

Add a rounded triangle snout. The ears and limbs are the same shape.

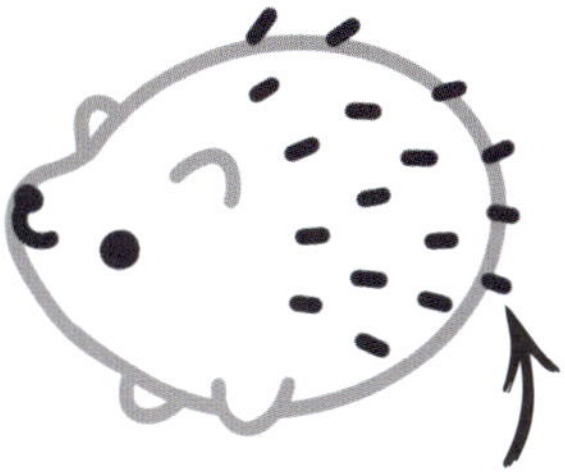

Draw lots of little lines for the spines.

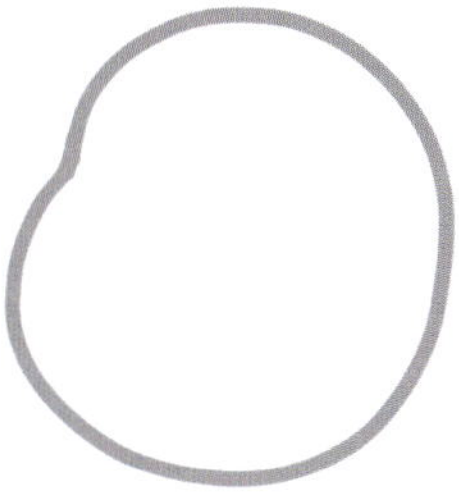

This hedgehog is about to curl into a ball. Draw a fat jelly bean shape.

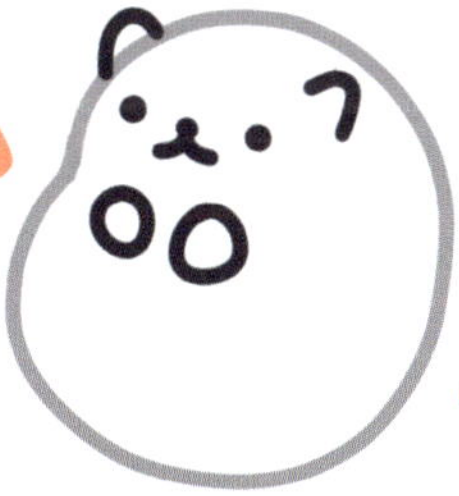

Hedgehogs like to eat worms and caterpillars.

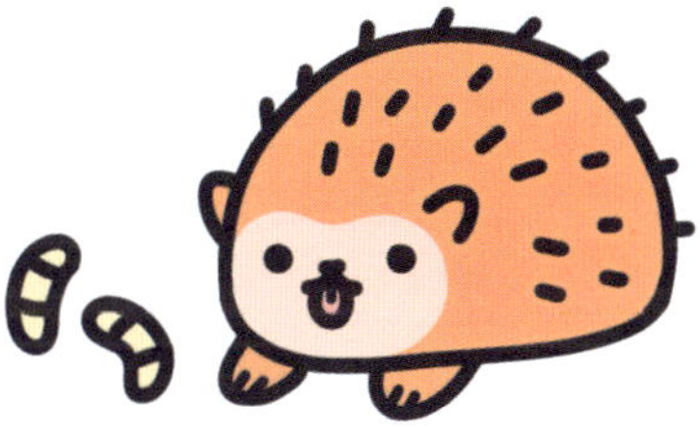

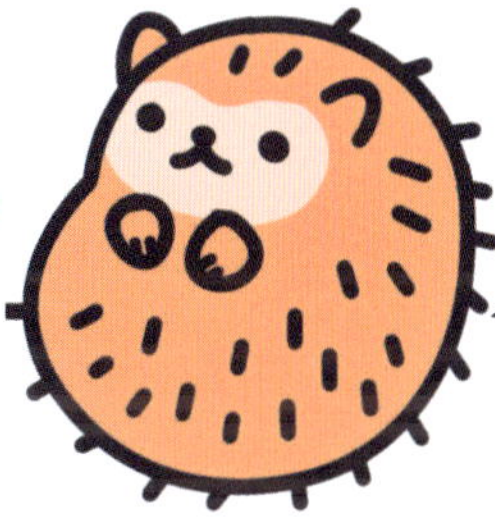

Add the face at the top left. The arms are folded so they look like circles.

Add the spines all over the hedgehog's body.

Mouse

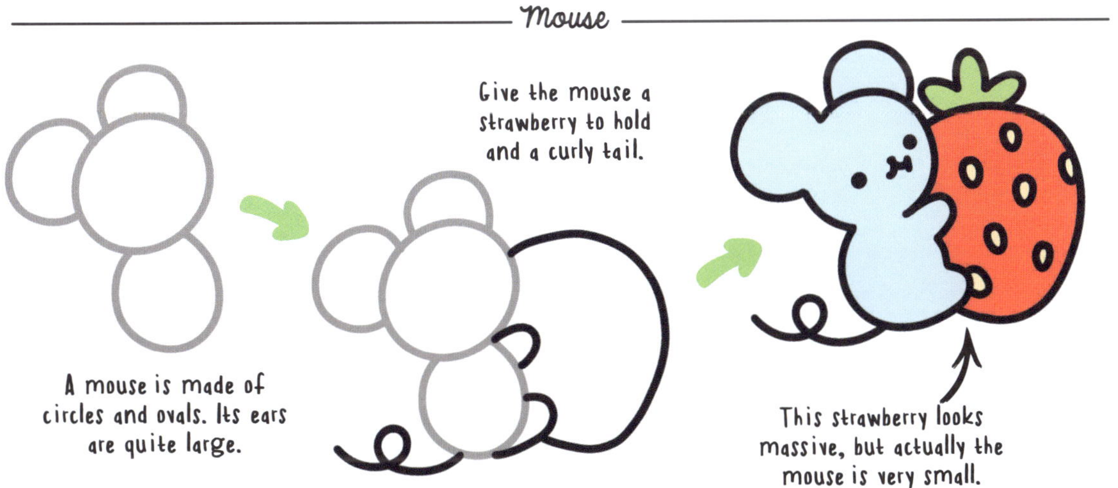

A mouse is made of circles and ovals. Its ears are quite large.

Give the mouse a strawberry to hold and a curly tail.

This strawberry looks massive, but actually the mouse is very small.

RACCOONS

Raccoons are food raiders and are great at finding things in the wild. Their long claws allow them to hold on to objects, unlike most other animals.

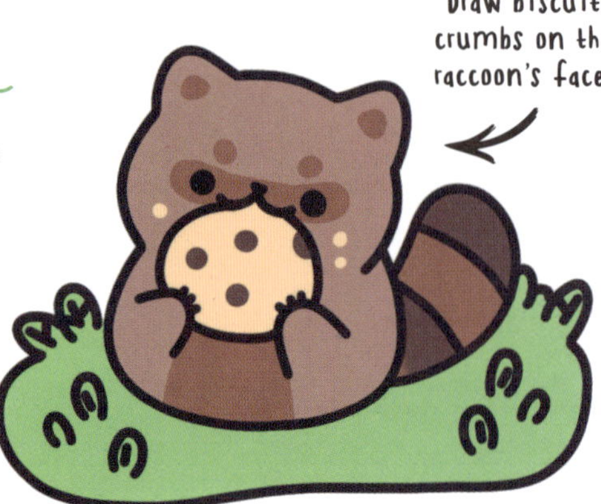

Draw biscuit crumbs on the raccoon's face.

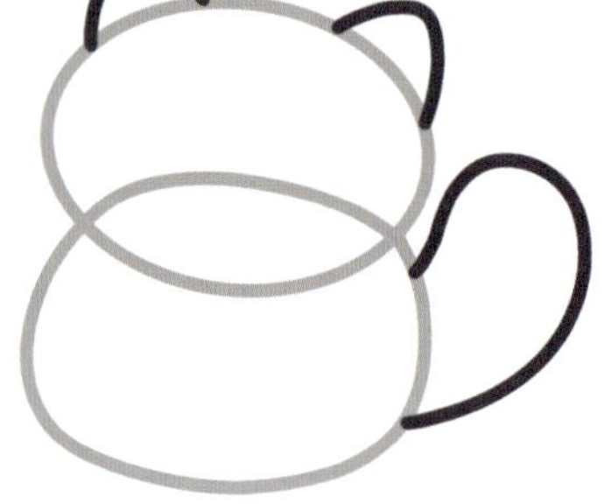

I always start my raccoon drawings with two ovals. Then I add the triangle ears and a big tail.

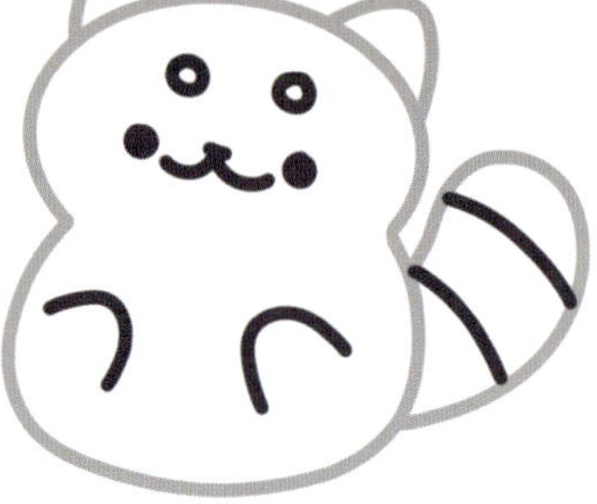

Add a face and draw the hands pointing upwards so it can hold the biscuit.

Pay attention to the pattern on the raccoon's face and tail.

Don't forget to draw those long nails!

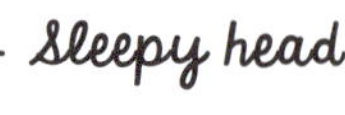

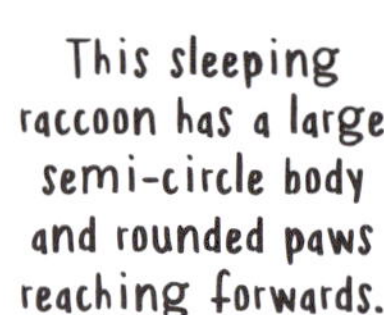

This sleeping raccoon has a large semi-circle body and rounded paws reaching forwards.

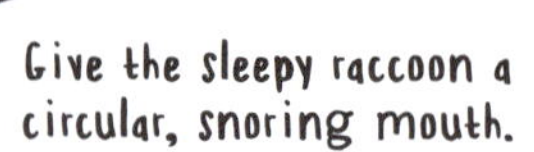

Give the sleepy raccoon a circular, snoring mouth.

Raccoons are also notorious climbers! Draw this one snoozing on a branch. Add some 'Z's to show it's asleep.

SNAKES

Snakes are super-cute reptiles with beady eyes. Their unique body shape means they can take on all manner of poses, plus you can play with the patterns on their skin.

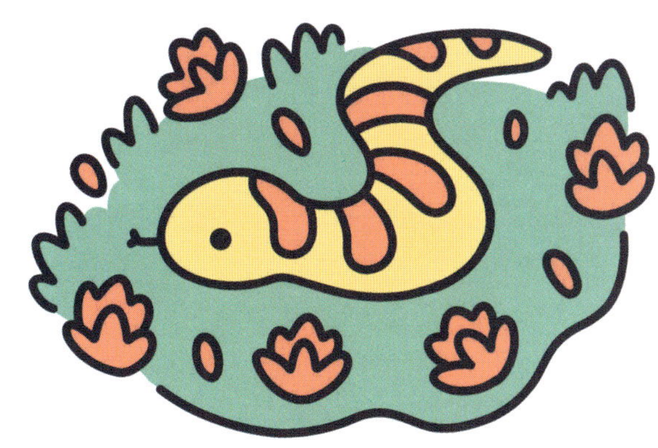

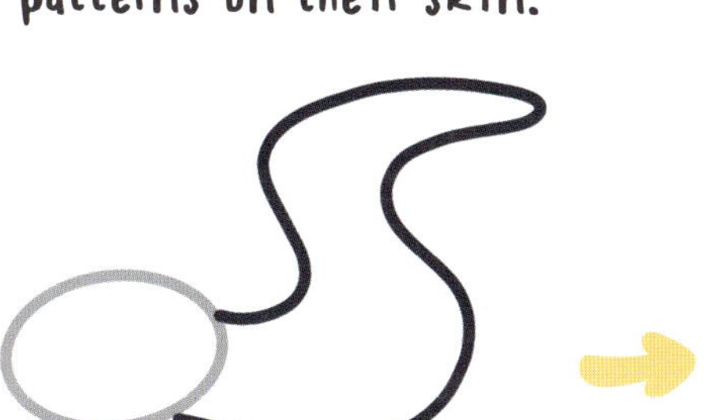

Draw a wide oval head and a long, slithering body, with a pointed end.

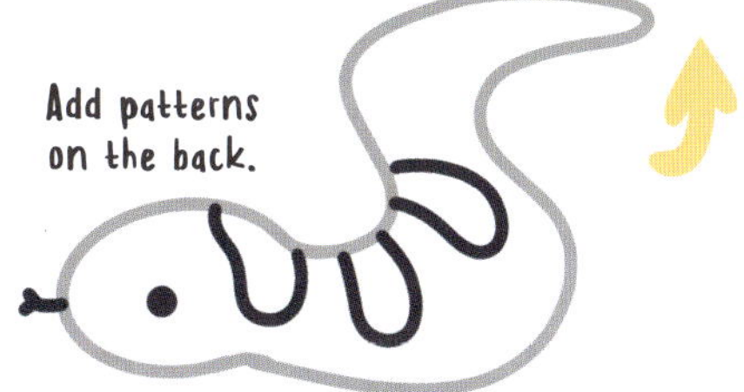

Dot in an eye and give your snake a tongue.

Sitting snakes

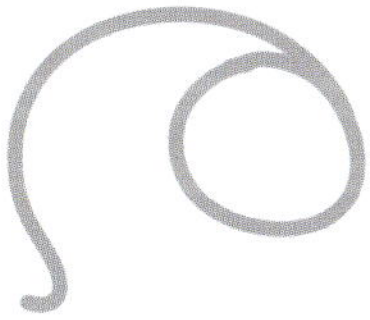

If you are experimenting with different body positions for your snake, still start with an oval head.

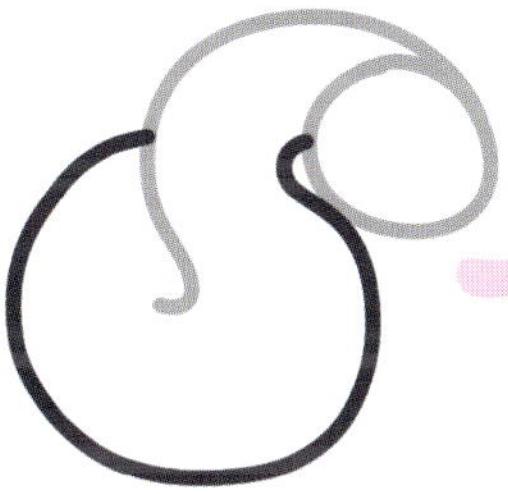

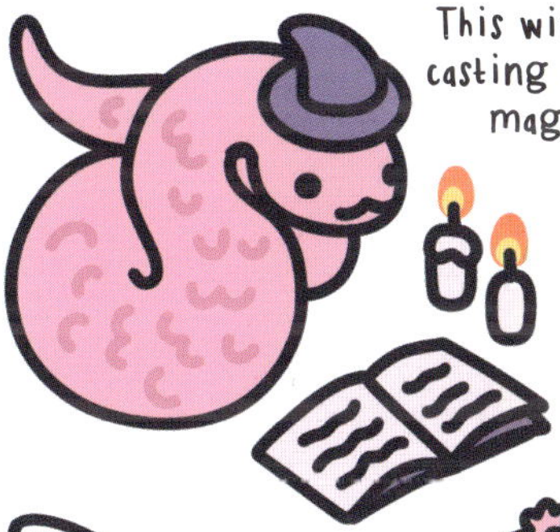

This wizard snake is casting spells from a magical book!

You can make really unique snake designs inspired by your favourite plants or mushrooms.

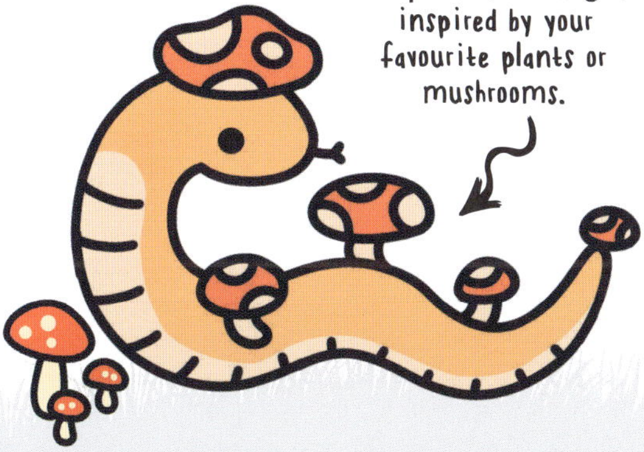

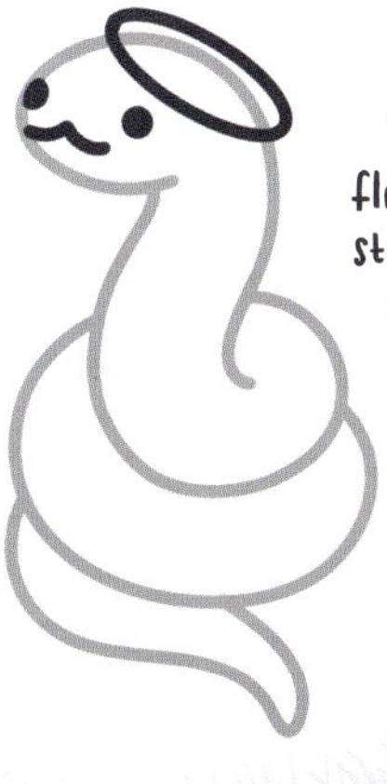

To draw a flower crown, start with an oval base.

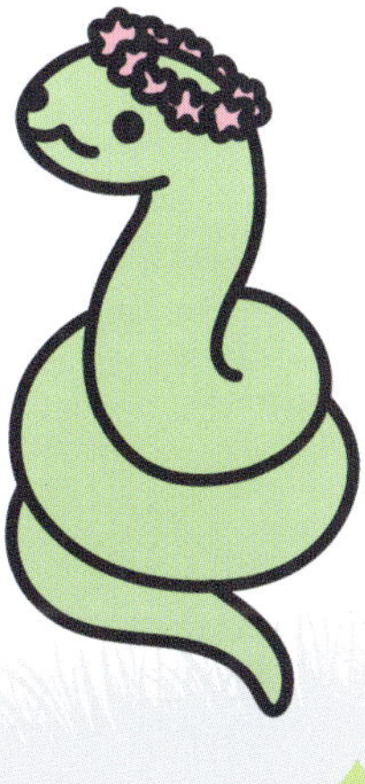

LADYBIRDS

While most ladybirds are red or orange, some types are pink, tan and even blue. Their spots fool predators into thinking they are poisonous.

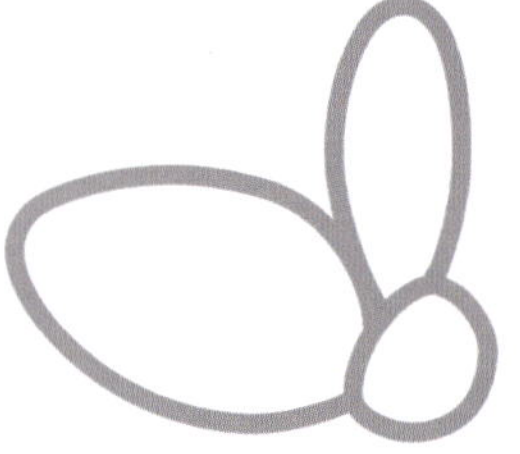

Draw a small gumdrop head and two pointy ovals for wings. The wing closest to you is bigger than the back wing.

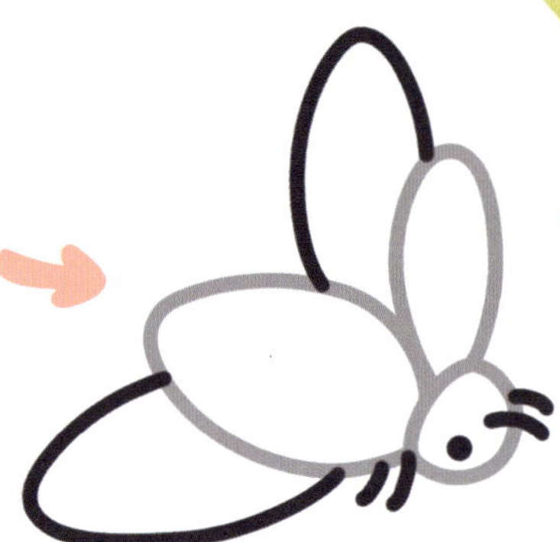

Add more pointed ovals for the inner wings. Add the antennae and an eye.

Finish by adding spots on the front wings and lines on the inner wings.

Stand up

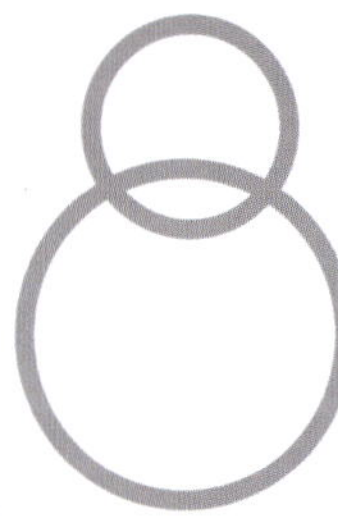

Start with a small circle for a head and a larger circle for the body.

Add two legs and a triangle shape where the bug's wings meet. Add spots, eyes and antennae.

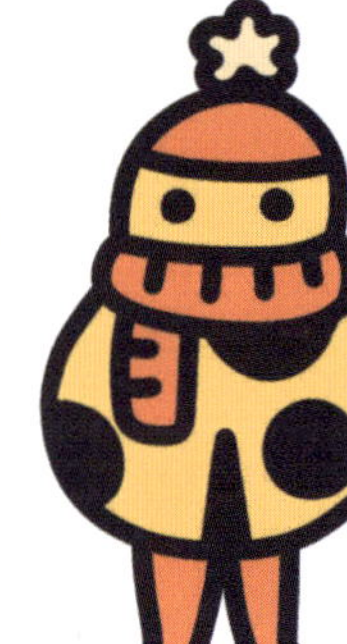

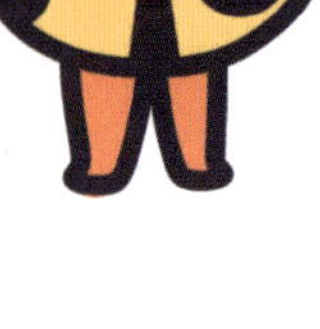

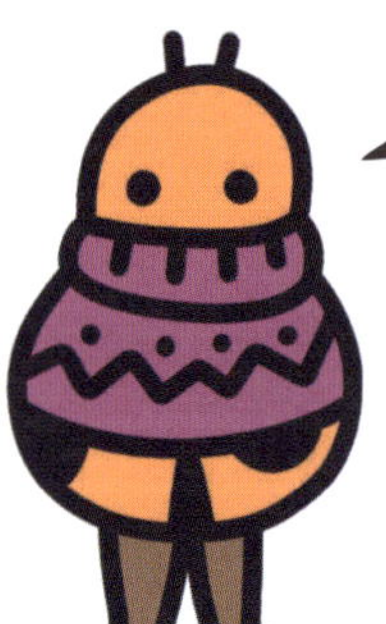

You could give your ladybirds some clothes.

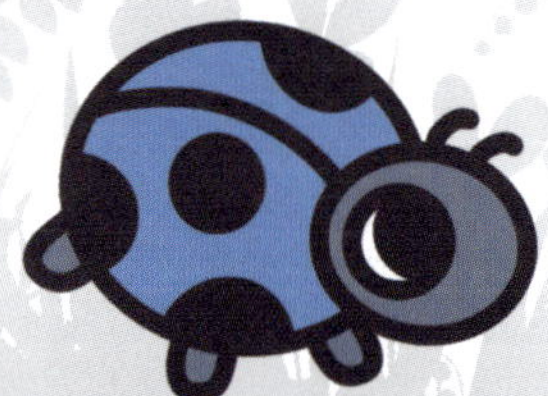

The base of a ladybird consists of mostly circles and ovals.

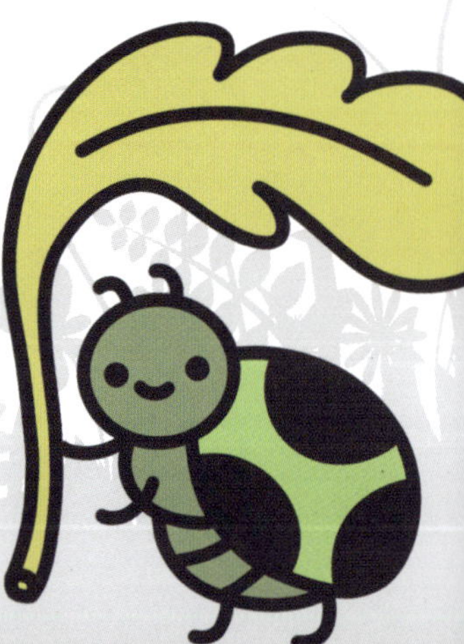

BEES

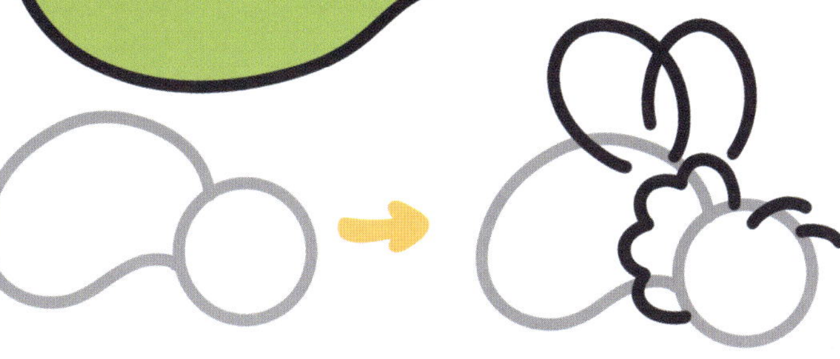

Bees can be drawn in various ways, with base shapes usually consisting of circles and jelly bean shapes!

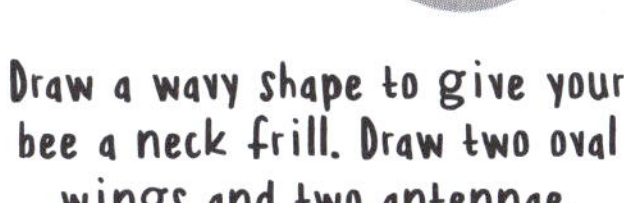

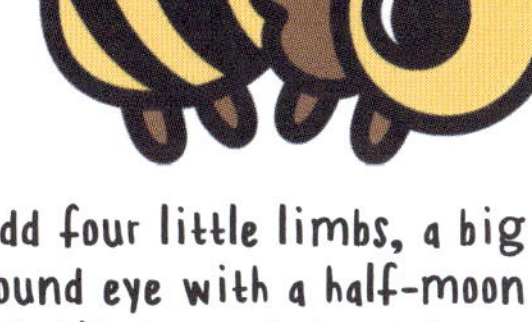

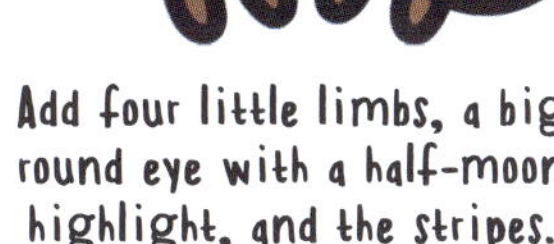

Draw a circle head and a jelly bean body.

Draw a wavy shape to give your bee a neck frill. Draw two oval wings and two antennae.

Add four little limbs, a big round eye with a half-moon highlight, and the stripes.

Simply stripy

You can also draw bees without giving them separate heads.

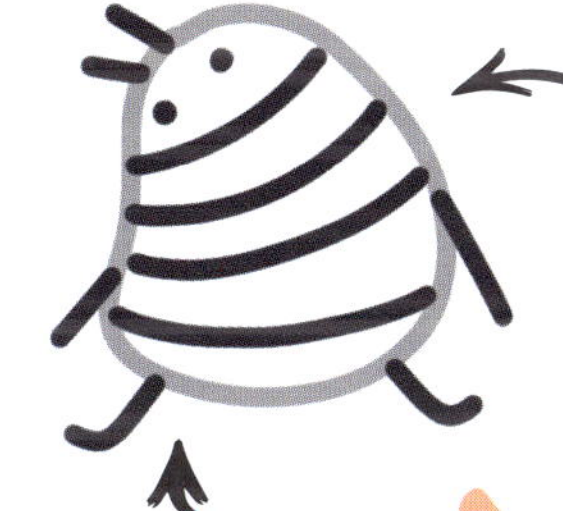

Draw simple line limbs and antennae. Dot in the eyes and add the stripes.

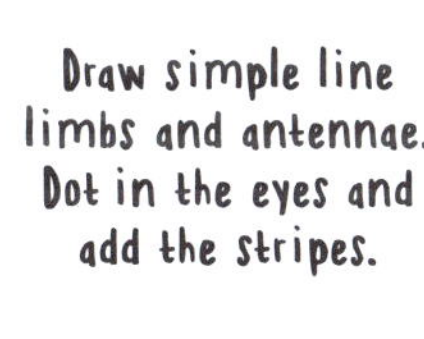

Think of this base as a triangular jelly bean.

Make the wings small and round.

Draw a jellybean and a curved wing.

Add a second wing, stripes and little limbs. You could even add a honeycomb.

WOLVES

Wolves are depicted as the scary bad guy in fairy tales, but we're here to make them lovable and cute!

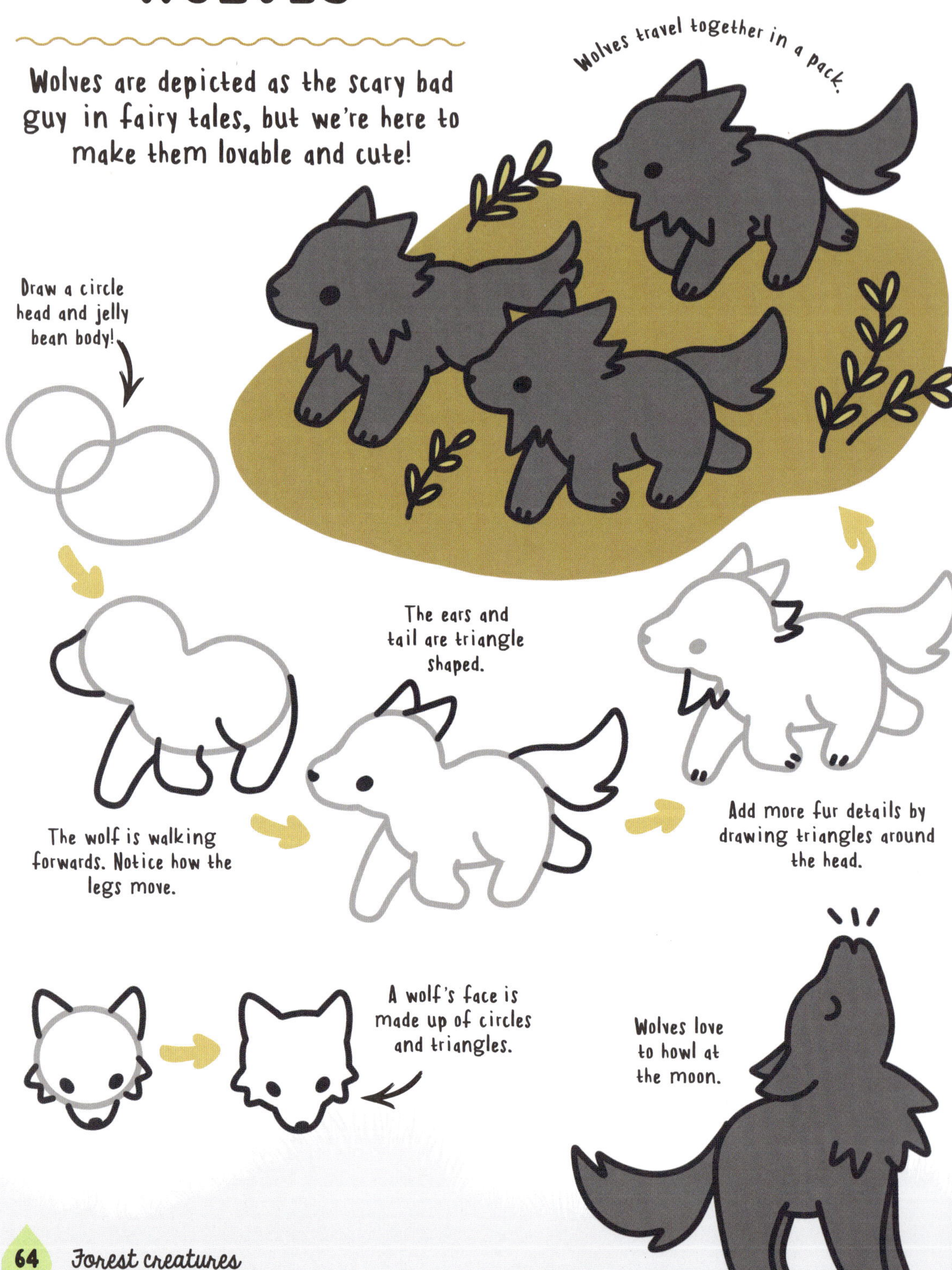

Lone wolf

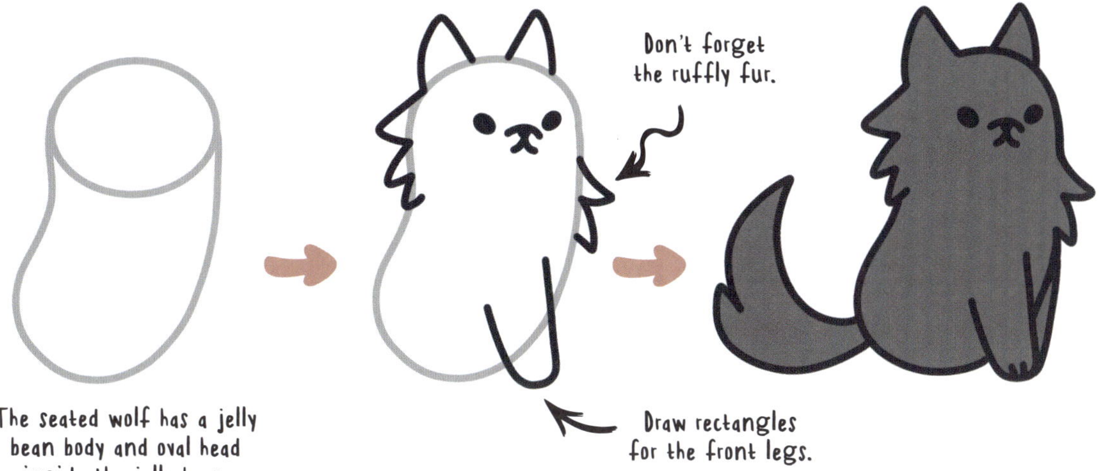

The seated wolf has a jelly bean body and oval head inside the jelly bean.

Sleeping wolf

Draw the front legs extending out and the back legs close to the body.

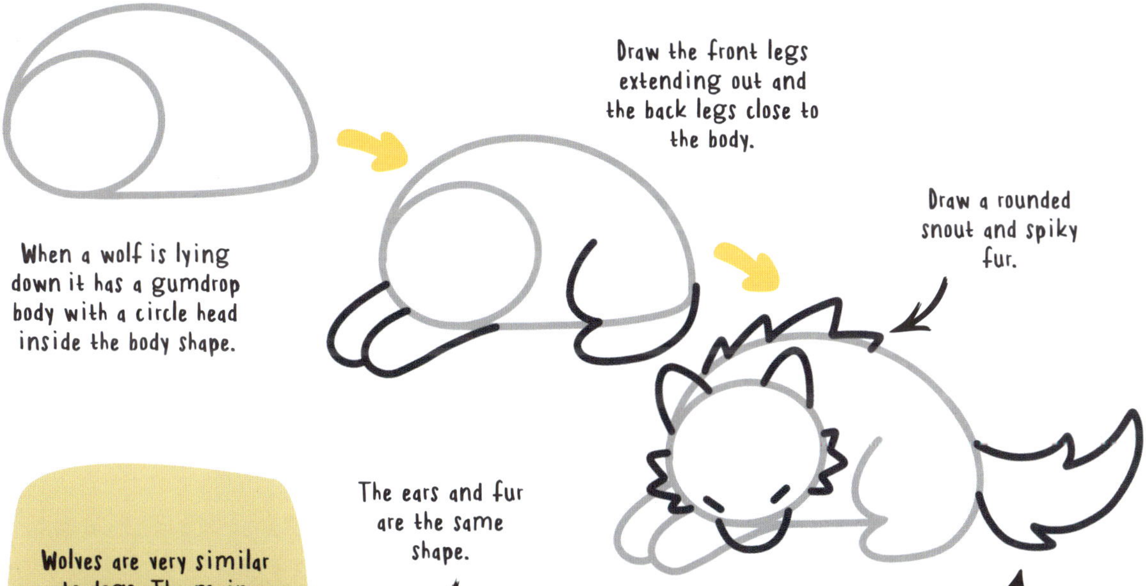

When a wolf is lying down it has a gumdrop body with a circle head inside the body shape.

Draw a rounded snout and spiky fur.

The ears and fur are the same shape.

The fur on the tail also looks spiky.

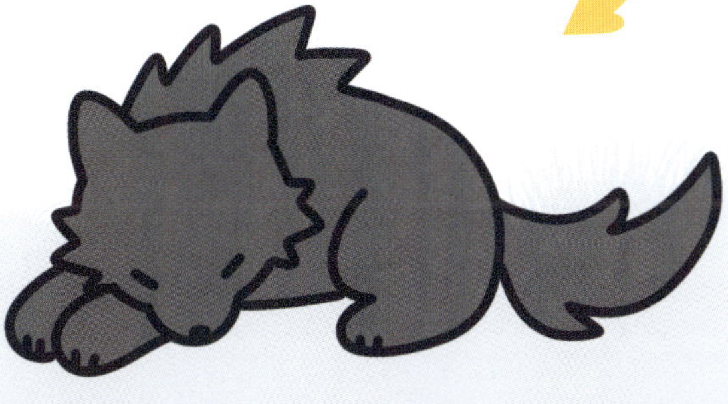

Wolves are very similar to dogs. The main differences are their ruffly fur, long noses and pointy ears.

DEER

Deer are shy creatures, so you'll have to be very quiet if you want to spot one. You can choose to draw your deer with or without antlers.

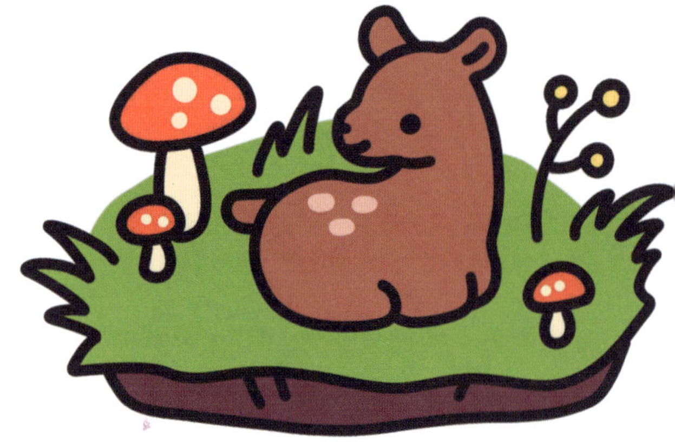

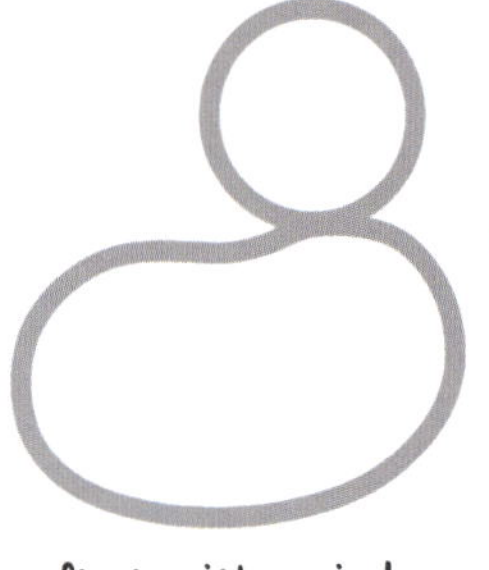

Start with a circle head and a jelly bean body.

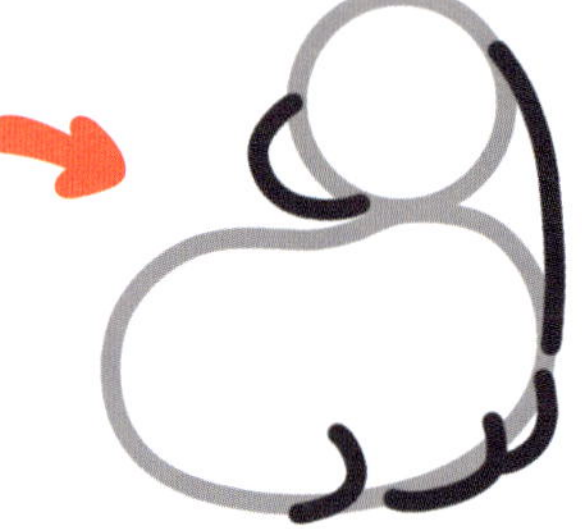

Connect the shapes by drawing the neck. Add curved lines to represent the limbs and snout.

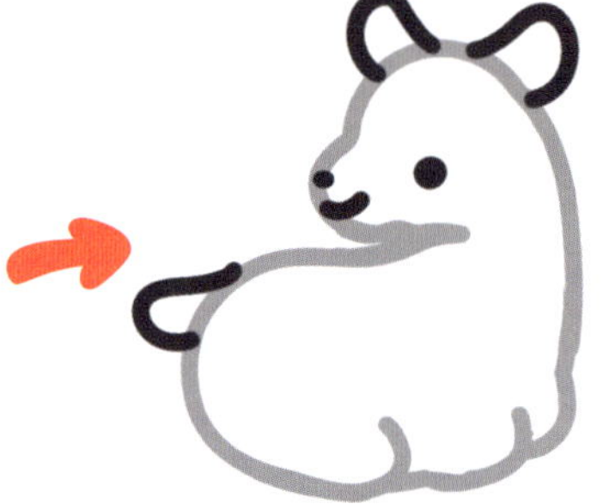

Add rounded ears, a little tail and facial features.

You can add a spotted pattern on the rump if it is a fawn. Adult deer do not always have spots.

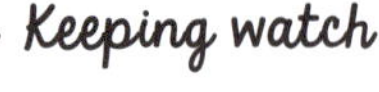

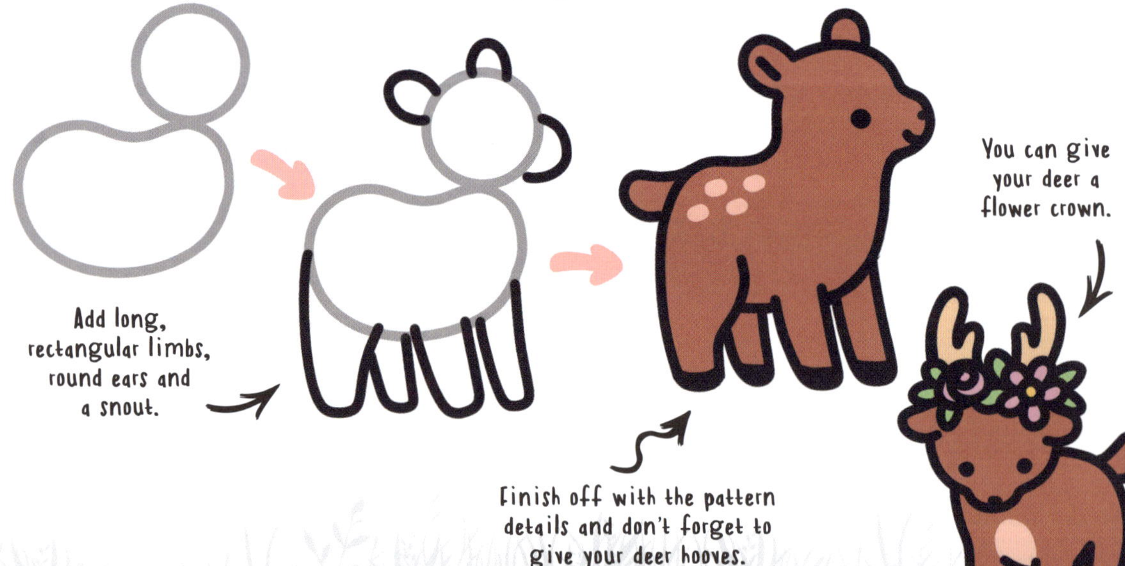

Add long, rectangular limbs, round ears and a snout.

Finish off with the pattern details and don't forget to give your deer hooves.

You can give your deer a flower crown.

Antlers

Antlers are simple to draw when you break them down.

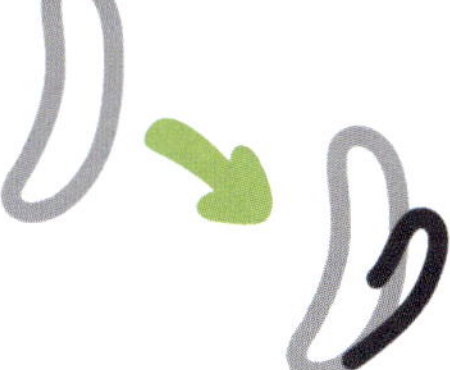

Start with a long stick, then keep adding more stick shapes to the sides.

Deer in action

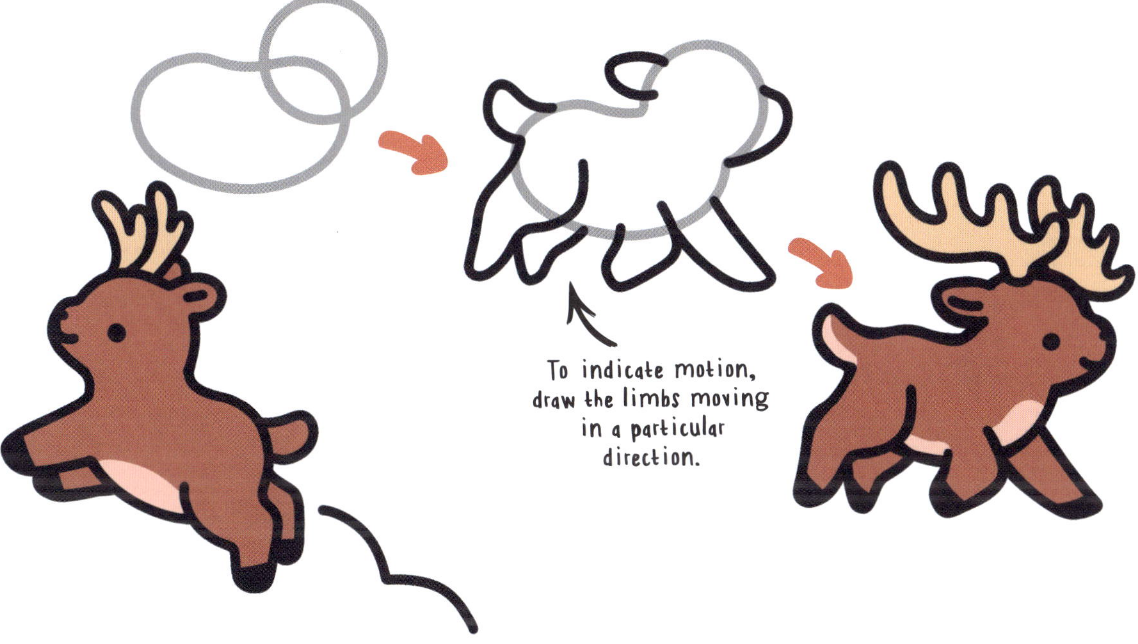

Hiking deer

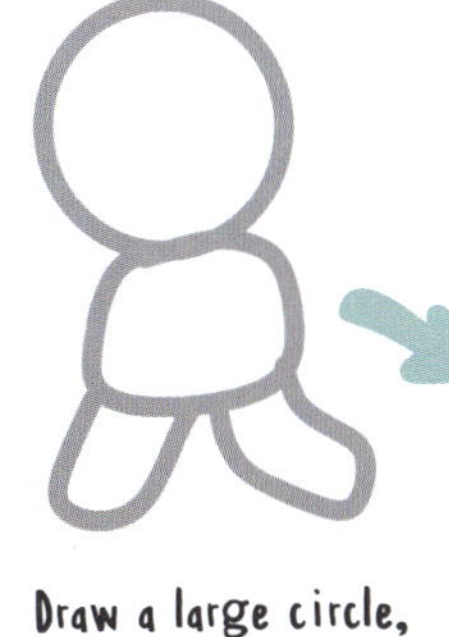

Draw a large circle, a smaller square body and legs.

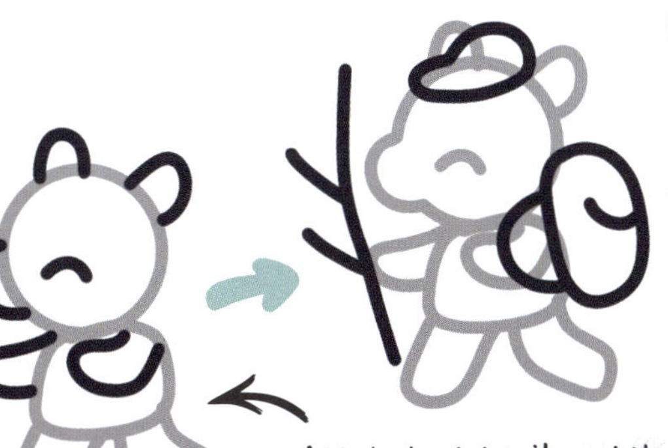

Add the head details and the arms, bending the front one at the 'elbow'.

Give this adventuring deer a cap, walking stick and backpack.

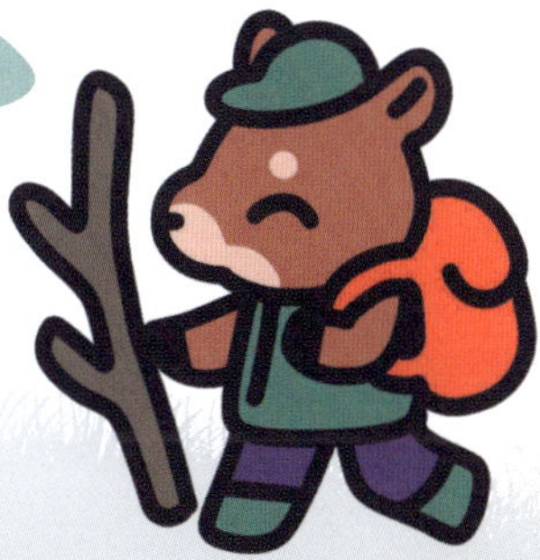

SNAILS

Snails carry their homes on their backs. They're fun to draw because you can decorate their homes with cool patterns or little trinkets.

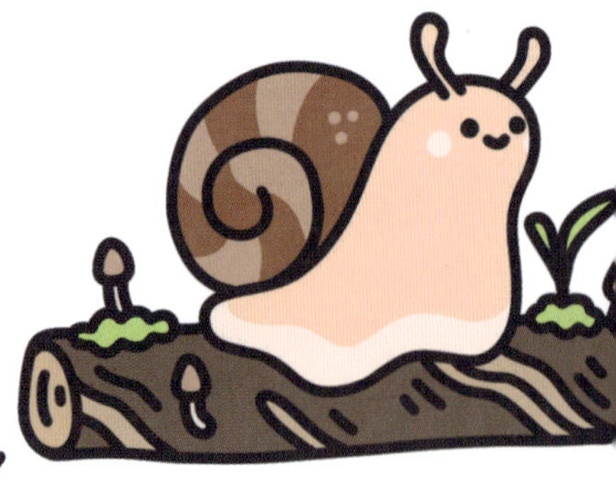

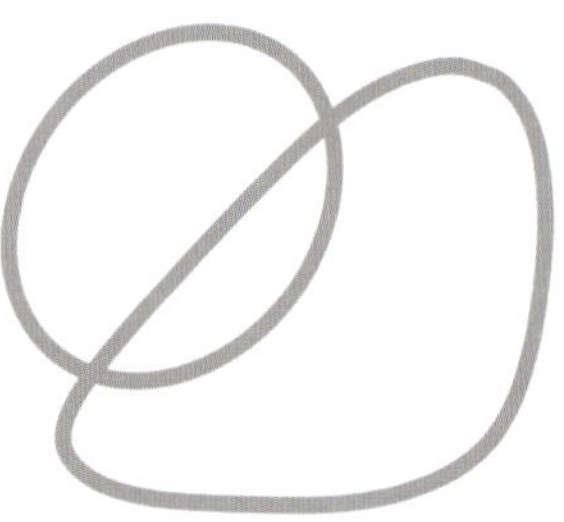

The shell is an oval and the body is a rounded triangle.

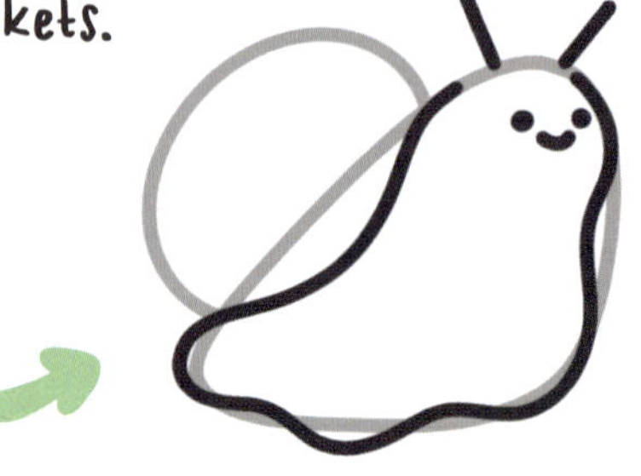

Fill in the rounded triangle with wavy lines to define the body. Add antennae and a face.

Draw a spiral in the shell, then add the shell pattern. Finish by filling out the antennae.

Try drawing different antennae for each snail. They could be short and stubby or long like bunny ears.

Flower shell

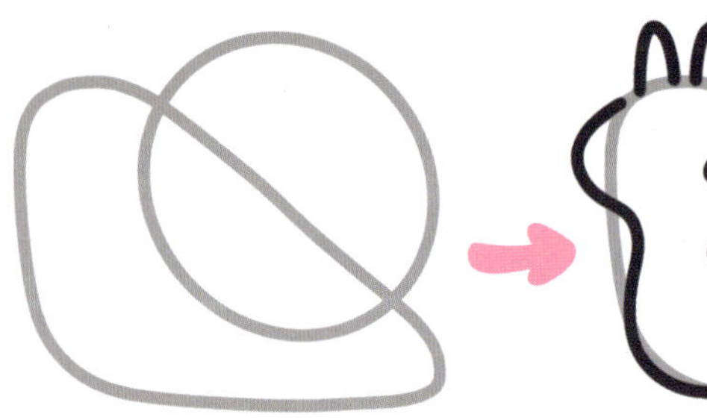

Draw the outline of a flower motif inside the circle shell.

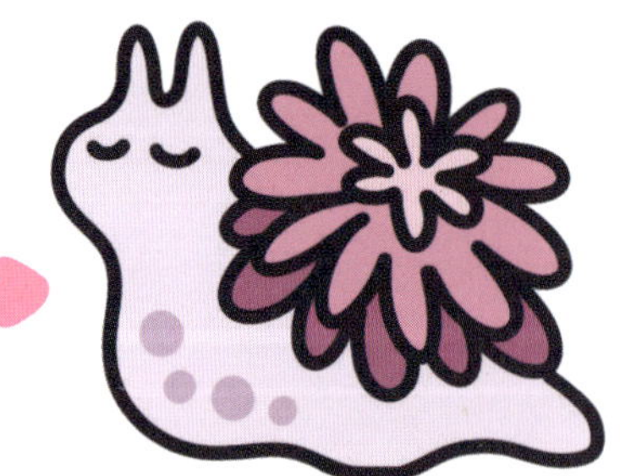

Add two more flower motifs and a pattern on the body too.

Or you could add small flowers to the shell.

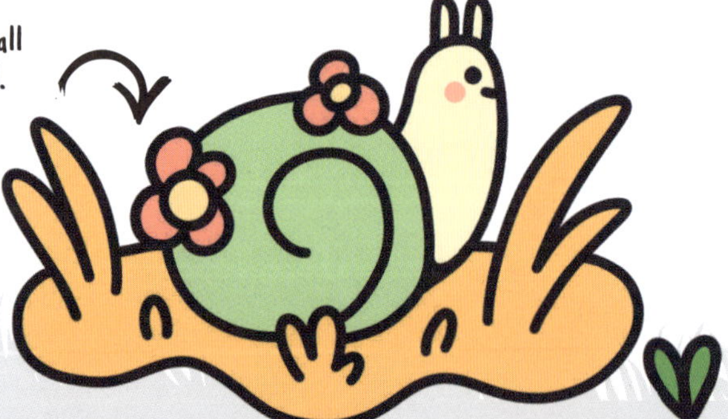

Snail trail

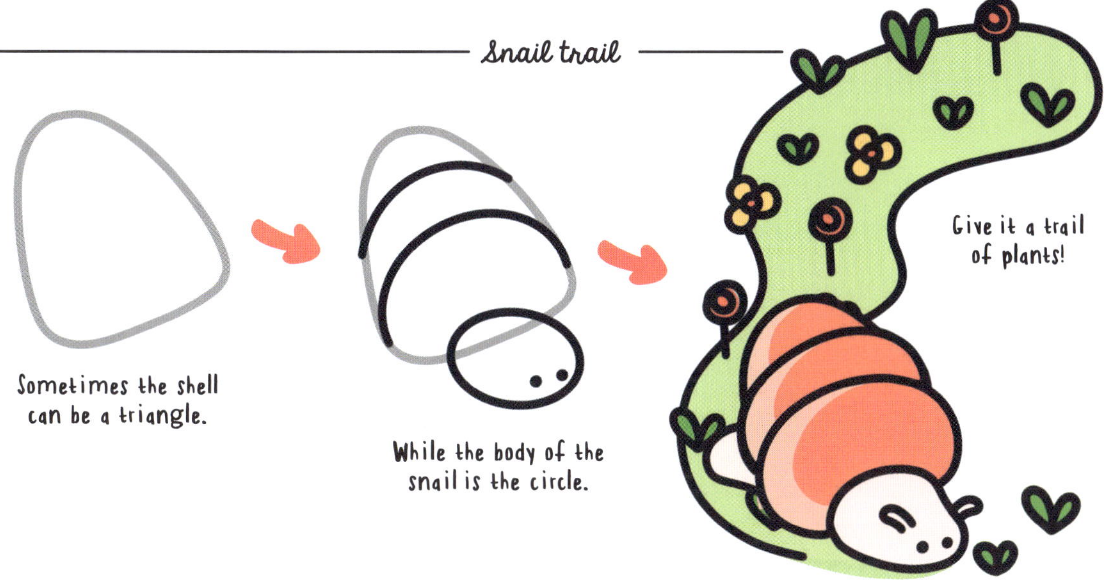

Squashed bodies

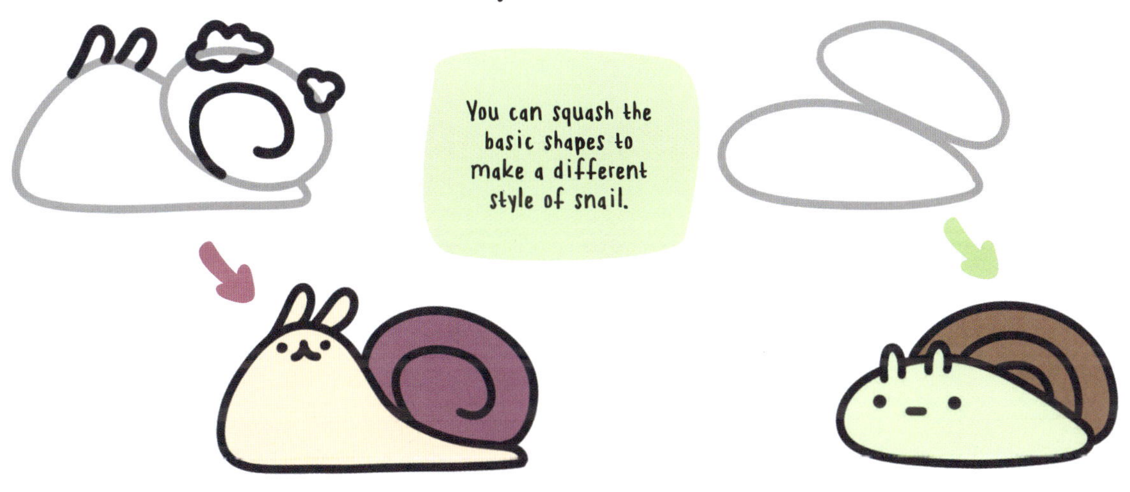

Shell accessories

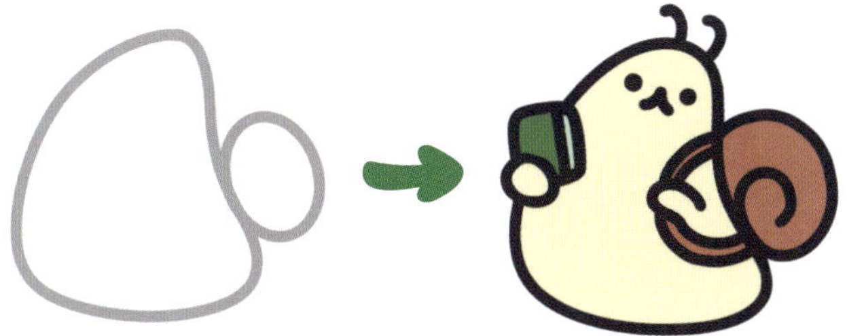

You can make the shell a backpack. Give this studious snail a book too!

BEARS

Bears live in forests and grasslands and need a lot of body fat to get them through the hibernating months. Don't be afraid to draw a really round bear!

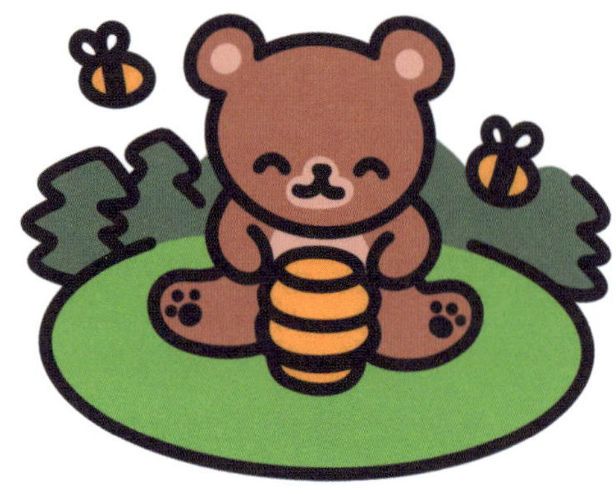

Give your bear a honeycomb to hold, cute paw details and a smiling face.

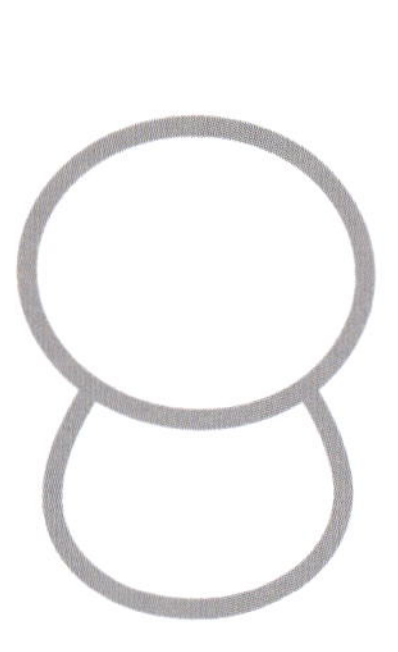

Start with a large oval head and a smaller gumdrop body.

Draw the arms close to the body and the legs pointing outwards and flat on the ground.

Don't forget the little round ears.

Your choice of colour will distinguish what type of bear you are drawing: perhaps a grizzly bear, black bear or a panda? Pandas live in bamboo forests.

Teddy bears

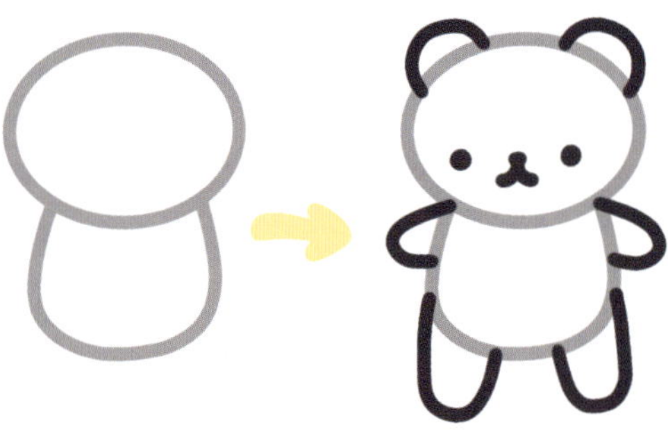

Add legs pointing downwards from the bottom of the gumdrop body.

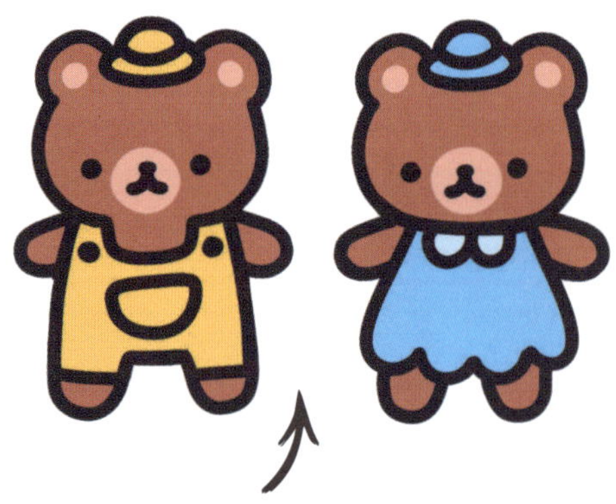

You can give teddy bears character by adding cute outfits.

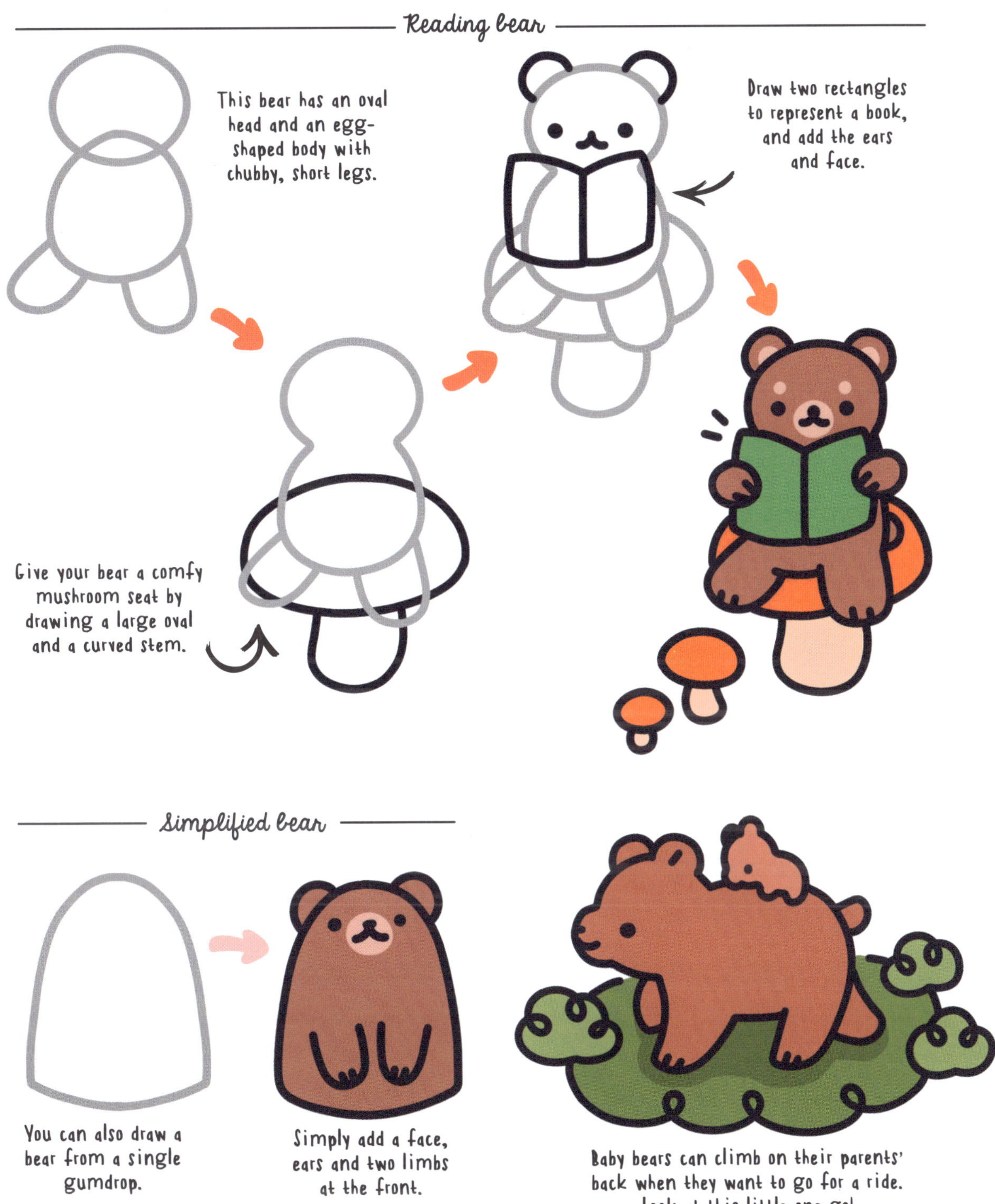

Reading bear

This bear has an oval head and an egg-shaped body with chubby, short legs.

Give your bear a comfy mushroom seat by drawing a large oval and a curved stem.

Draw two rectangles to represent a book, and add the ears and face.

Simplified bear

You can also draw a bear from a single gumdrop.

Simply add a face, ears and two limbs at the front.

Baby bears can climb on their parents' back when they want to go for a ride. Look at this little one go!

SQUIRRELS

Squirrels can jump more than ten times their length, and use their fluffy tails like parachutes that help them to balance when they leap from tree to tree.

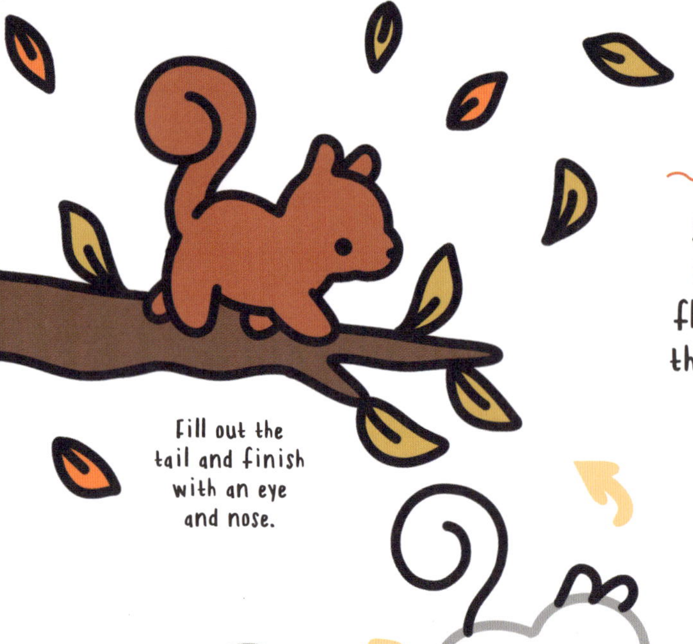

Fill out the tail and finish with an eye and nose.

Start with a round head and oval body.

Add the limbs, snout and ears. To start the tail, draw a curved line that spirals at the top.

Spiral

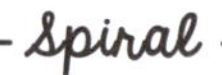

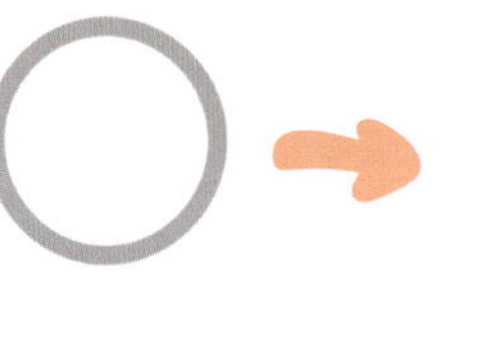

One way to draw a spiral is to start with a circle . . .

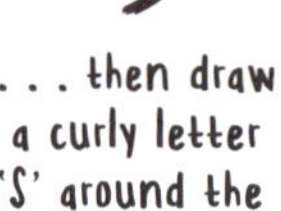

. . . then draw a curly letter 'S' around the circle.

Collecting nuts

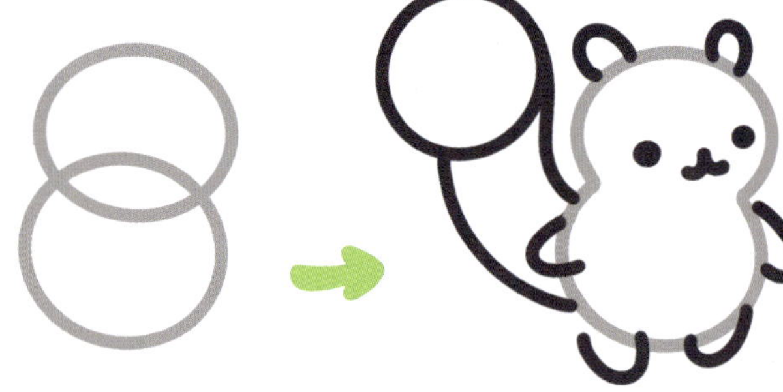

For this squirrel, start with an oval head and a circle body.

This time try a bushy tail. Add short limbs, ears and a face.

Give your squirrel a sweater and acorn-inspired hat, and a basket to collect nuts in.

Climbing squirrel

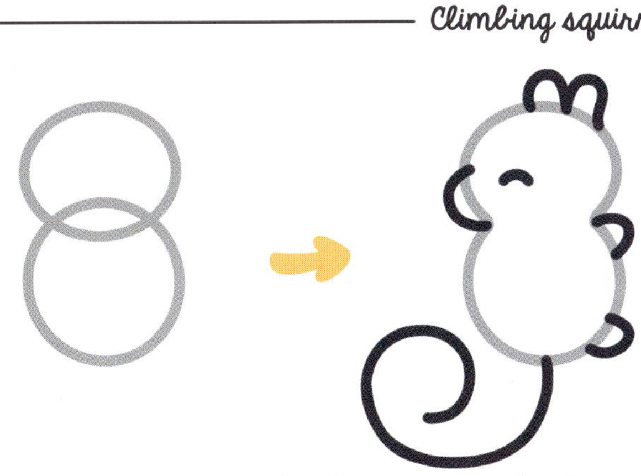

Give this squirrel a closed eye, a spiral tail . . .

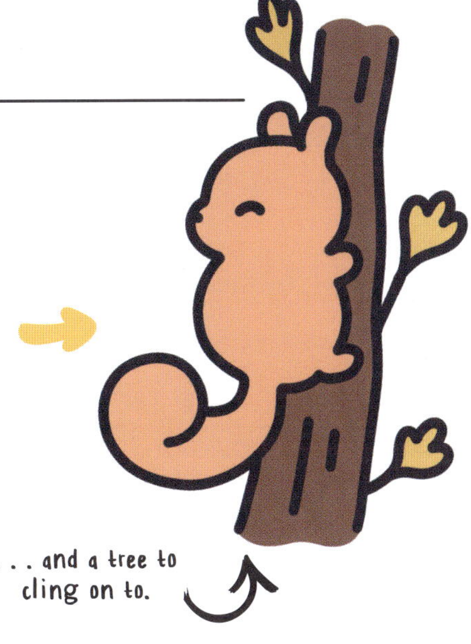

. . . and a tree to cling on to.

Seated snack

Add short limbs, a little snout and two small ears.

For a seated squirrel, start with two circles. The head circle is off-centre to the body.

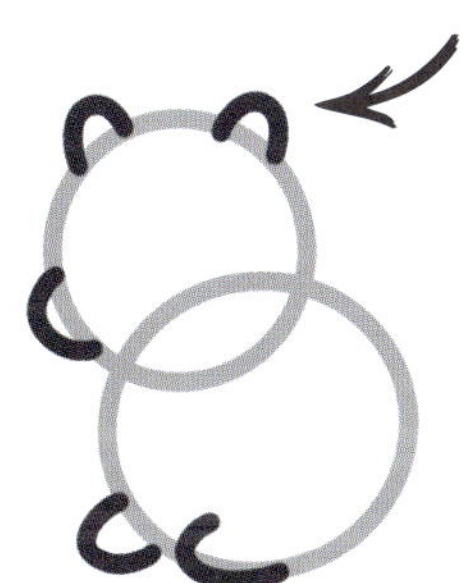

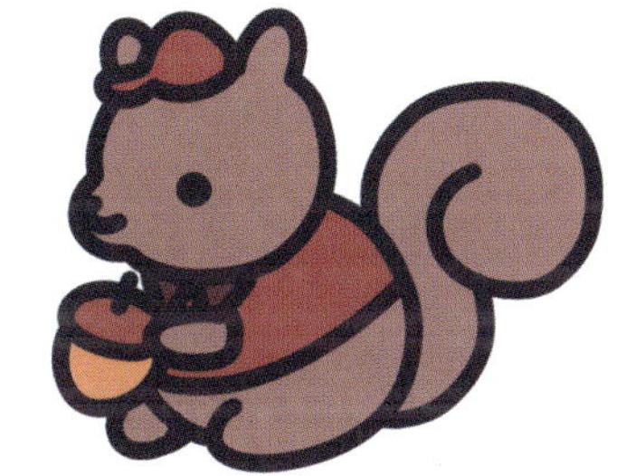

Add a spiral tail, a cap and sweater, and a yummy acorn snack!

Sleepy squirrel

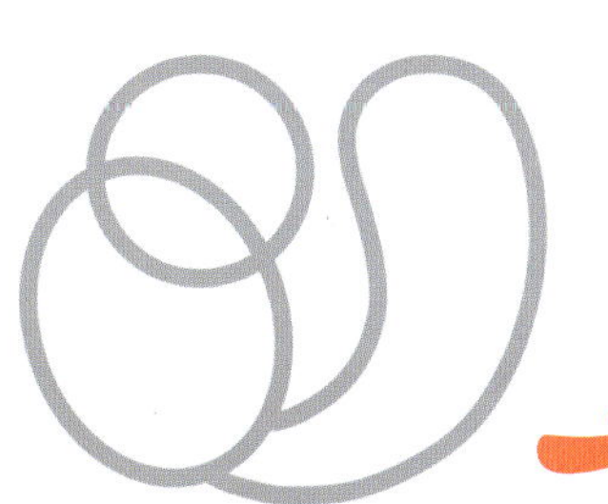

This sleepy squirrel has a bushy tail with a circle head and oval body that curve towards the tail.

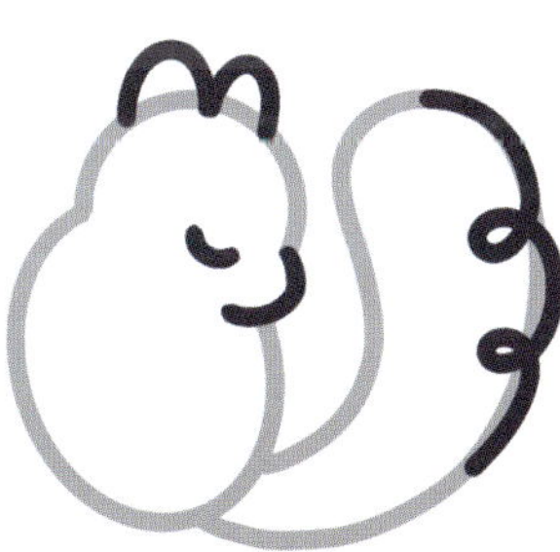

Give the tail a fluffy feel by adding some loops.

Surround your squirrel with acorns and leaves.

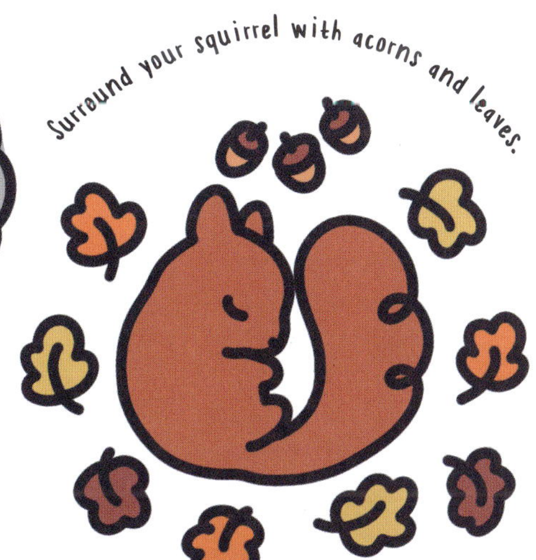

FROGS AND TOADS

Many types of frog live in jungles around the world, and toads like the dank undergrowth of woodland environments. You can make different types of frogs and toads using these simple shapes.

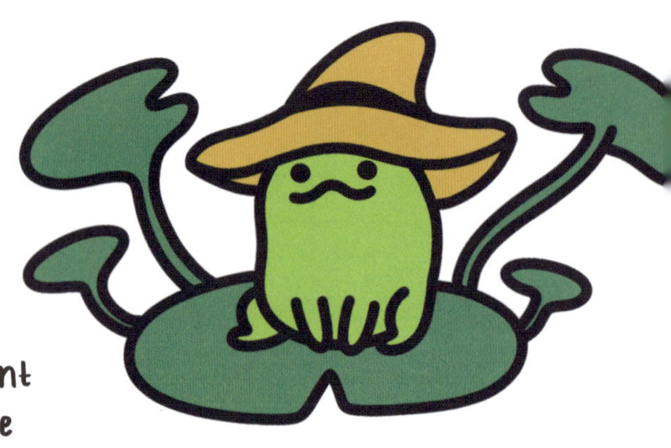

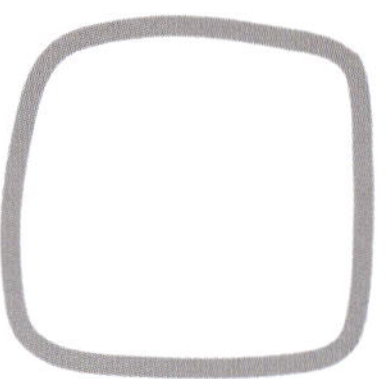

Start by drawing a square.

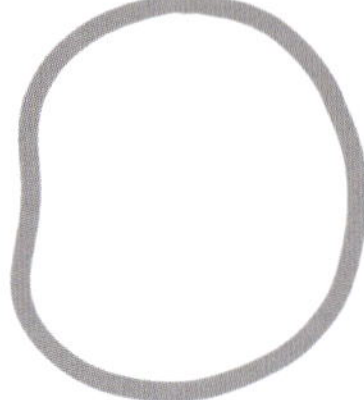

Draw a jelly bean.

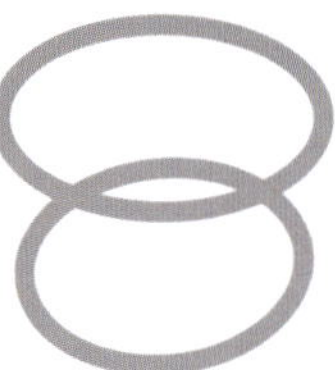

Draw an oval body and a thinner, wider oval head.

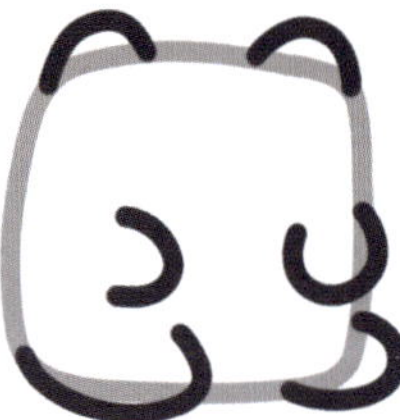

Add stubby, round limbs and draw the eyes at the top corners of the square.

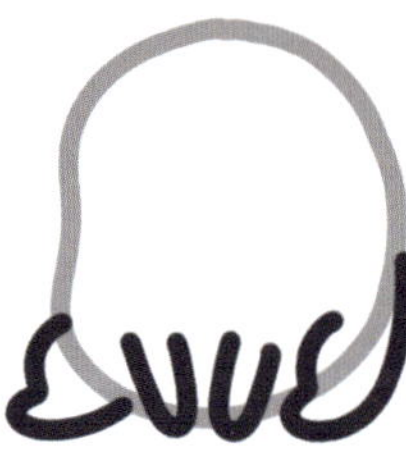

Draw the limbs at the bottom of the body.

Add thin limbs and eyes close together on top of the head.

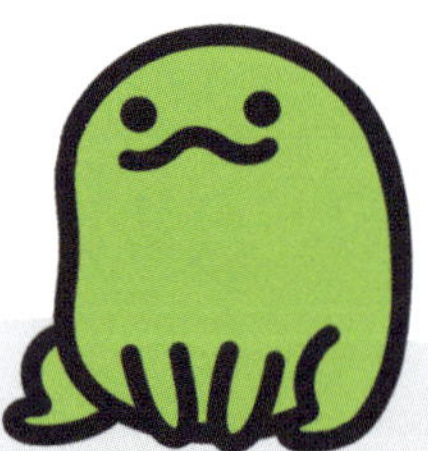

Rain-forest frog

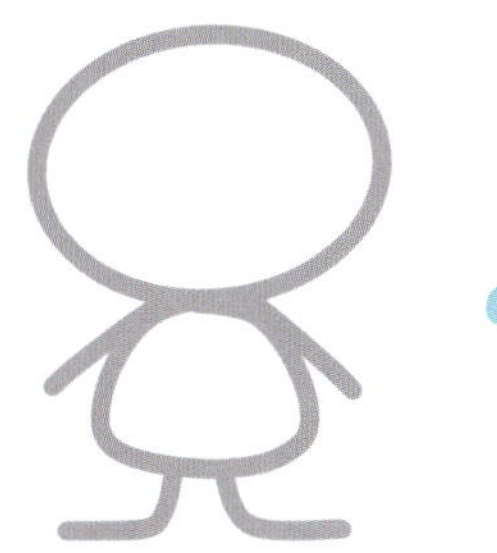

Start with a large oval head and a smaller gumdrop body. Add lines for the limbs.

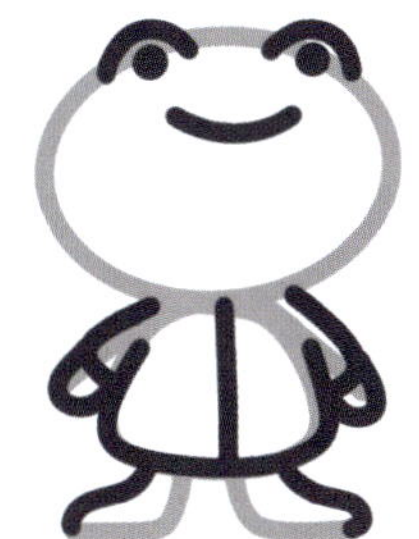

Put the eyes at the top of the head and fill out the limbs. Give your rain-forest frog a raincoat.

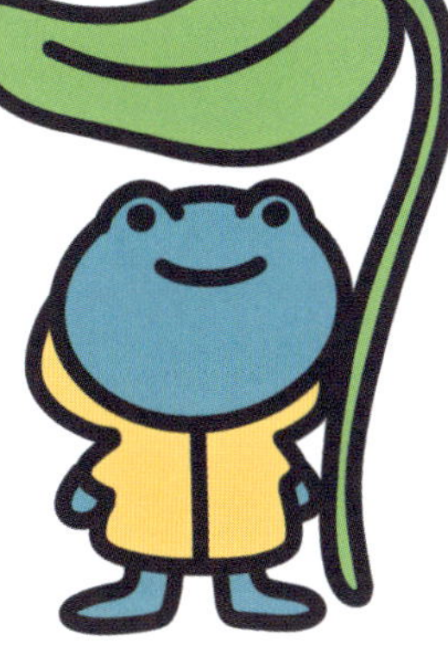

Draw a big leaf for your frog's umbrella.

Stubby toad

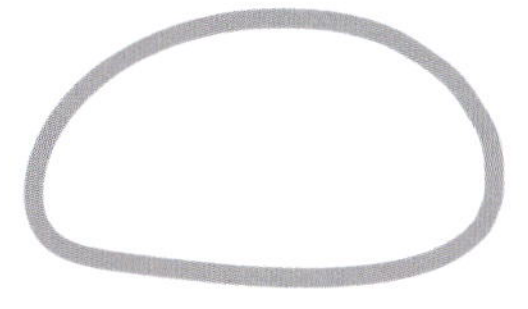

Did you know that toads have shorter legs than frogs? Start this toad with a rough semi-circle.

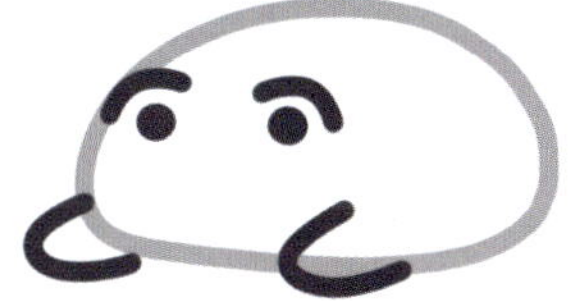

Add limbs in front of the body. Dot in the eyes and add a curved line above each eye.

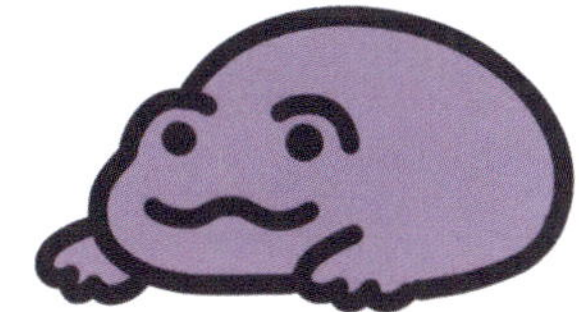

Add a mouth and the toe details.

Floating frog

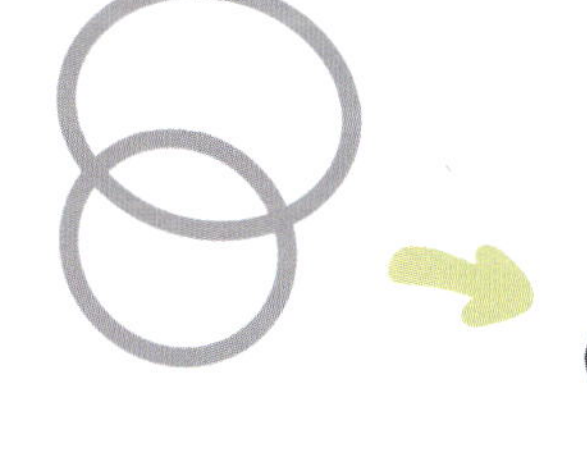

This frog is chilling out. Start with an oval head and a smaller circle body.

Draw the limbs spread out like a star shape, and the eyes closed.

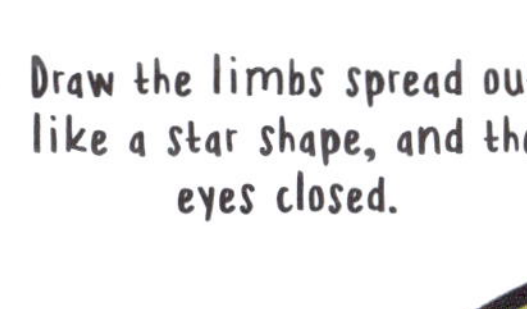

To draw a lily pad, start with a circle, then 'cut out' a triangle.

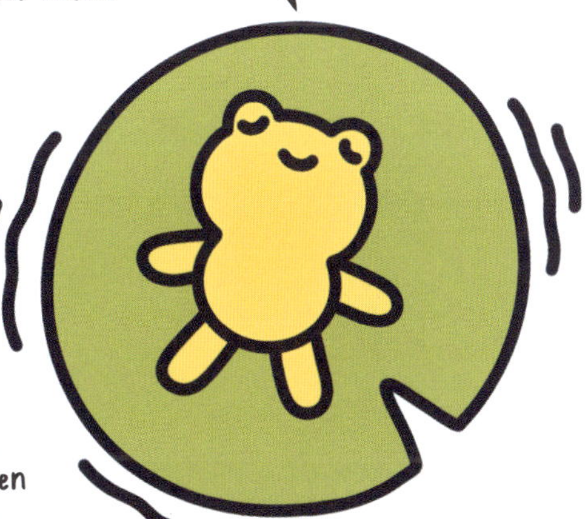

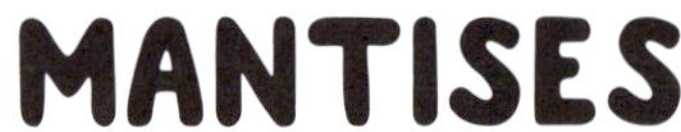

MANTISES

Mantises are insects well known for their folded praying arms, which is why they are also known as praying mantis.

Draw a tall semi-circle for the body and a wide egg shape for the head. Draw a curved line to begin the top limb and a zigzag for the lower limb.

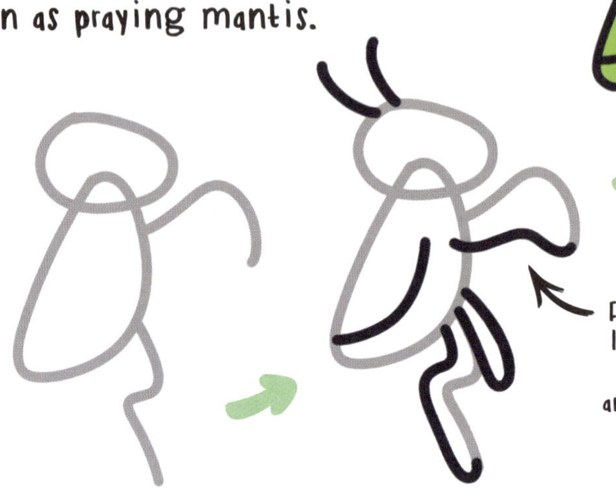

Fill out the limbs. Add antennae and a wing.

Look at me!

You can use the same shape for the 'arms', but draw them outstretched.

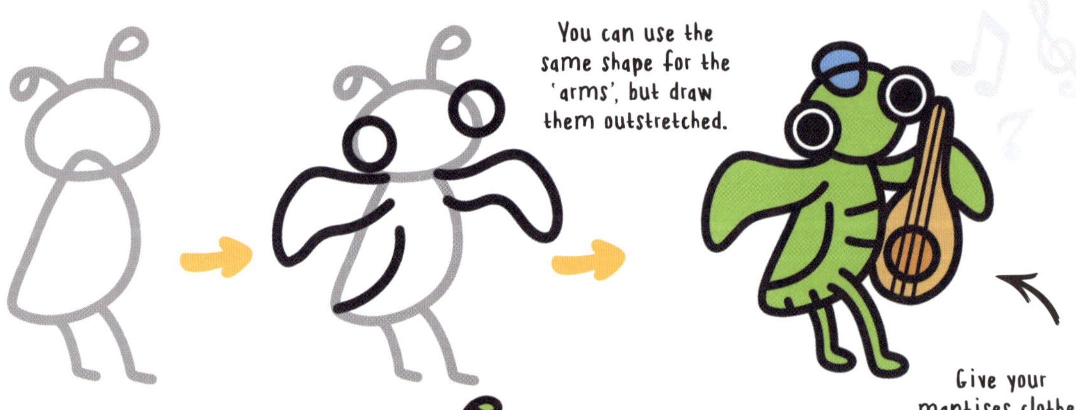

Give your mantises clothes to wear or things to hold.

To draw a mantis with its head facing you, simply adjust the shape of the head.

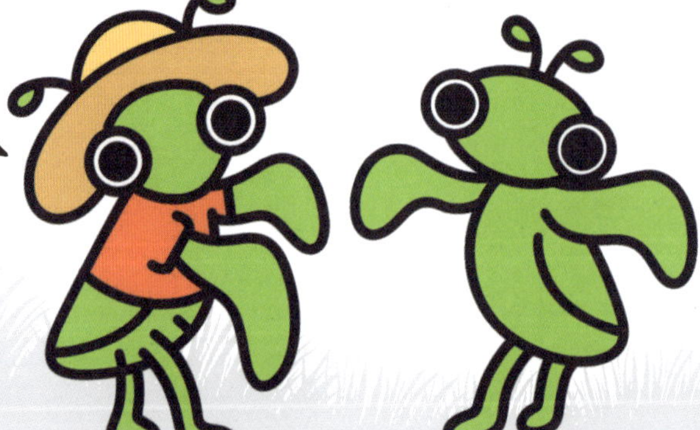

Draw the eyes sticking out from the sides of the head.

ROLY-POLY BUGS

Roly-poly bugs have a hard outer casing like armour, and can roll up into balls to protect themselves from predators.

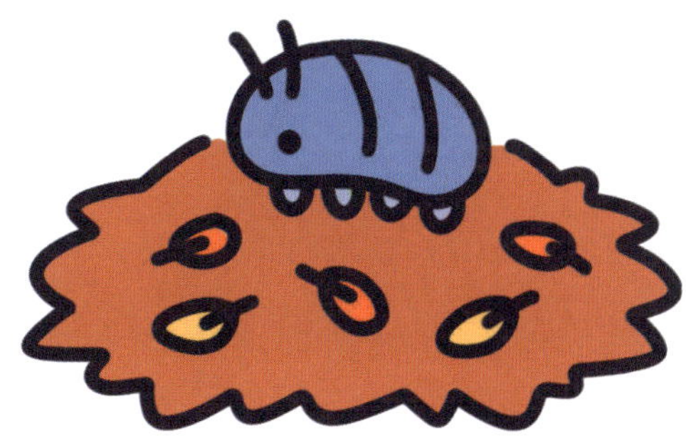

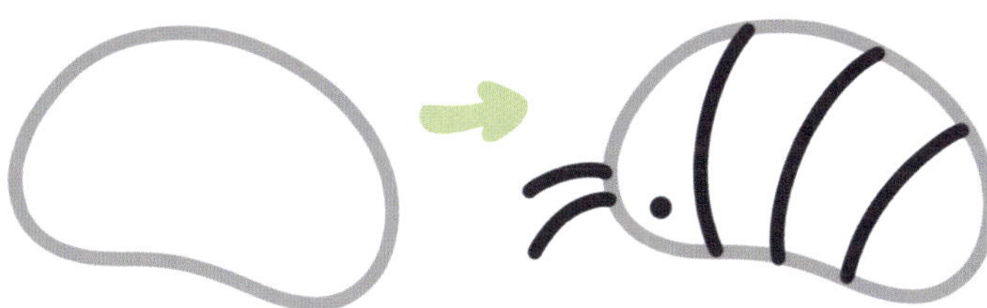

Start with a simple jelly bean.

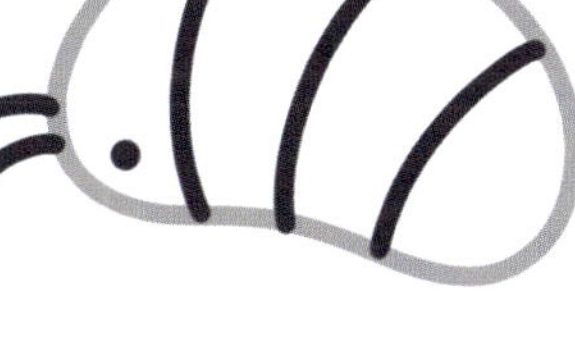

Add in curving horizontal lines and dot in an eye. Add two antennae.

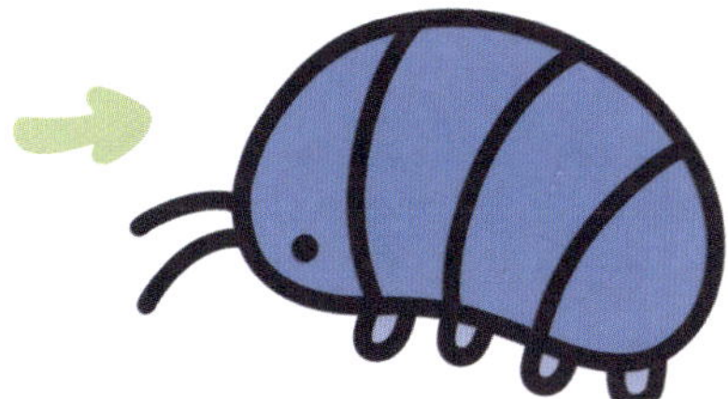

Finish by adding the little legs.

Roll away

Draw an oval with horizontal lines.

Add the legs, antennae and flowers.

When roly-poly bugs curl up into a ball, they can roll around and travel quickly!

The base of the rolled-up pose is a circle.

NATURE DOGS

Nature dogs have evolved to suit their environment. In winter, nature dogs grow thick fur, while in spring and summer their coats can become flowery or leafy.

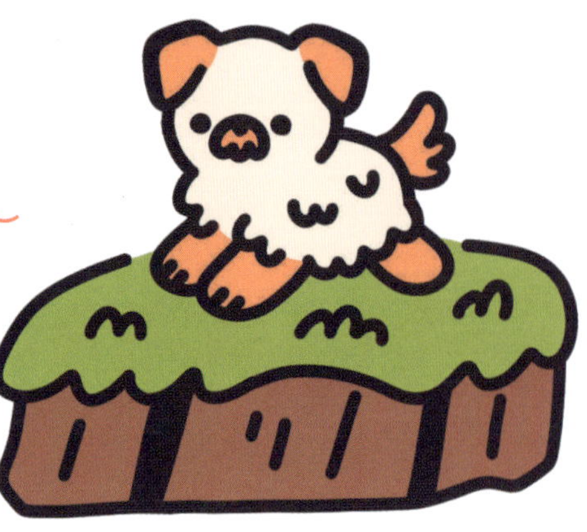

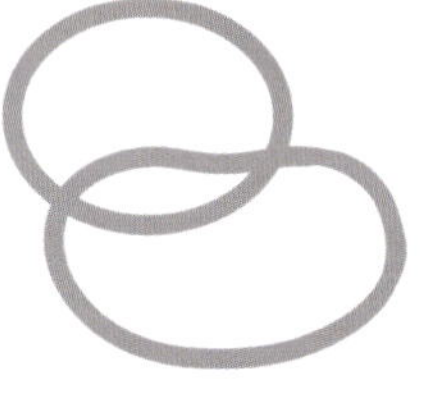

Draw a circle for the head and a jelly bean body.

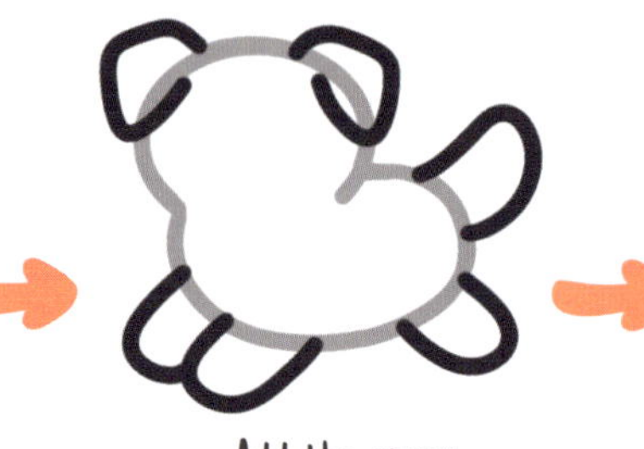

Add the curvy ears and limbs.

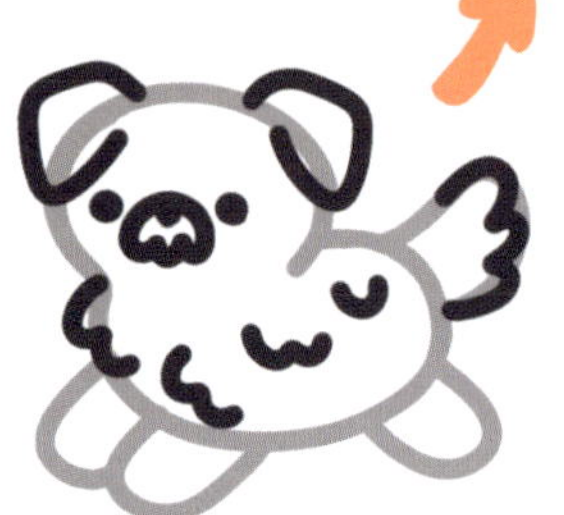

Finish with lots of wavy lines for the fuzzy fur.

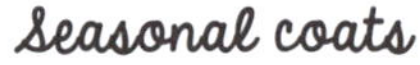

Seasonal coats

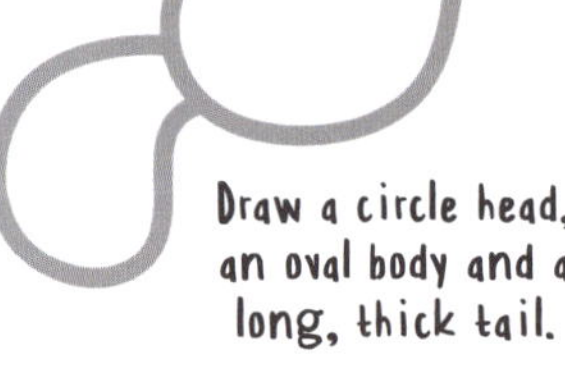

Draw a circle head, an oval body and a long, thick tail.

Add the curvy ears and just two limbs, plus a fuzzy detail on the head.

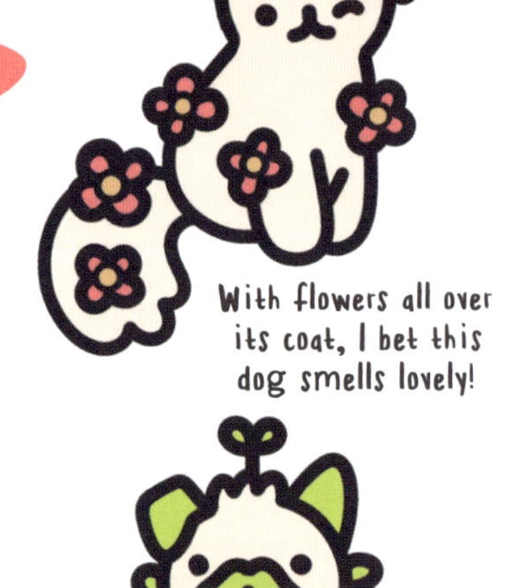

With flowers all over its coat, I bet this dog smells lovely!

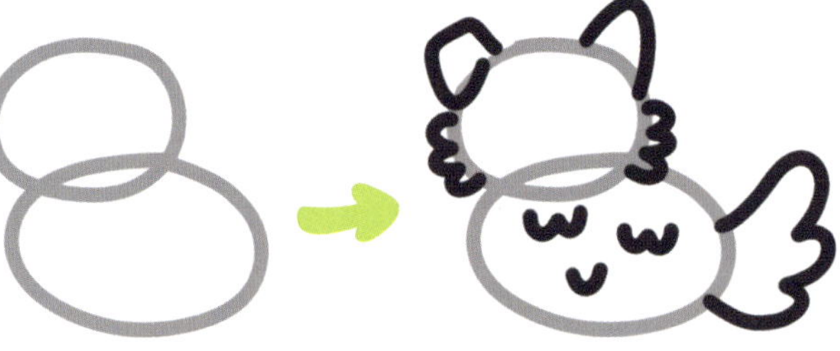

Start with two ovals for this lying-down pose.

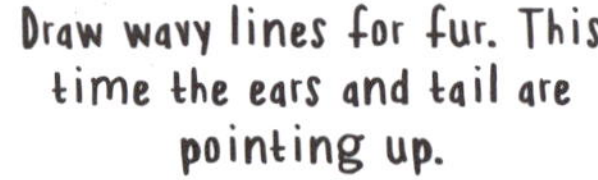

Draw wavy lines for fur. This time the ears and tail are pointing up.

Add a leafy moustache and leaf details all around.

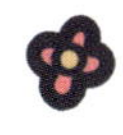

Rainy-day dog

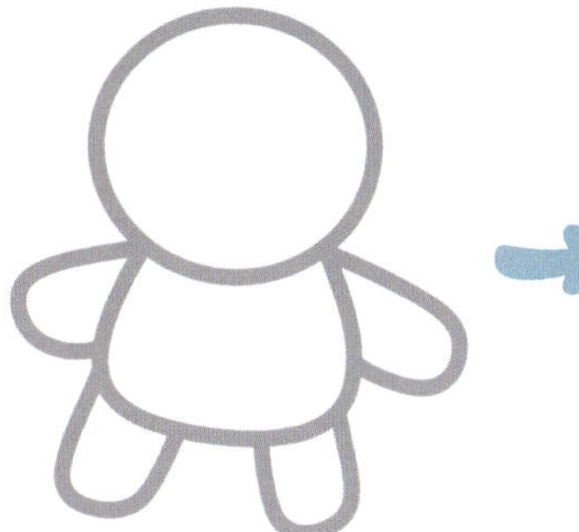

Draw a circle head and a gumdrop body. Add the limbs.

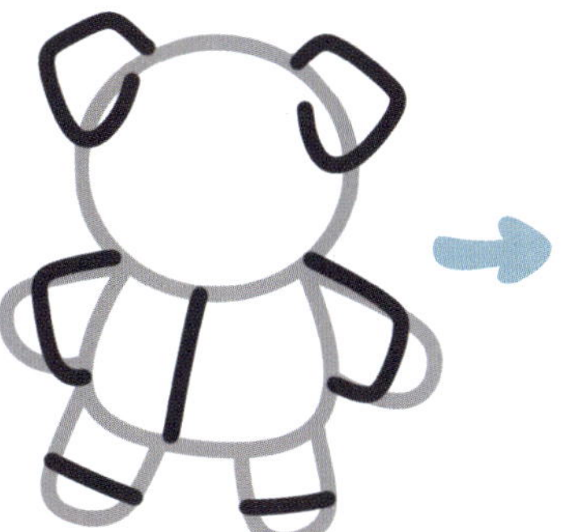

Just a few lines indicate the trousers and jacket. Add the ears.

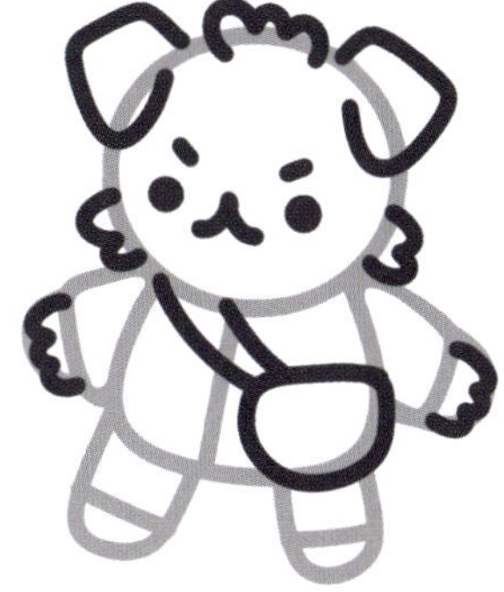

Draw in some fuzzy details, a useful little bag and the facial features.

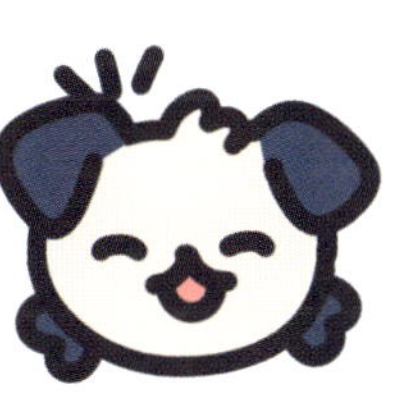

Happy face

You can even have fun dressing your nature dogs, to protect them from the rain or sun.

Surprised face

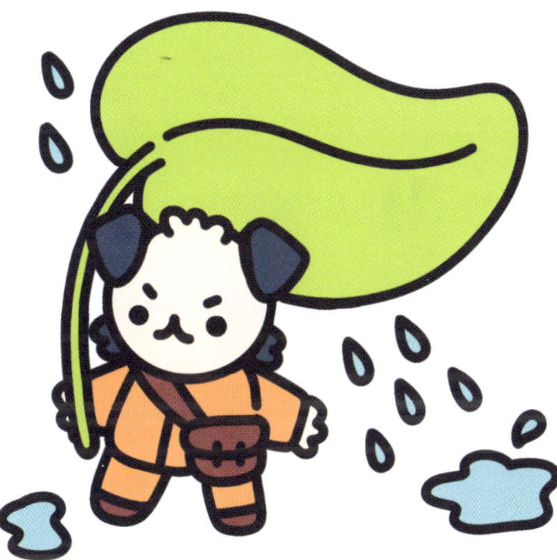

Forest fashion

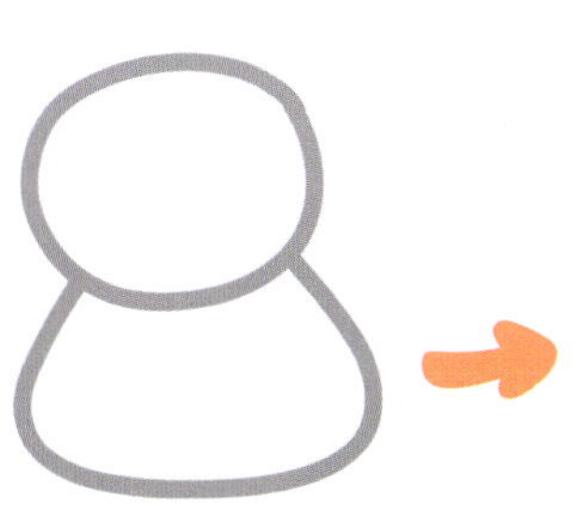

Squash up the gumdrop body.

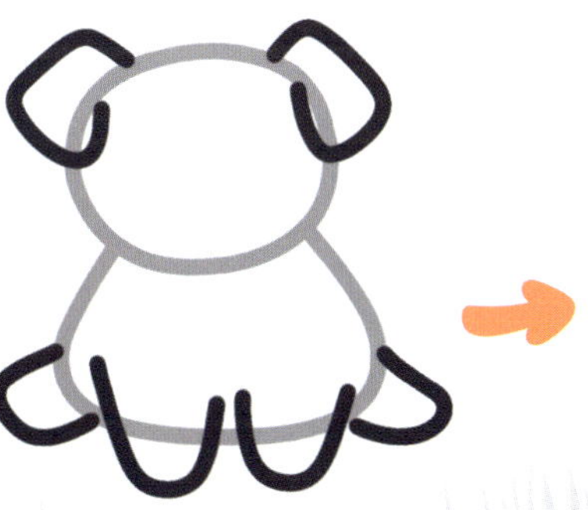

Notice how the back legs point outwards.

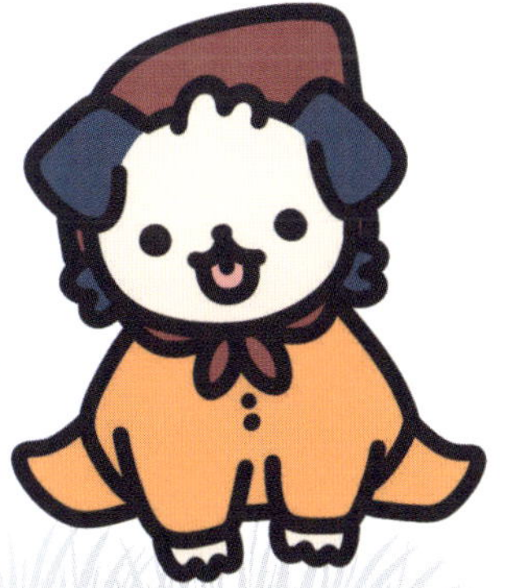

A few simple lines and dots are all that is needed to indicate the clothes.

UNICORNS

Unicorns can be quite shy, so forests are great places for them to live.

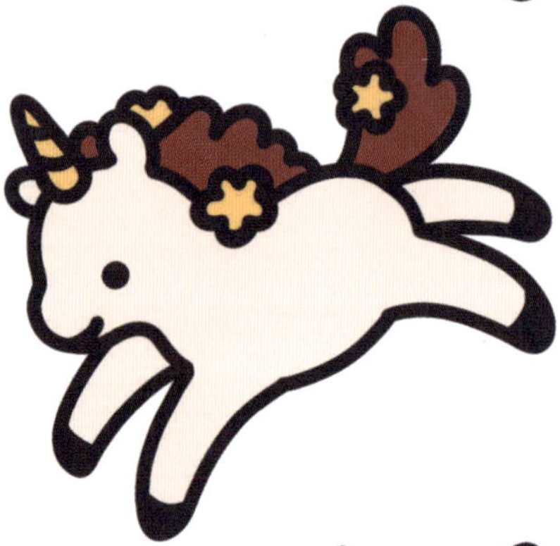

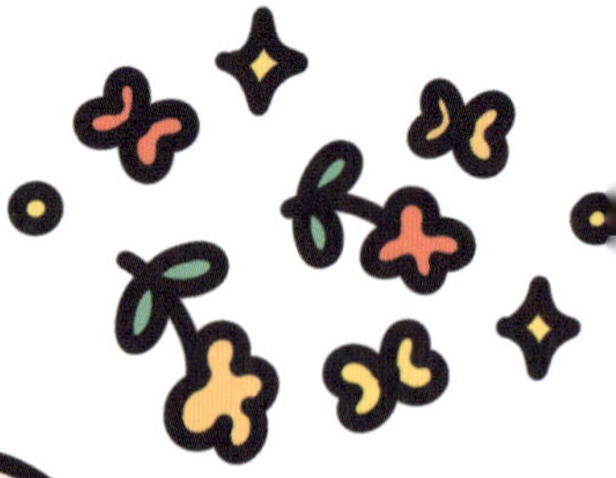

Add flower decorations too, if you want!

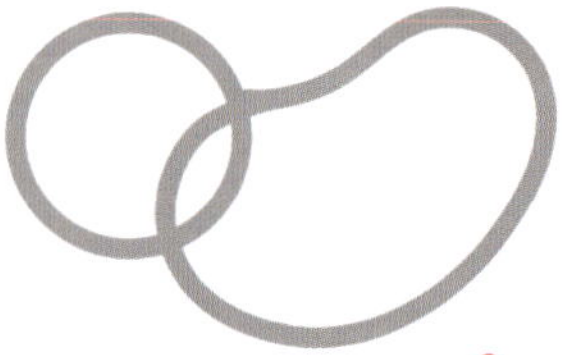

Start with a circle head and a jelly bean body.

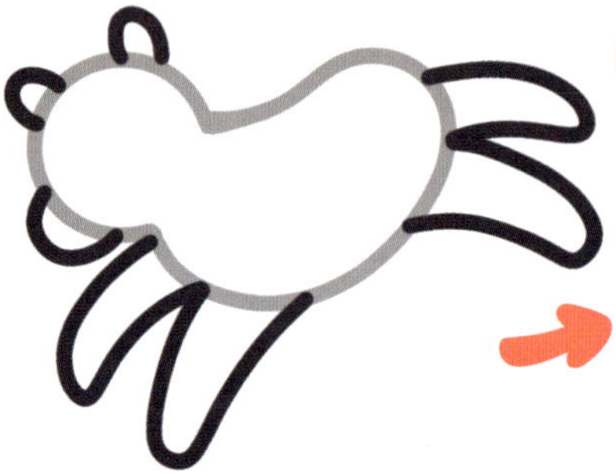

When in a jumping pose, the limbs are curved rectangles. Add ears and a nose too.

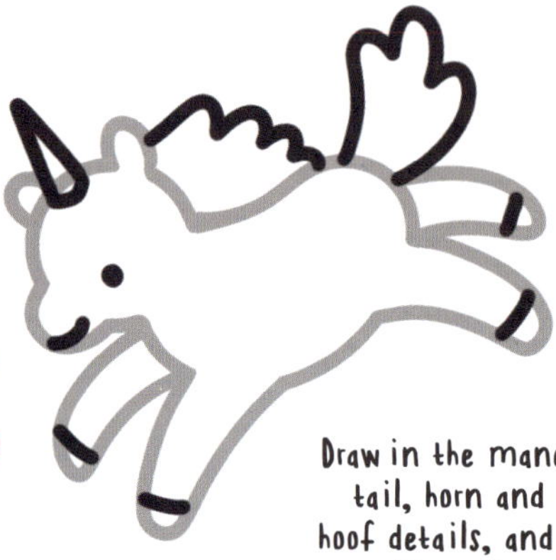

Draw in the mane, tail, horn and hoof details, and a smiling face.

Floral calm

Make the mane and tail big and bushy looking.

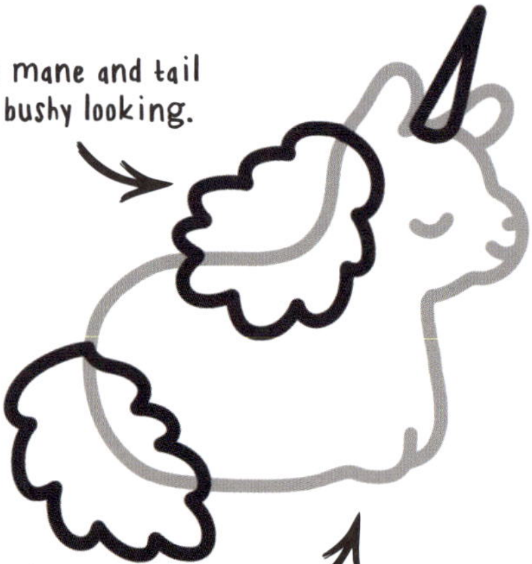

Add flowers to the mane and tail, and colour them green to look like leaves.

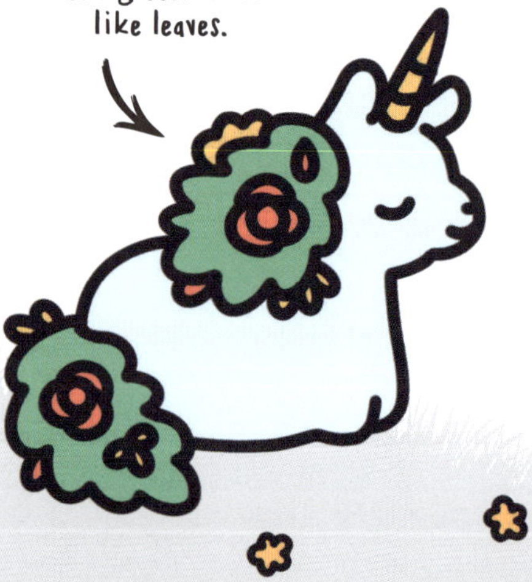

The legs of a seated unicorn are tucked under the body.

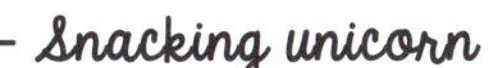

Snacking unicorn

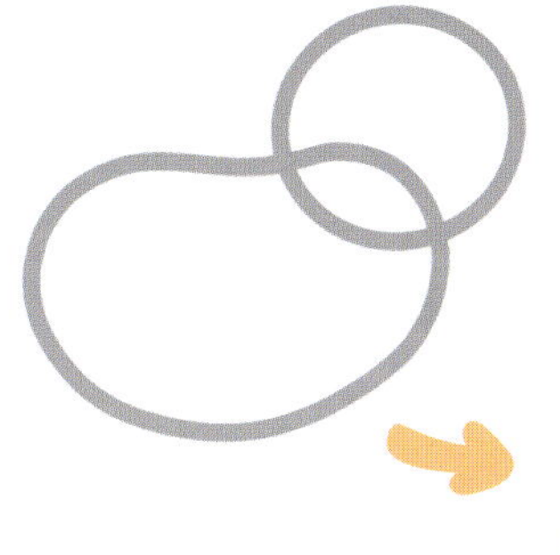

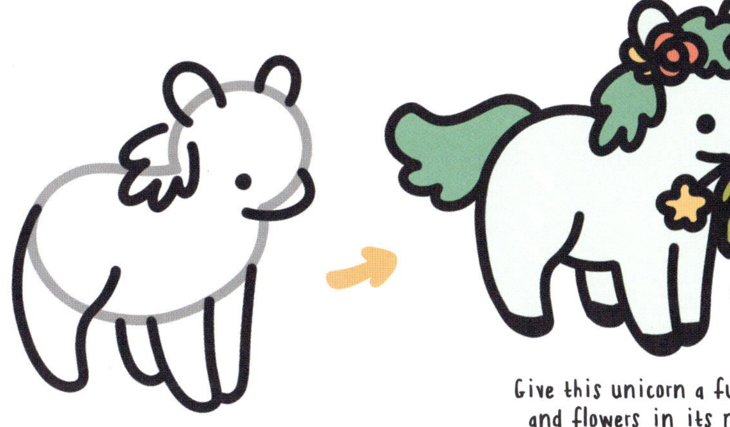

Add rectangular and curved legs to the jelly bean body.

Give this unicorn a full tail and flowers in its mane and in its mouth. Yum!

Out for a stroll

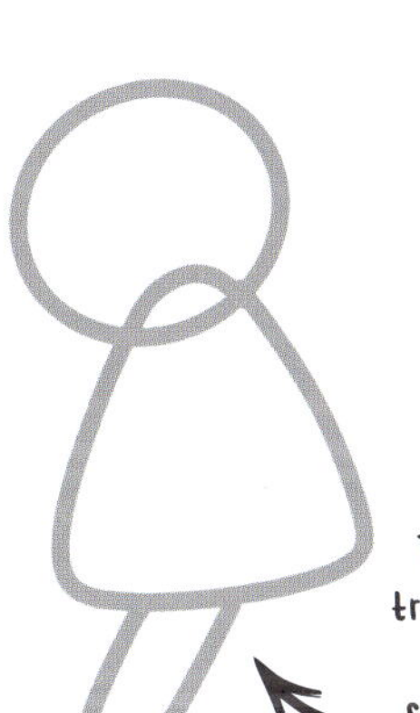

This time draw a triangle body shape, round head and straight front leg.

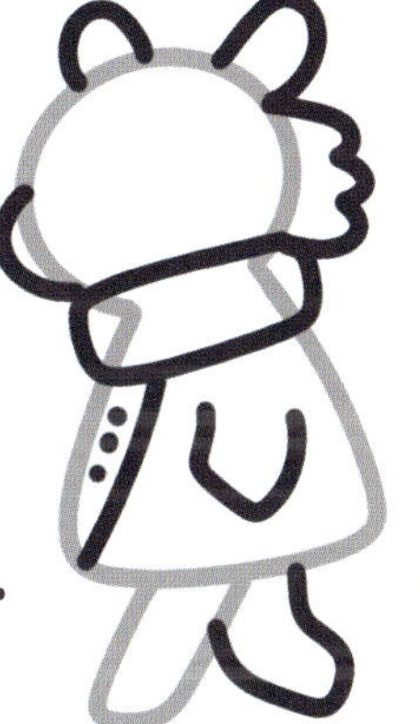

Bend the back leg to show the unicorn is walking. Give your character a warm coat and scarf.

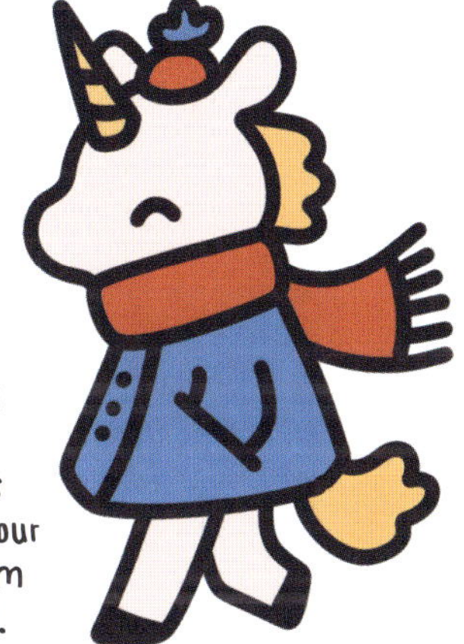

Mini unicorn

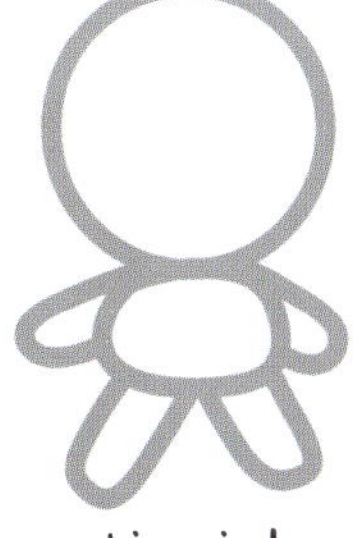

Draw a big circle and a squashed oval body. Add the little limbs.

Add the nose, tail and a cool outfit.

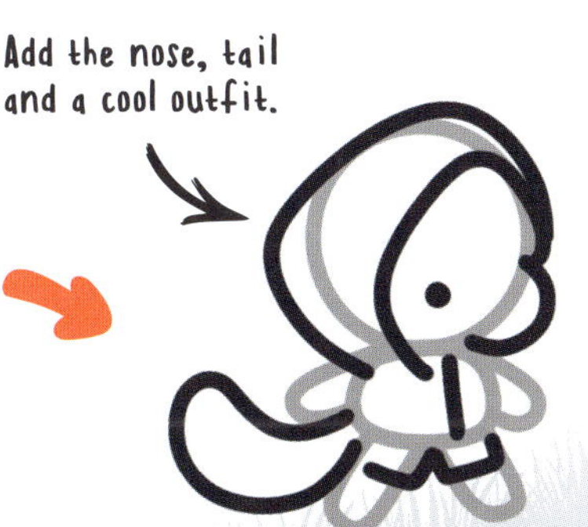

The ears stick out from the hood.

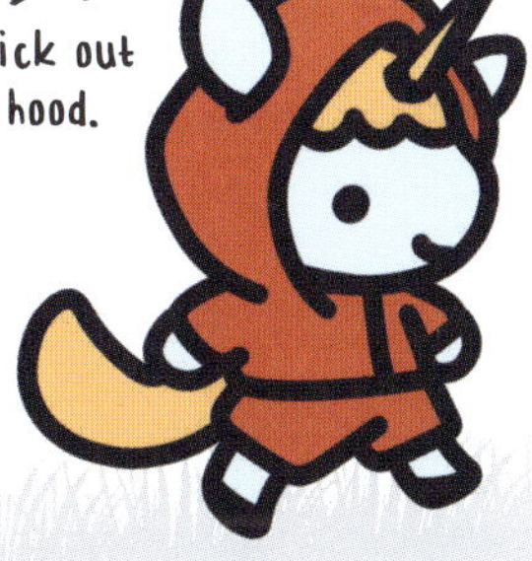

DRAGONS

Dragons have evolved over thousands of years to suit their environments. Sometimes their colours help them with camouflage.

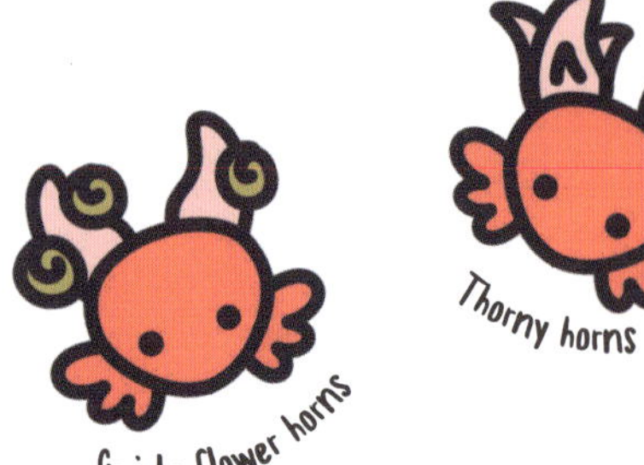

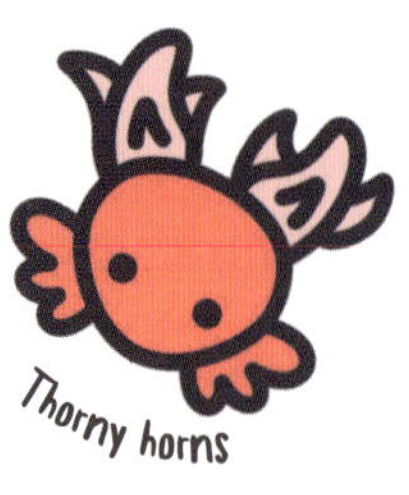

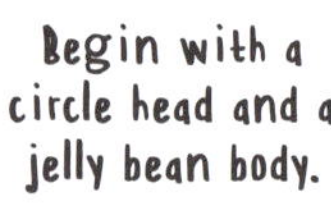

Begin with a circle head and a jelly bean body.

Connect the head with the body, then add horns, a tail and two short legs. Draw the outlines for the wings.

Refine the wing shapes and add the finishing touches.

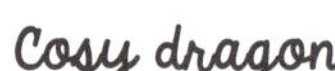

Cosy dragon

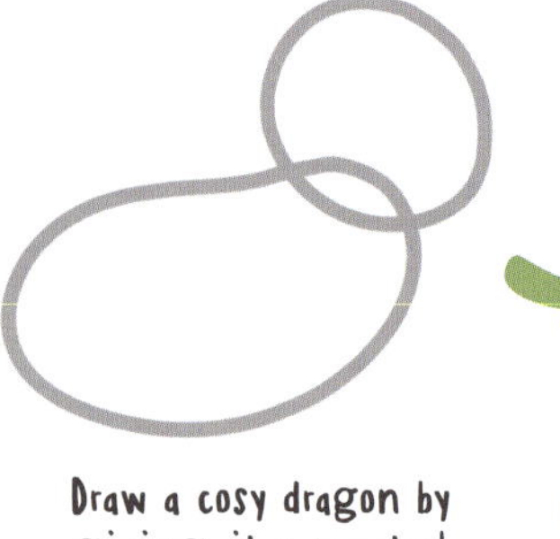

Draw a cosy dragon by giving it a sweater! Add the clothing on top of the jelly bean body.

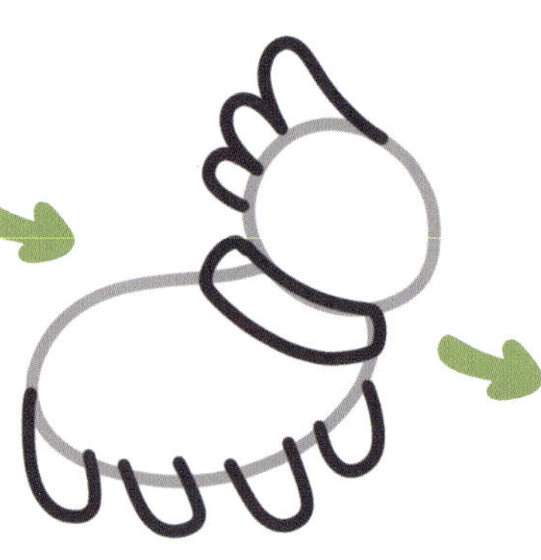

The tail and wings are similar shapes: they curve upwards and look like antlers.

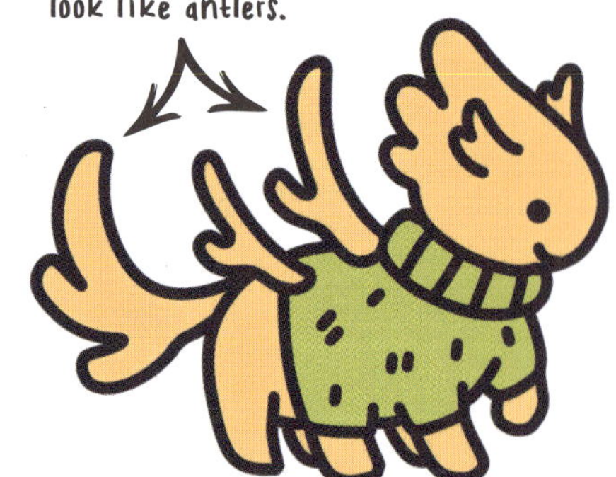

Water dragon

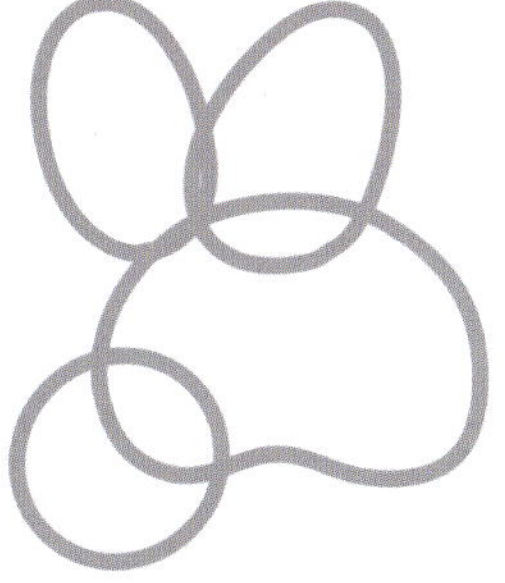

This dragon starts with a jelly bean, a circle and two egg-shaped wings.

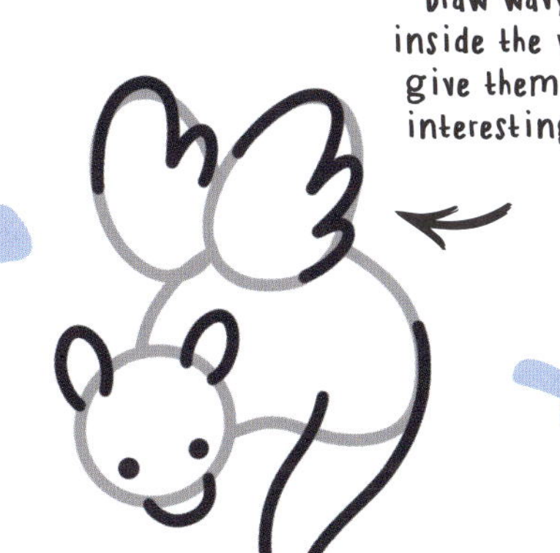

Draw wavy lines inside the wings to give them a more interesting shape.

The antlers and scales on the back have a wavy, watery quality.

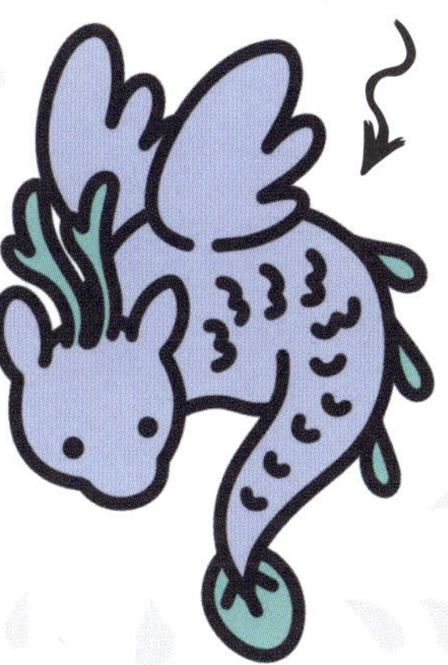

Flying long dragon

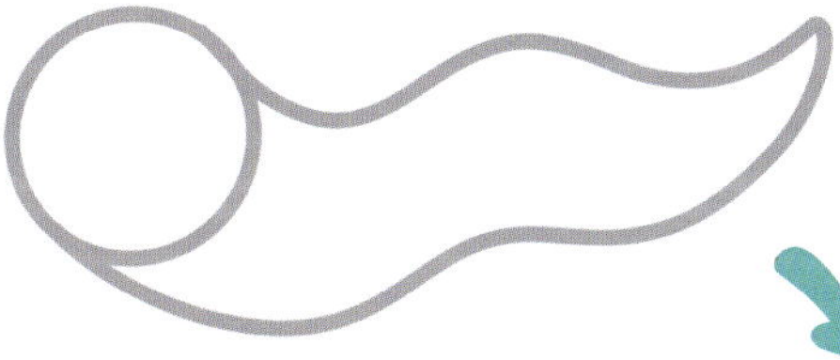

Start with a circle, then draw a wavy worm shape extending out from it.

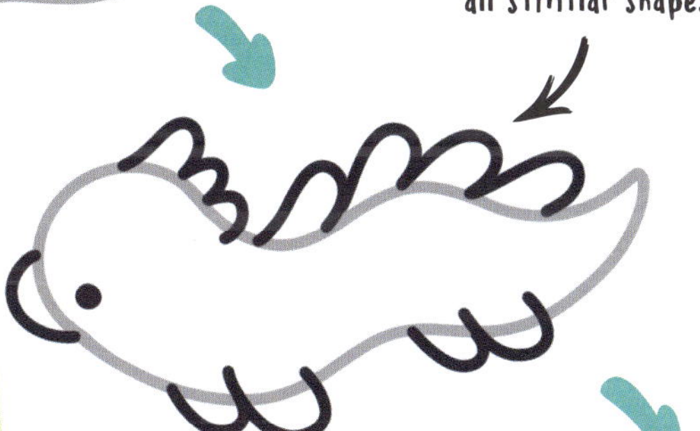

This next step is fun because the face, limbs and scales are all similar shapes.

The tail is like a bunch of leaves.

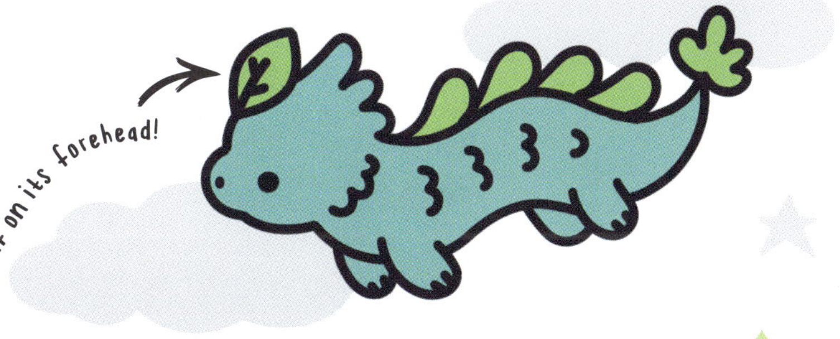

Add a cute leaf on its forehead!

Dragons come in all shapes and sizes. Some look a bit like other mammals, some look more like reptiles, and others are a mix of the two!

FUZZY WUZZIES

The fuzzy wuzzy is a sassy, nocturnal, moth-like creature that loves to show off its wings, and is always excited to meet new friends.

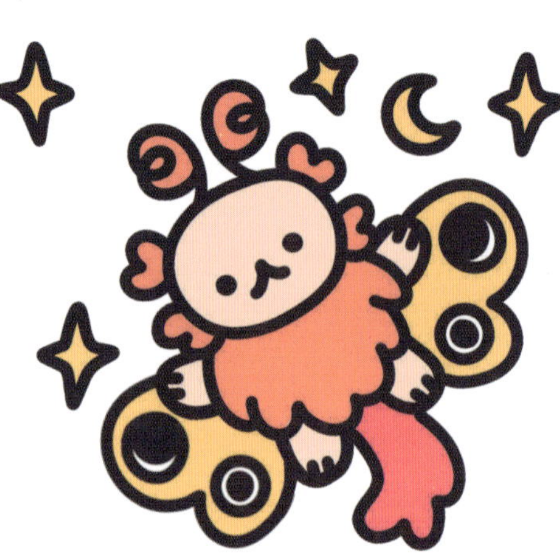

Start with a circle head and a gumdrop body.

Draw in the curved limbs and line antennae.

Draw heart shapes for the wings and ears.

Embellish the antennae with looping lines and draw the face.

Add a long tail, a fuzzy body and a pattern on the wings.

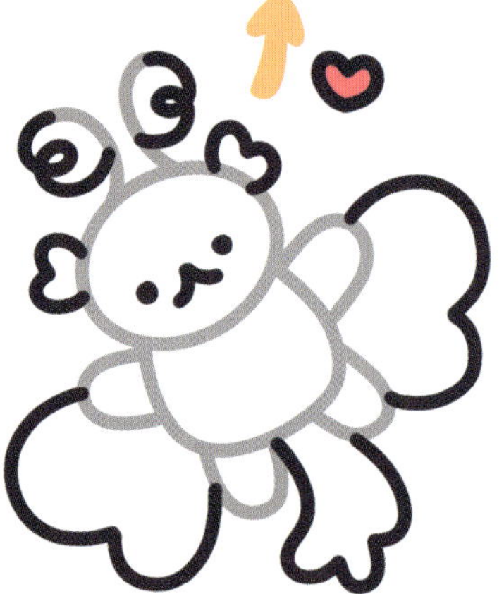

Look at my wings

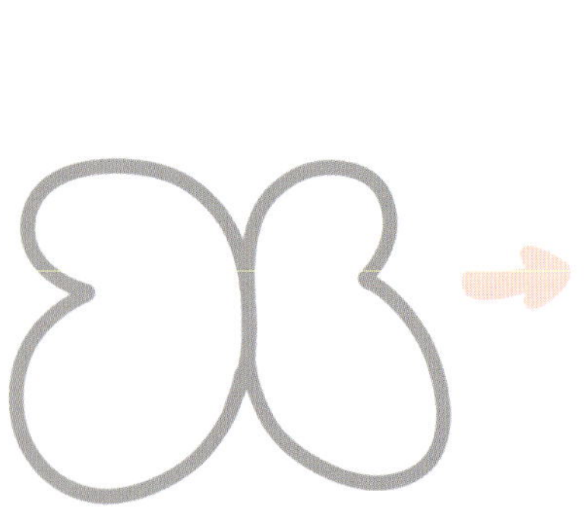

For this pose, start with the wings, which are like squashed heart or jelly bean shapes.

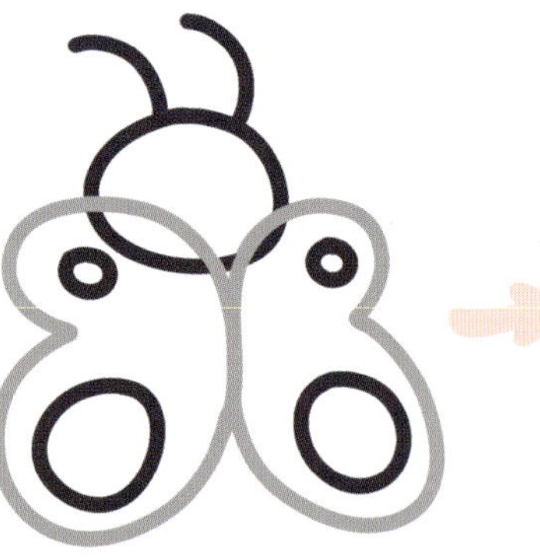

Add a circle head and antennae lines, and large and small circular wing details.

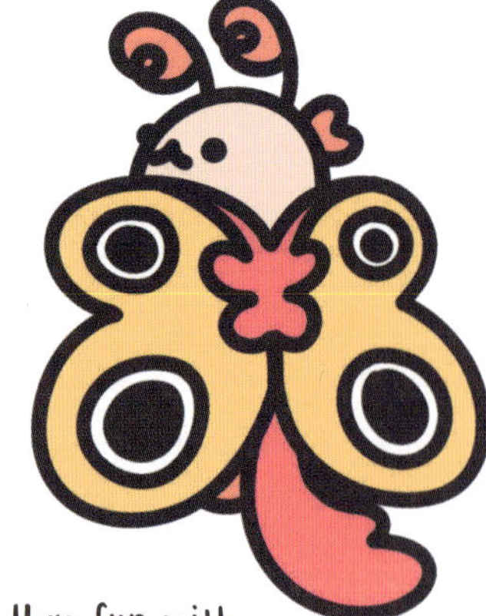

Have fun with the finishing touches.

Play with poses

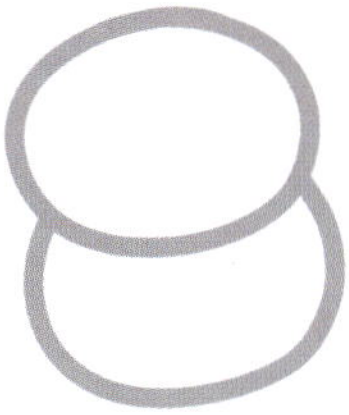

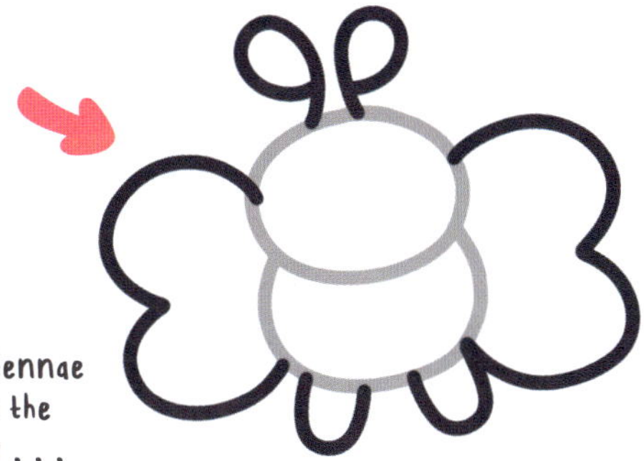

Add wings, antennae and limbs to the gumdrop body . . .

Try star-shaped eyes and mouth.

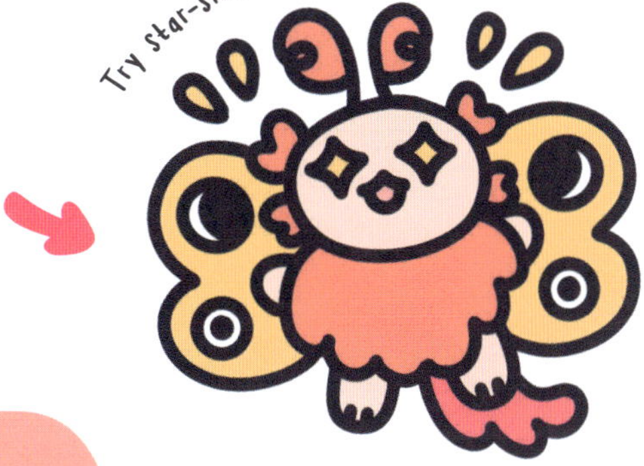

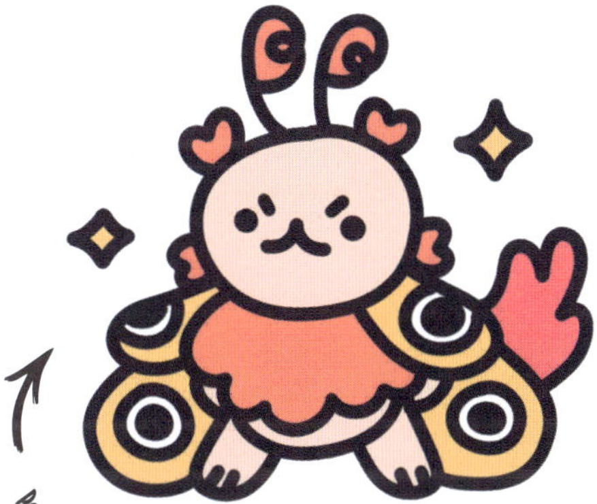

. . . then have fun with different poses and facial expressions.

Position the wings downwards and add eyebrows for a confident pose.

Tilt the head to show curiosity.

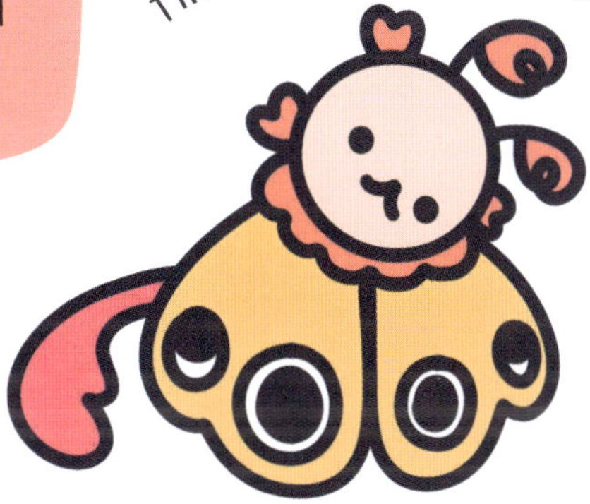

Sleepy time

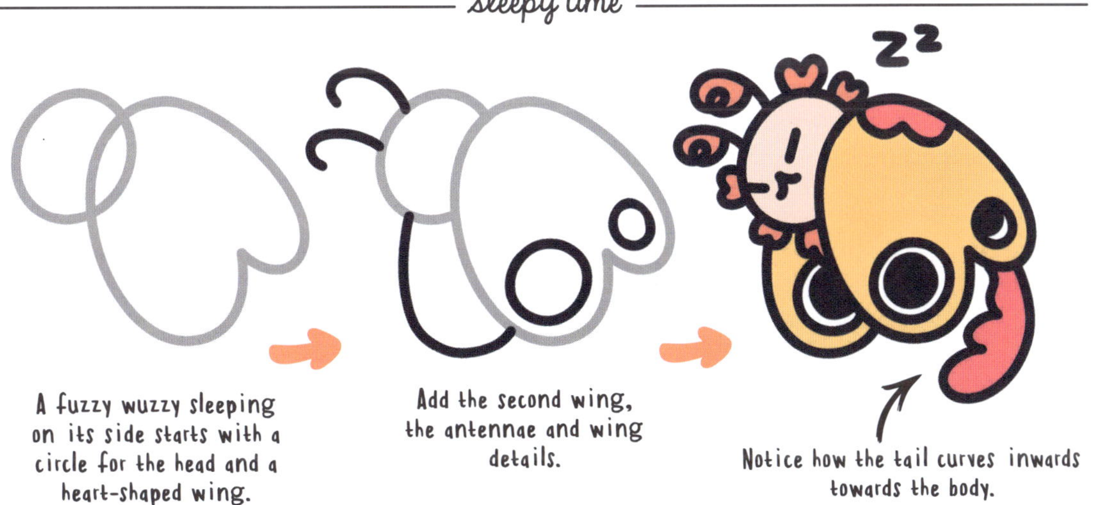

A fuzzy wuzzy sleeping on its side starts with a circle for the head and a heart-shaped wing.

Add the second wing, the antennae and wing details.

Notice how the tail curves inwards towards the body.

GROBBLES

Grobbles are mischievous creatures that like to disguise themselves in plant and animal costumes, and play tricks on each other.

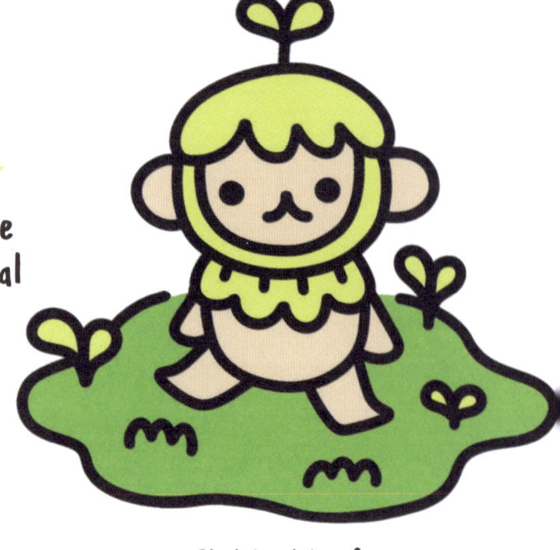

The base is made up of circles and round rectangles.

Use wavy lines to draw a plant-inspired hat and neckpiece.

Finish with a face.

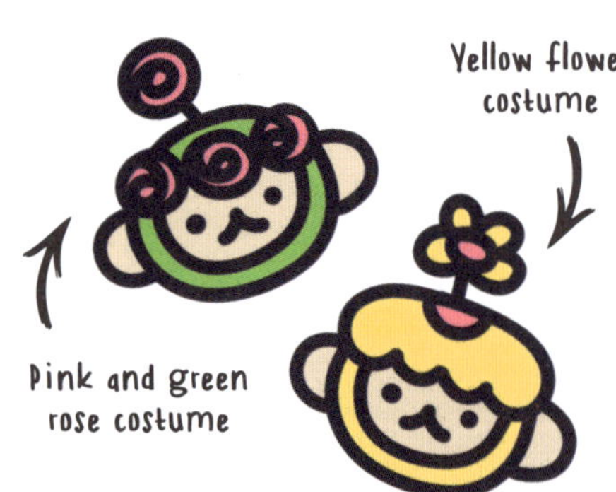

Yellow flower costume

Pink and green rose costume

Sneaky grobble

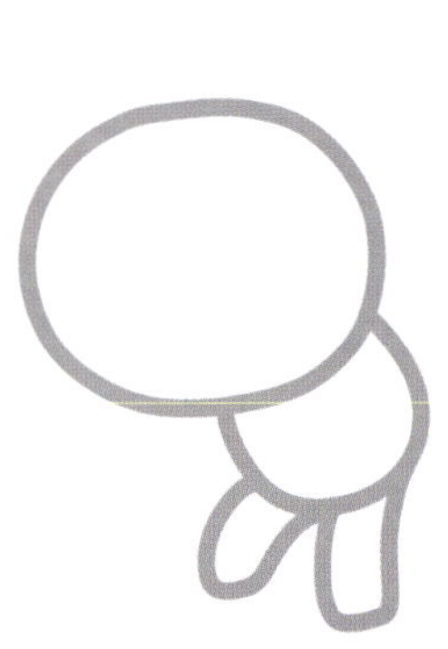

The secret to this pose is placing the body to the side of the head, instead of at the centre.

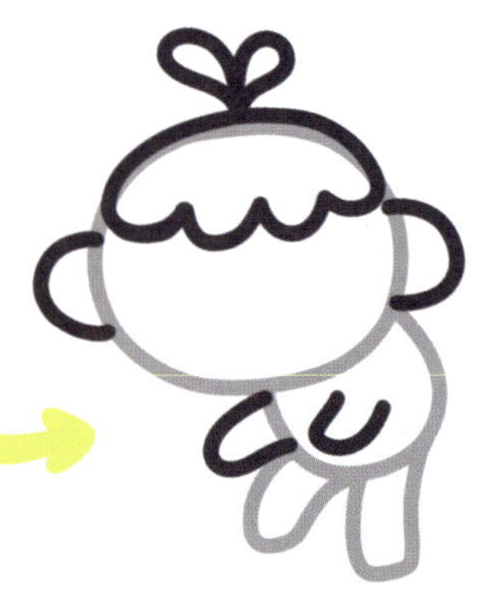

Add the ears and limbs and start adding the plant headdress.

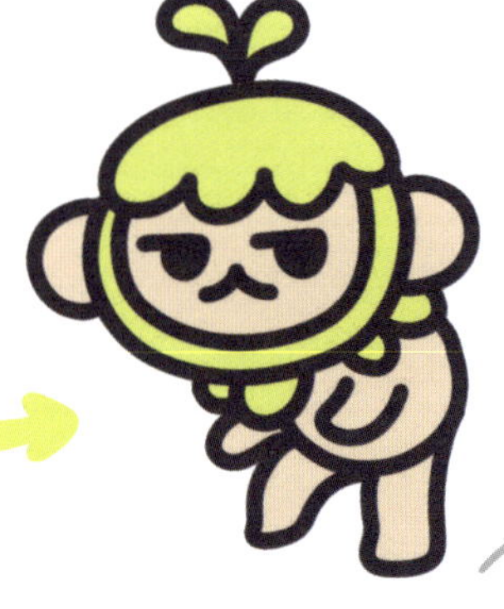

Draw big circles for eyes with lines across the top, for that sneaky facial expression.

This line shows the grobble is creeping up on someone.

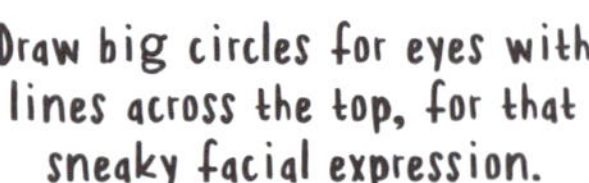

Flower flying

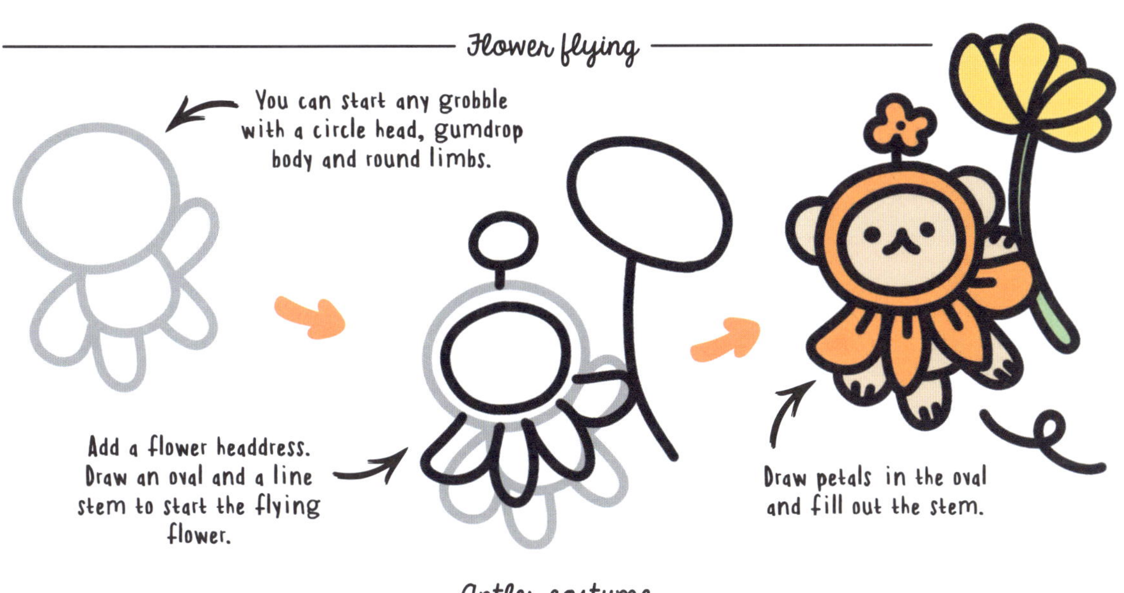

Antler costume

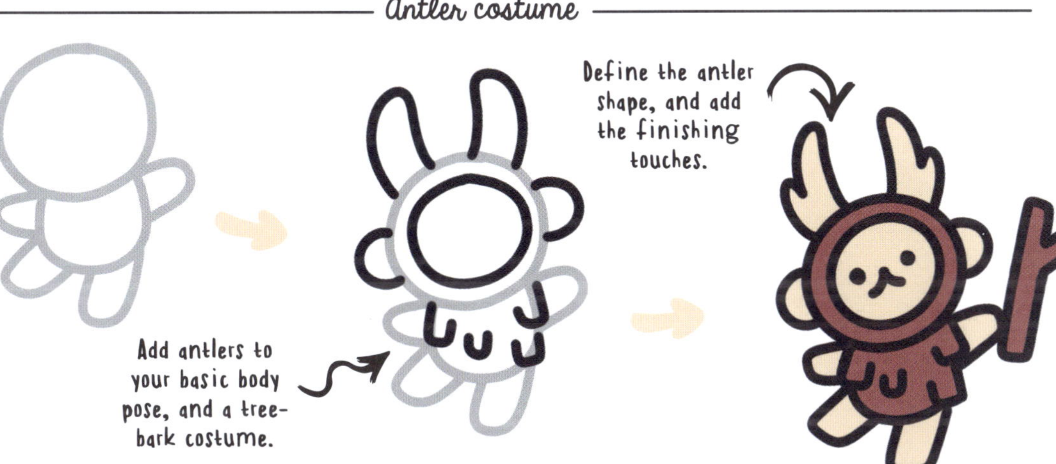

Mushroom costume

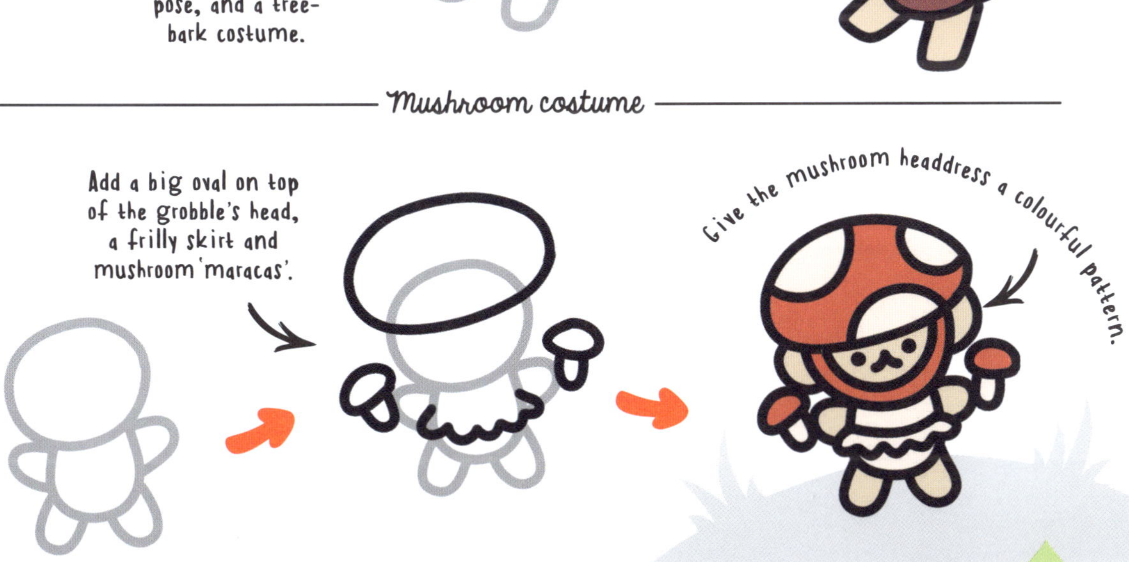

SHRUBBIES

These cute little forest creatures can change shape and colour depending on their surroundings. They mimic the shapes and shades around them, so they don't stand out.

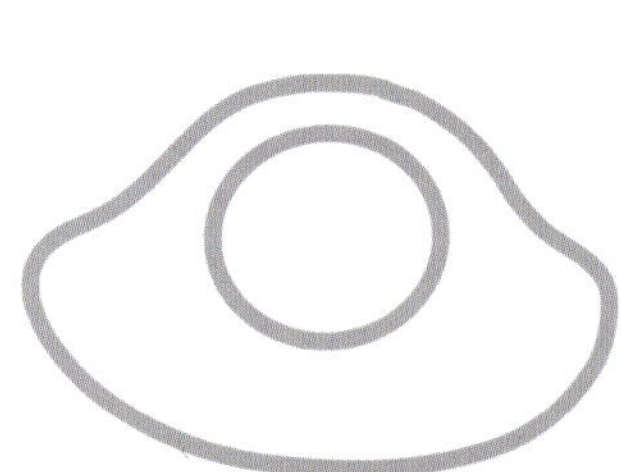

Start with a shape like a fried egg.

Draw a wavy line along the bottom edge of both shapes.

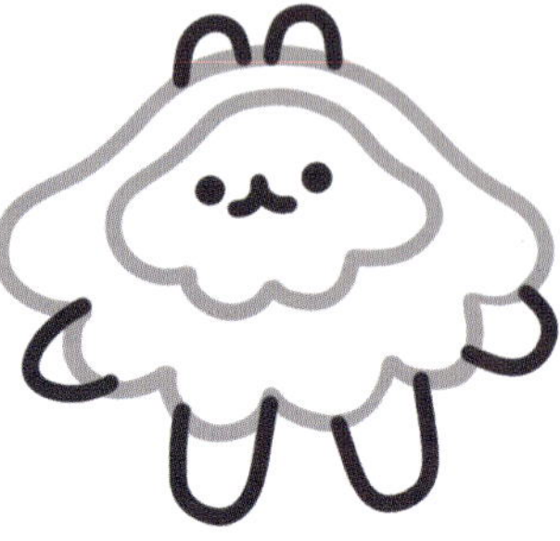

Fill in the details of the face, ears and limbs.

Bounce away

Draw a gumdrop with a smaller gumdrop inside for the face.

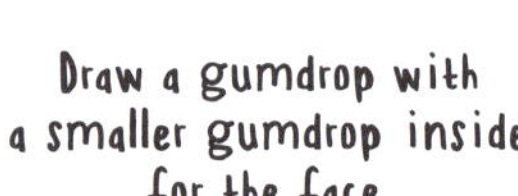

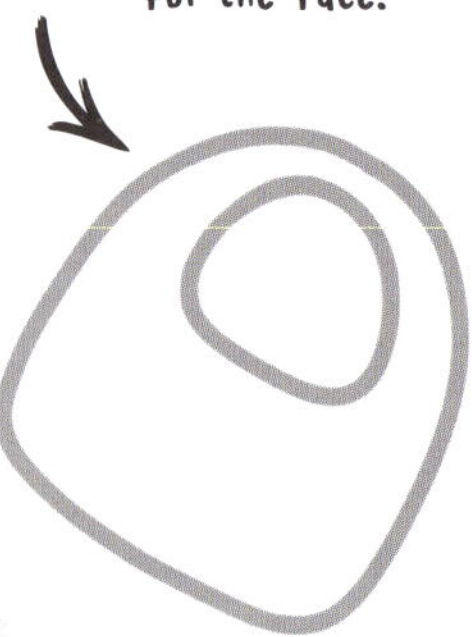

Add a wavy line along the bottom edge of the body and the face. Draw the ears, arms and facial details.

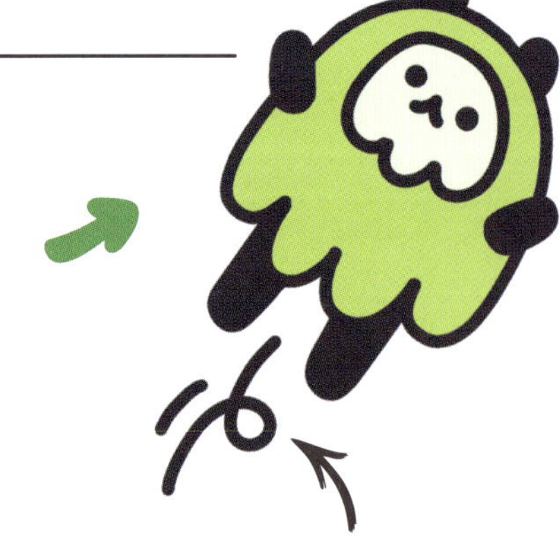

Add in long legs and motion lines to show the shrubbie is jumping up.

Spiky shrubbie

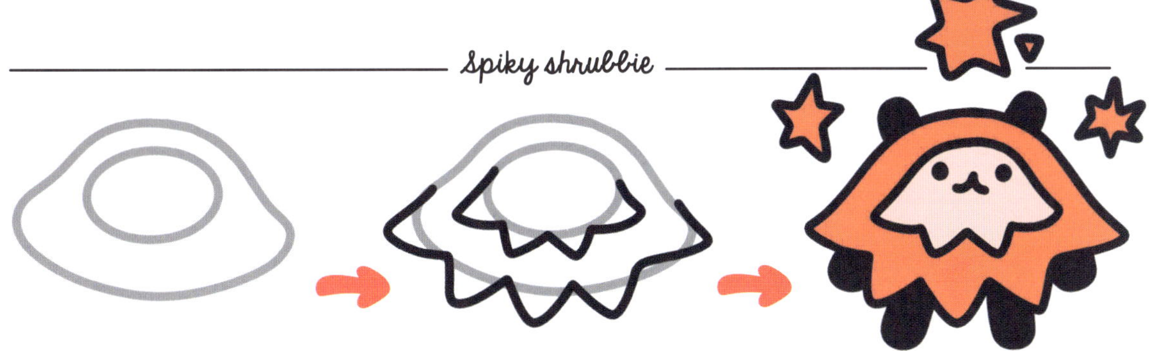

This shrubbie is spiky, so add pointy triangles instead of wavy lines to the fried-egg base shape.

Finish off with the face, ears and limbs.

Boxy shrubbie

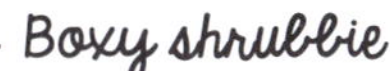

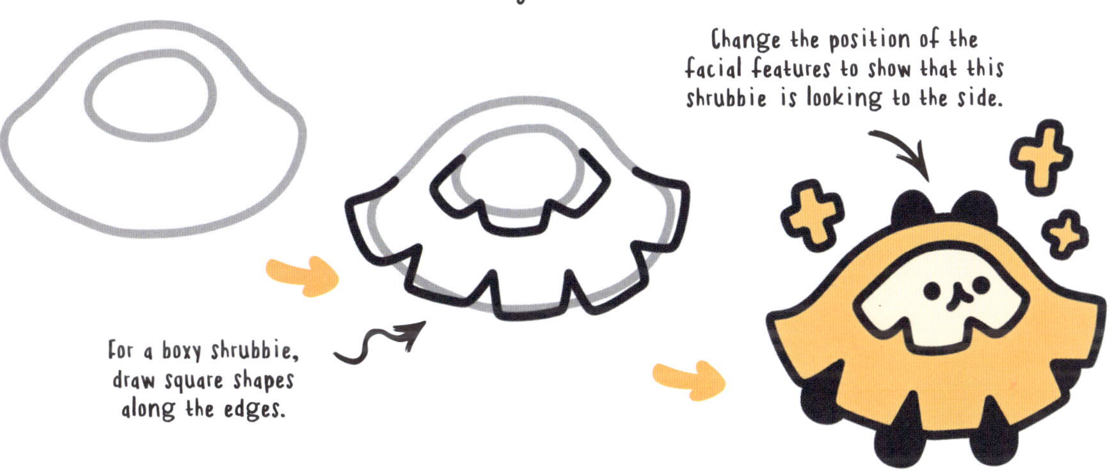

Change the position of the facial features to show that this shrubbie is looking to the side.

For a boxy shrubbie, draw square shapes along the edges.

Curly shrubbie

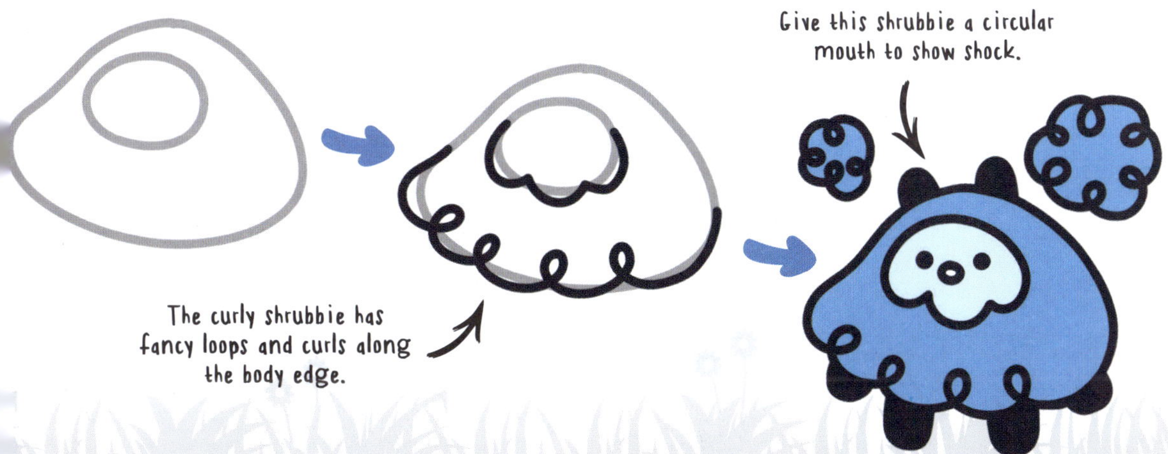

Give this shrubbie a circular mouth to show shock.

The curly shrubbie has fancy loops and curls along the body edge.

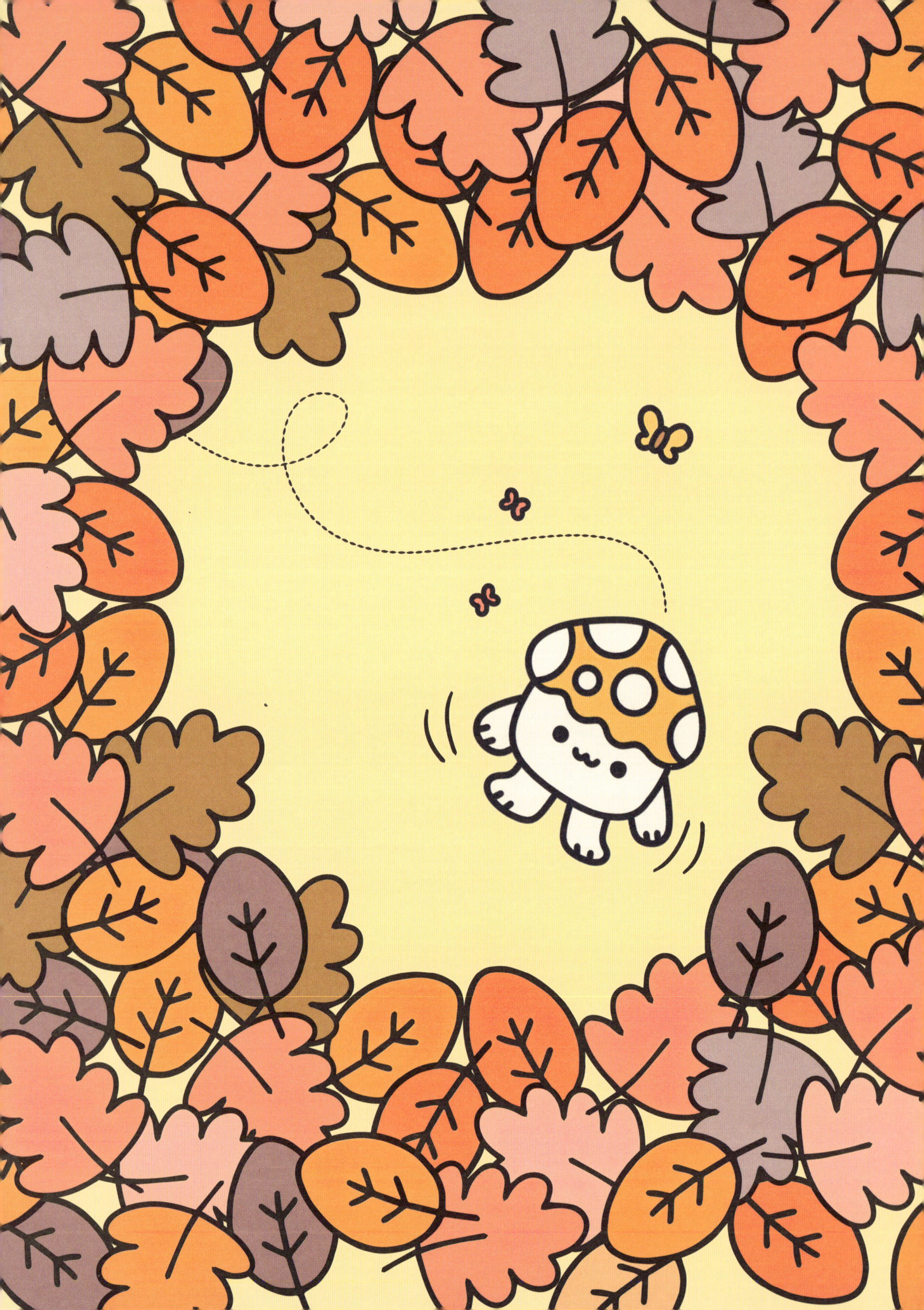

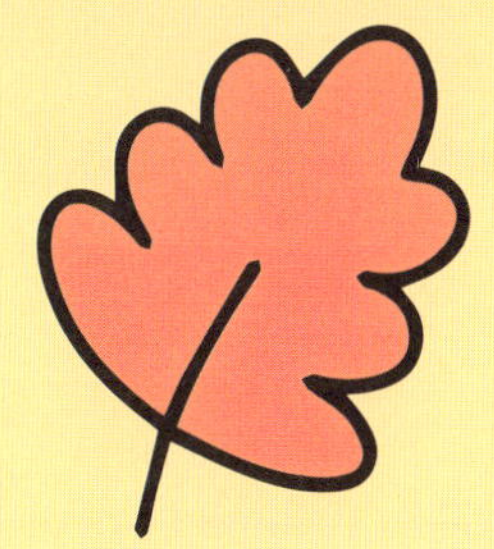

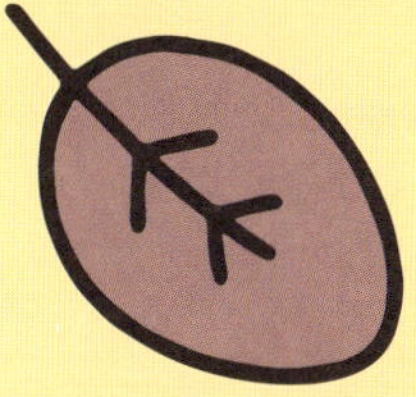

Chapter four

THE NATURAL WORLD

In this chapter you will find trees, bushes, acorns, mushrooms, and more! Create a beautiful forest for all your creatures to live in.

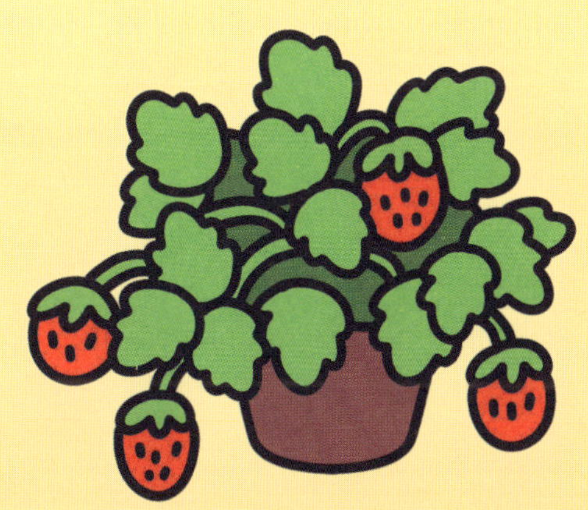

MUSHROOMS

Mushrooms are umbrella-shaped fungi, which come in different shapes, colours and sizes. They can grow from soil or even trees. Some mushrooms are poisonous.

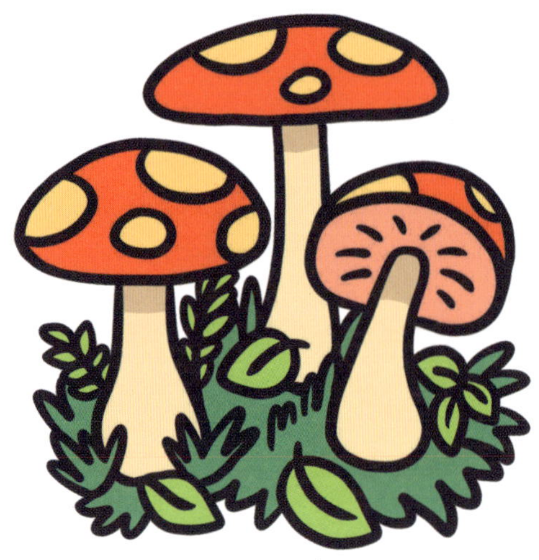

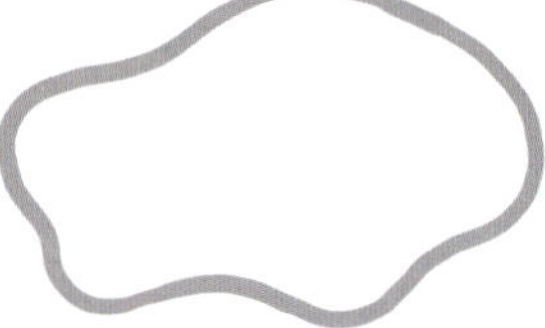

All mushrooms have a stem and a cap. For this type start with a wavy oval shape.

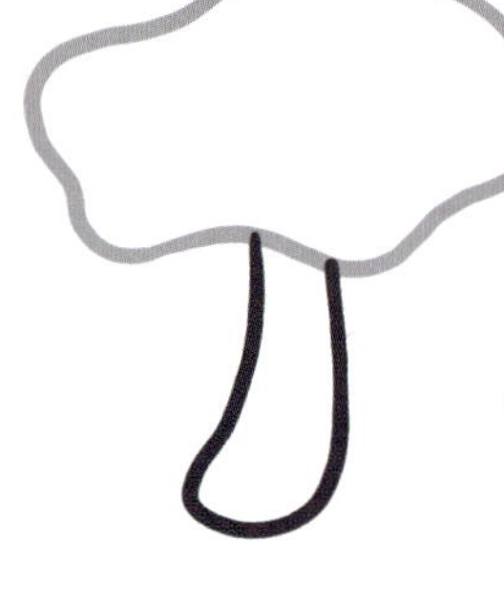

Add a long, thin stem below the cap.

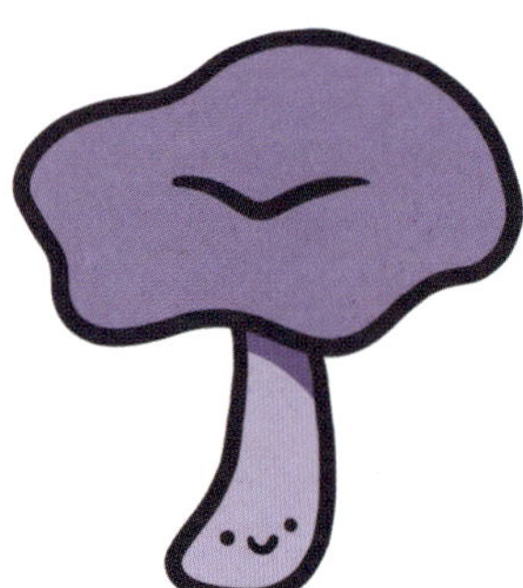

Finish with a cute face on the stem.

Mushrooms make great shapes for hats and dresses. Discover more ways to combine plants with people on pages 40–43.

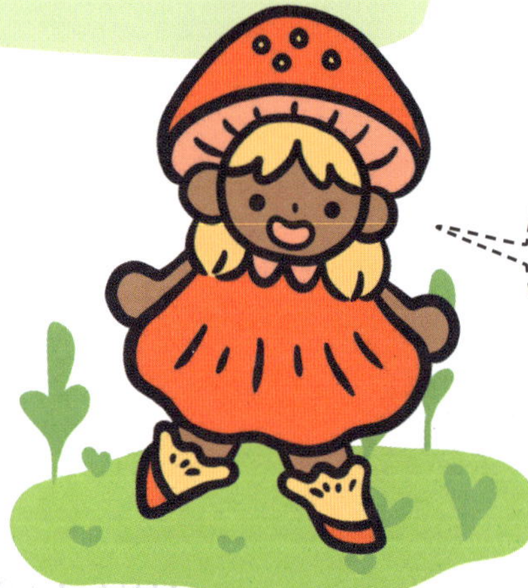

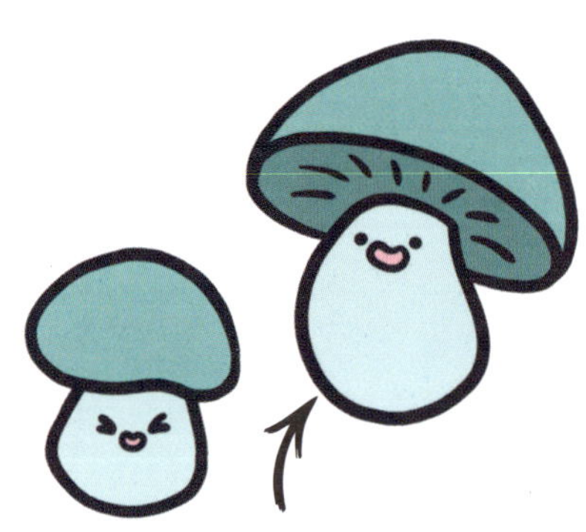

Some mushrooms have fatter stems and triangular caps.

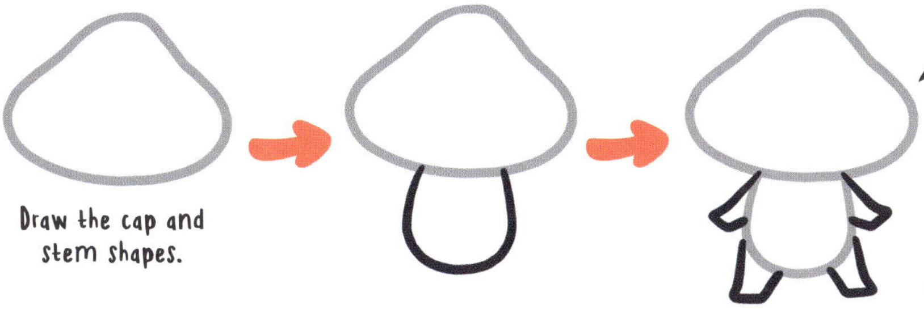

Draw the cap and stem shapes.

Add little arms and legs to turn your mushroom into a little character.

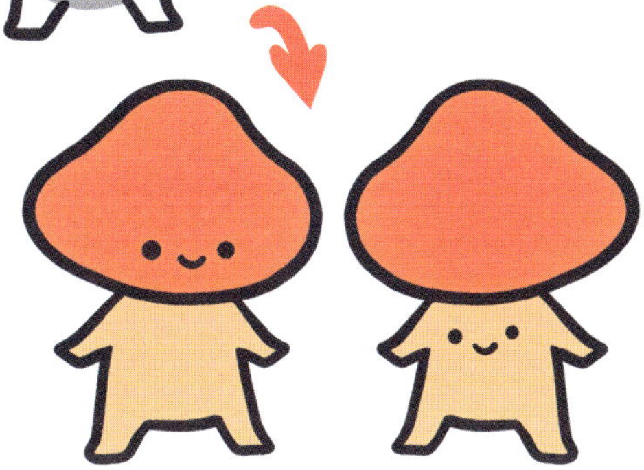

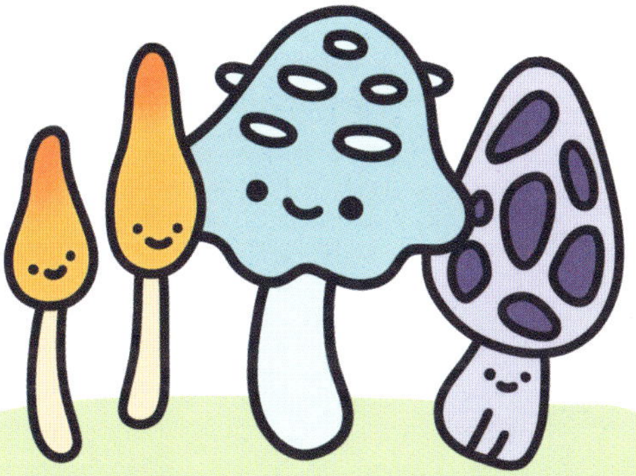

When you add patterns to your mushroom caps, don't forget that the textures can pop out from the surface.

You can choose to draw a face on the mushroom cap or the body. There's no right or wrong way!

Tree fungi

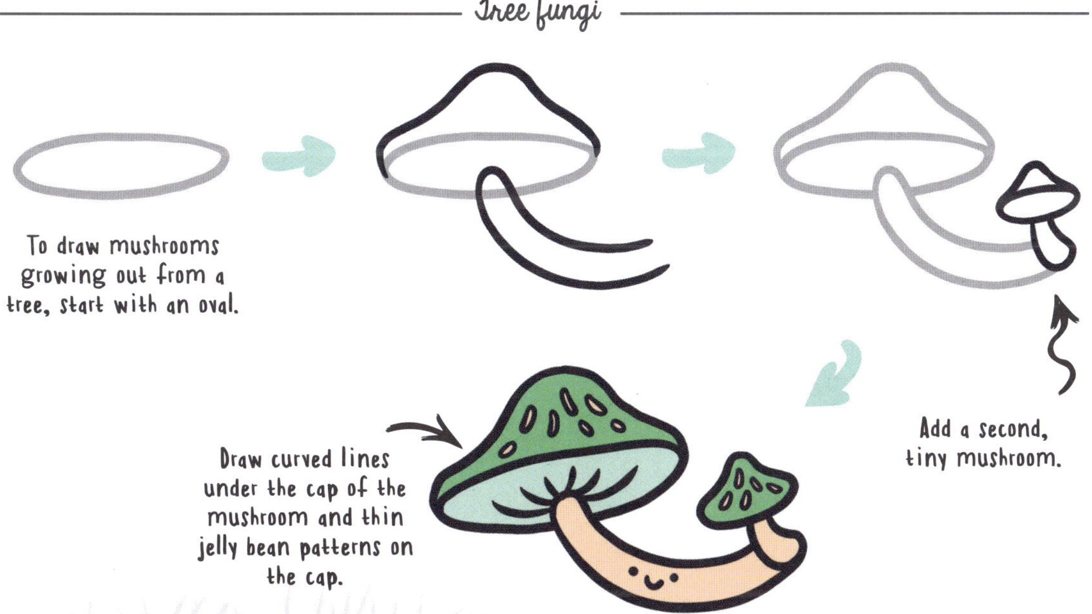

Hats

By drawing a face on the stem of the mushroom, your character instantly gets a cute hat!

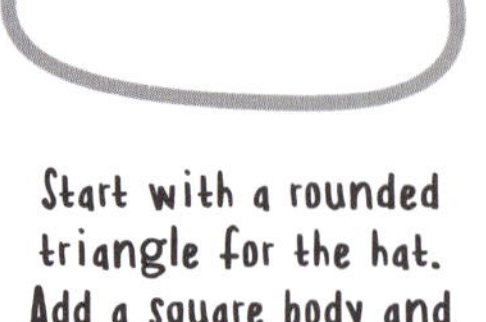

Start with a rounded triangle for the hat. Add a square body and rounded limbs.

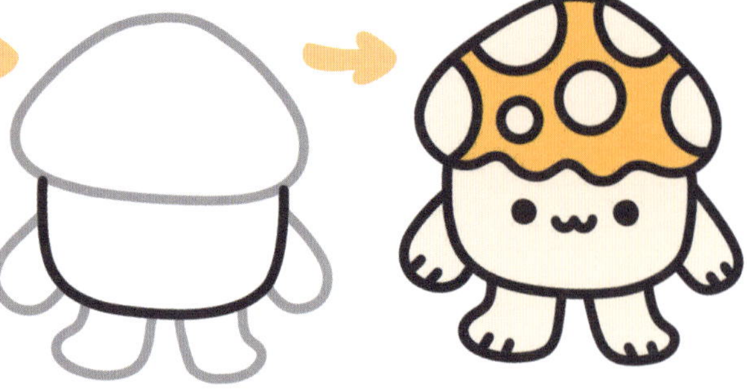

Give the hat a fun pattern.

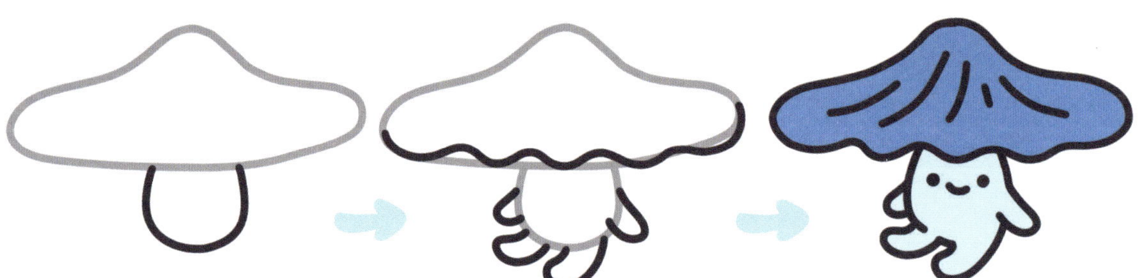

This hat is a wide, curvy triangle.

Add a wavy line at the bottom of the triangle. Give your character some arms and legs.

Draw in remaining details like the face and lines on the hat.

Enoki

Enoki mushrooms have unique caps.

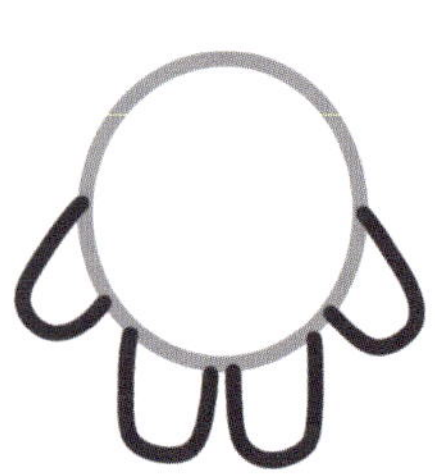

Start with a circle body and add limbs.

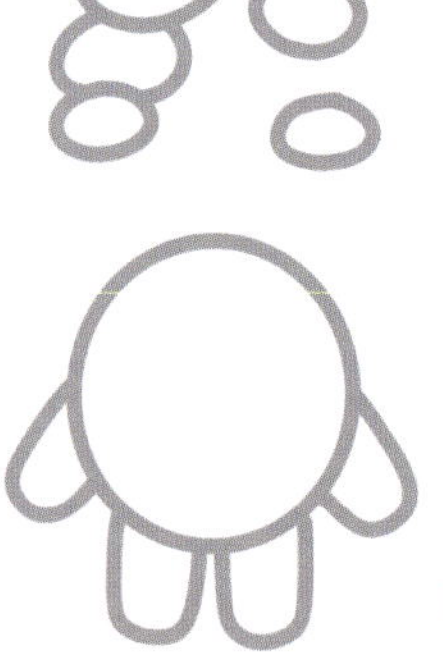

Draw small clusters of circles above the body.

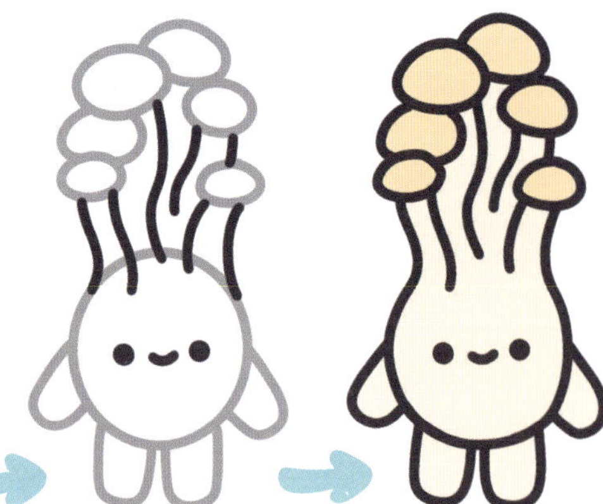

Add in lines to connect the clusters to the body.

When mushrooms grow in clusters, they emerge from a central point. You can always add more mushrooms to your cluster, just keep drawing them out from the sides.

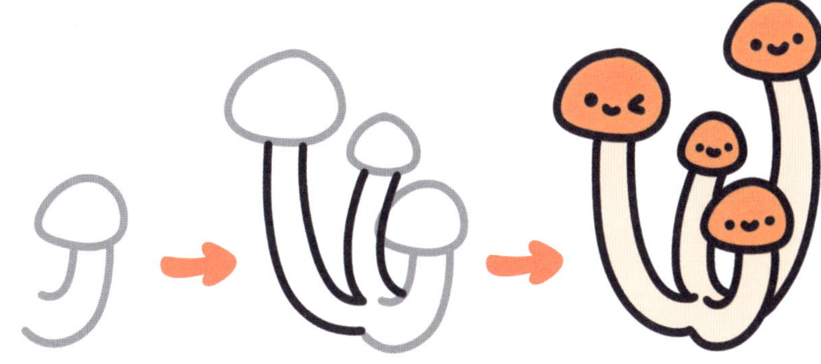

Begin with an oval cap and curved stem.

The new mushrooms are connected to the base of the first one.

Draw a different type of cluster with small caps and thick stems.

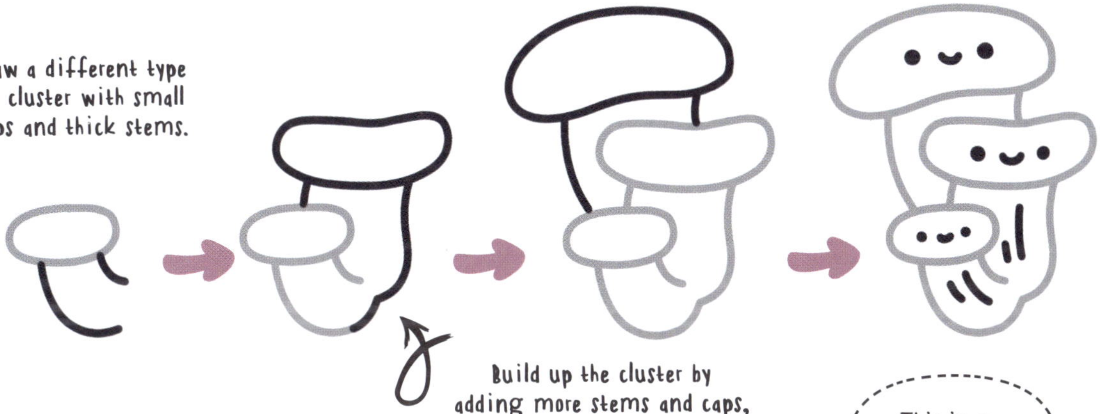

Build up the cluster by adding more stems and caps, making sure the stems are connected at the bottom.

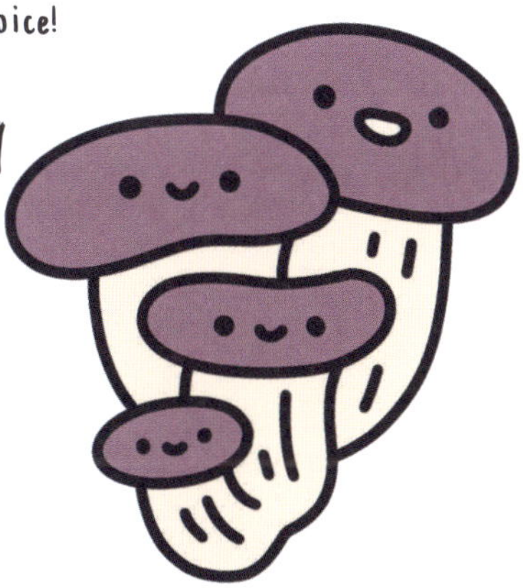

This is our cute mushroom family!

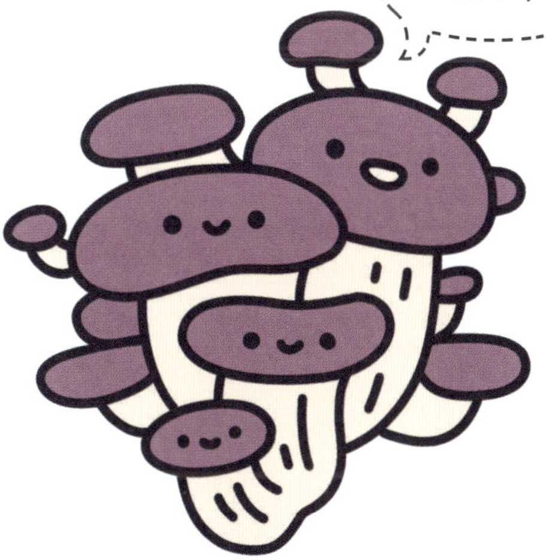

The faces can be different or the same, your choice!

VINES

Vines can grow really long, sometimes wrapping up and around trees or other plants, and sometimes hanging down. They can have different types of leaves and even flowers.

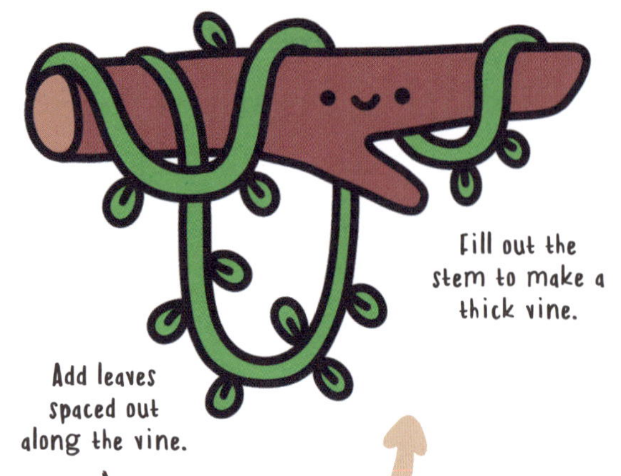

Fill out the stem to make a thick vine.

Add leaves spaced out along the vine.

Start by drawing a branch.

Draw a line wrapping around the branch and hanging down to start the vine.

Leafy vines

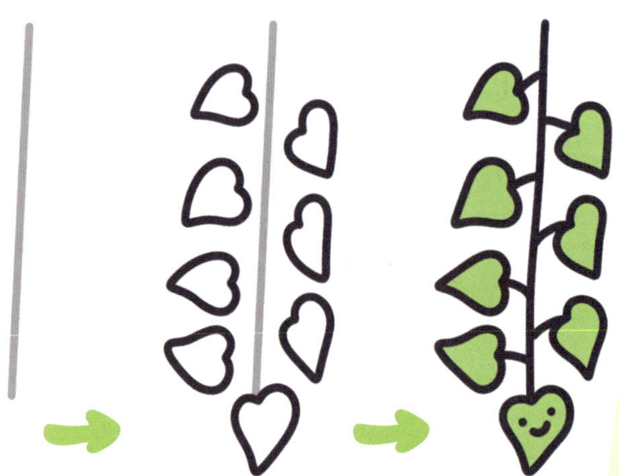

This vine starts out with a straight line.

Add heart-shaped leaves with smaller stems connecting them to the central line.

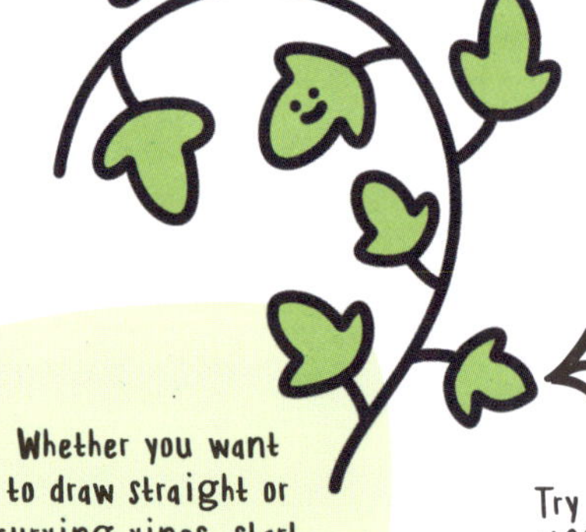

Whether you want to draw straight or curving vines, start with the central stem, then add leaves!

Try some different leaf shapes.

Trailing vines

Vines are popular houseplants. Draw a pot with a few lines for the central stems.

Add leaves and smaller stems. These leaves are rounded triangles.

To add flowers to your vines, draw looping wavy lines down from the stem and back up again.

Hanging vines

Hanging pots are perfect for vine houseplants. Start with a gumdrop.

Draw the stems coming out of the pot and draping downwards.

Now add in lots of oval leaves.

Draw the three cords that the pot hangs from.

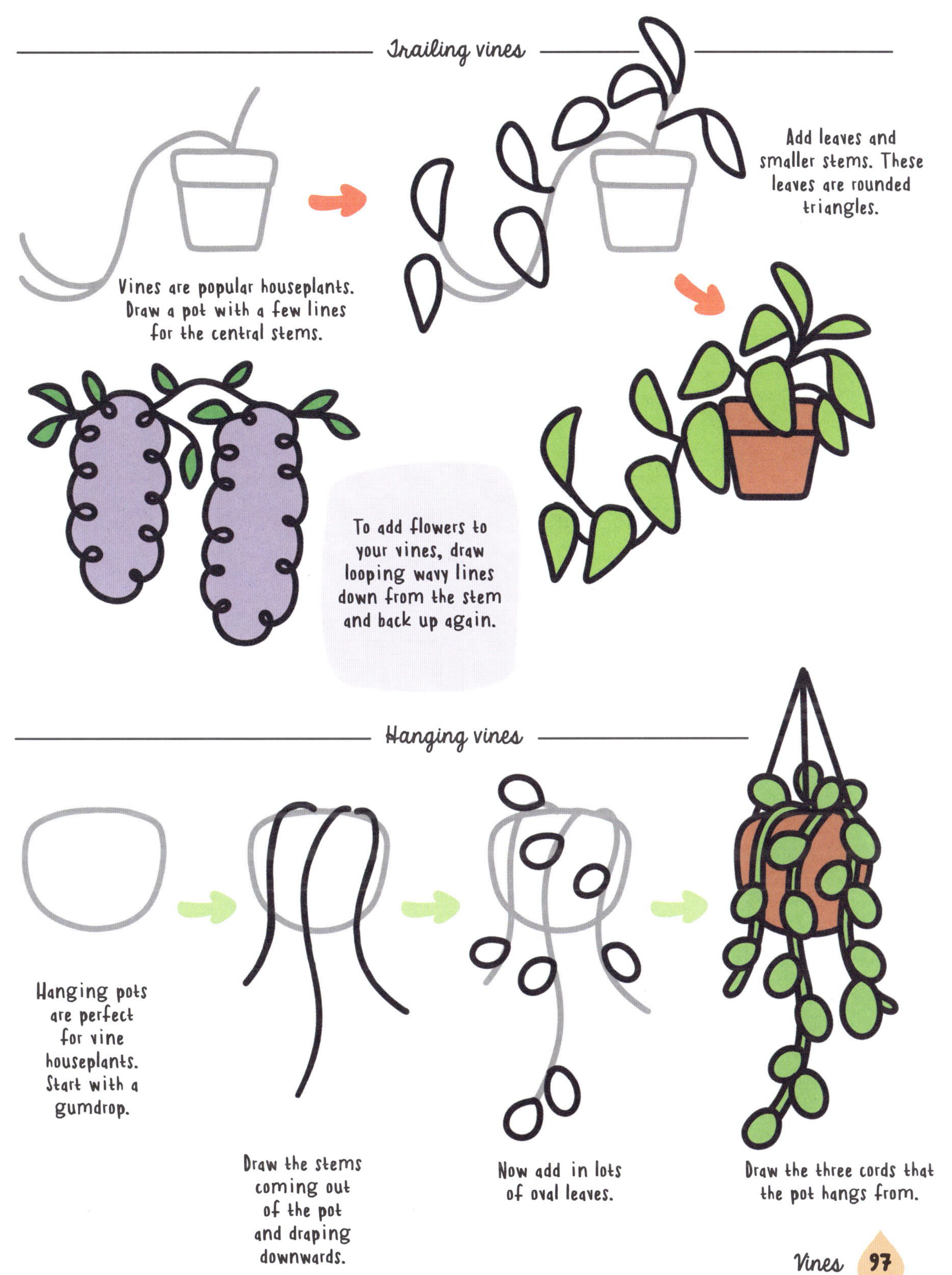

TREES

When drawing trees, you can always count on the fact that they have a single trunk at the centre with leaves coming out from the top. Experiment with different shapes for the treetops and leaves to draw different types of tree.

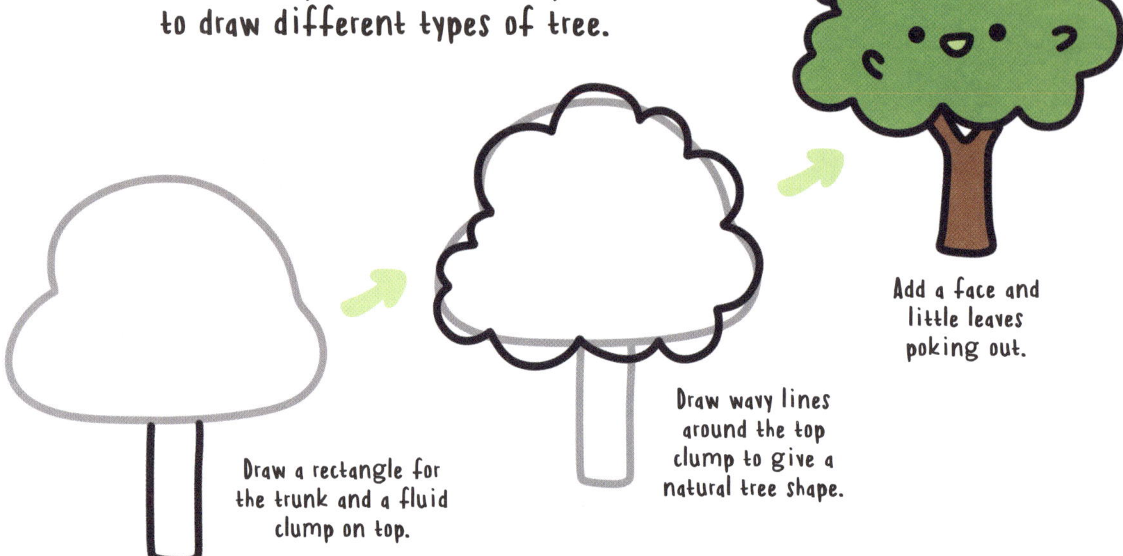

Evergreen

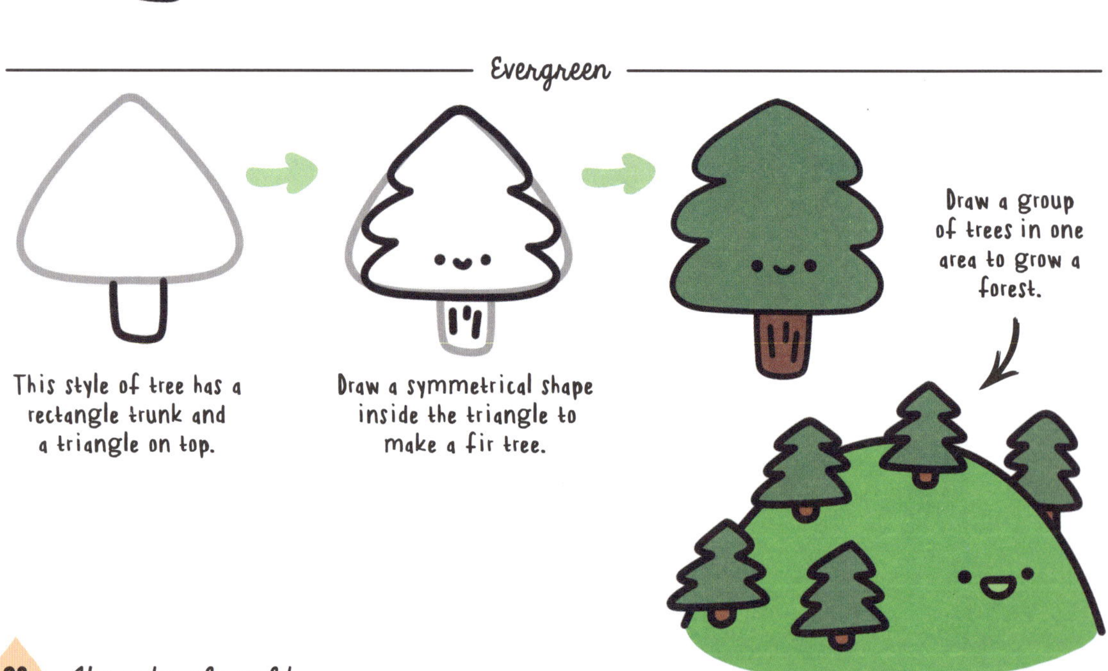

Willow

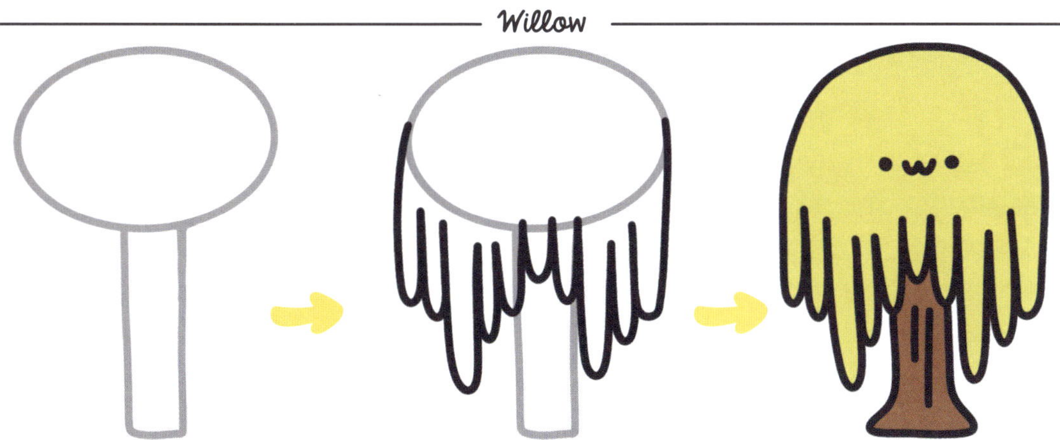

For this tree, draw an oval on top of the rectangle trunk.

The branches and leaves of a weeping willow hang down from the oval canopy.

Fruit trees

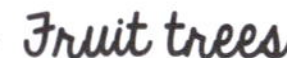

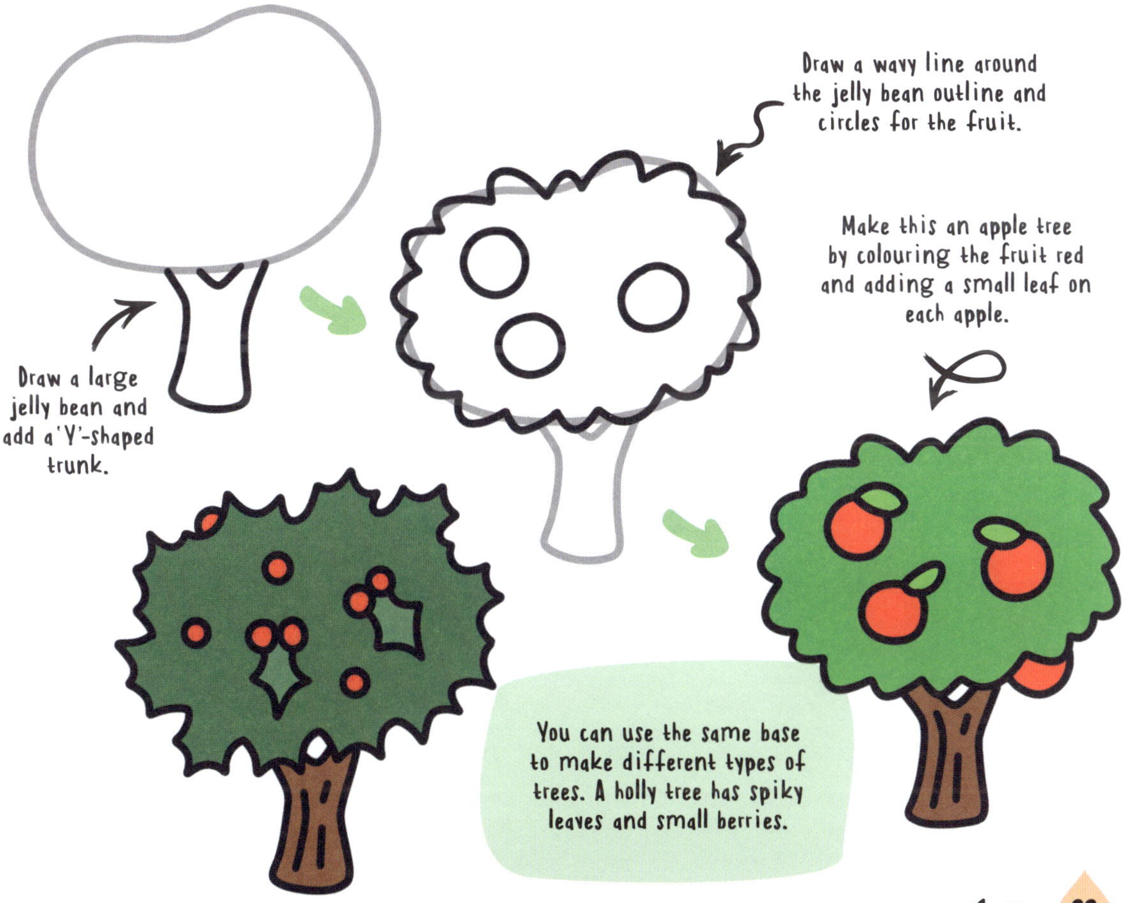

Draw a large jelly bean and add a 'Y'-shaped trunk.

Draw a wavy line around the jelly bean outline and circles for the fruit.

Make this an apple tree by colouring the fruit red and adding a small leaf on each apple.

You can use the same base to make different types of trees. A holly tree has spiky leaves and small berries.

FLOWERS

There are so many types of flowers and multiple ways to draw them (as separate flowers or combined bouquets). Here are some of my favourite species, drawn cute!

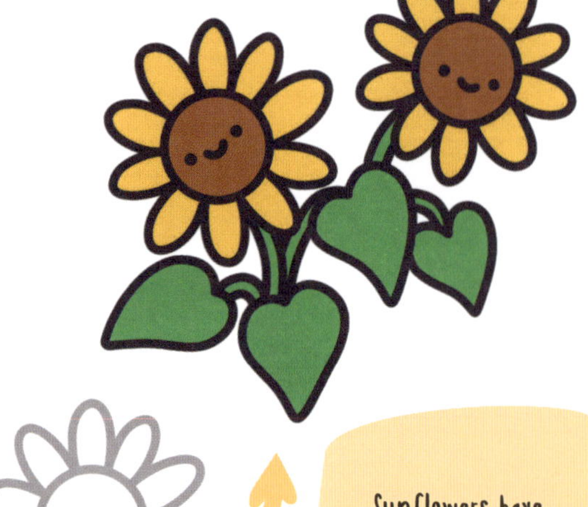

Start with a big circle. The stem comes out from the centre.

Draw long, rounded petals coming out from the circle.

The leaves are heart-shaped.

Sunflowers have yellow petals that make them look like the sun. Try drawing a sun with matching yellow rays shining out!

More flowers

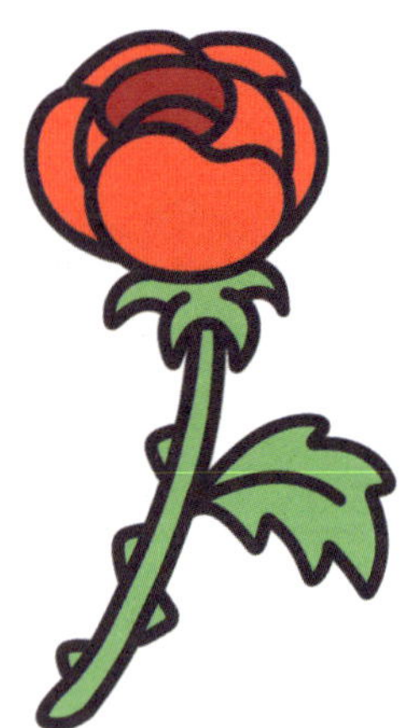

Roses have layered petals, spiky leaves and thorns on the stem.

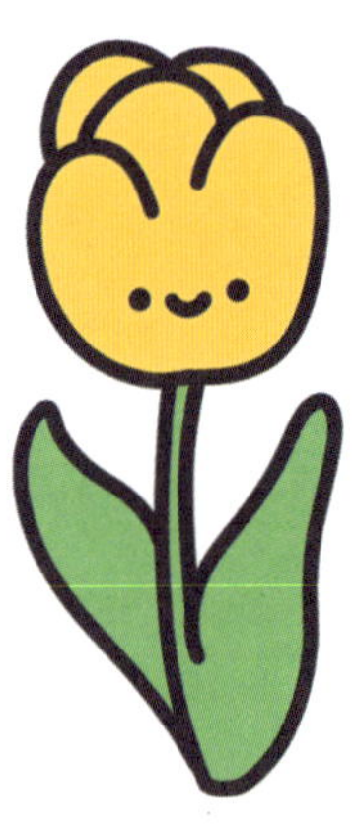

Tulips are my all-time favourites: they have oval petals.

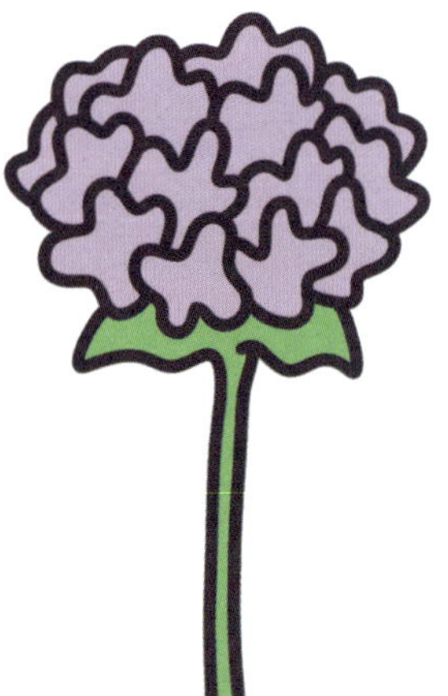

Hydrangea have clusters of small petals that look like stars.

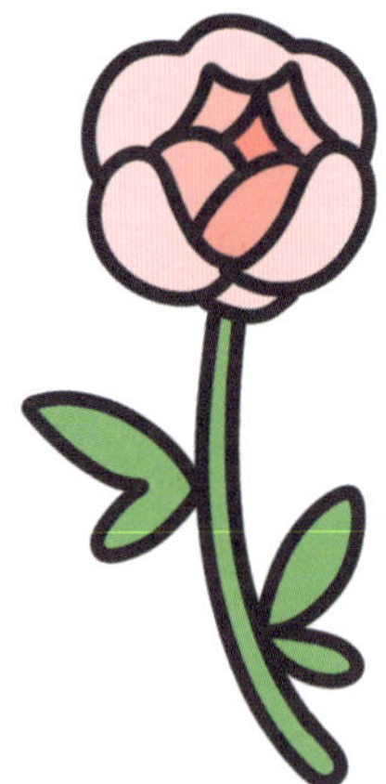

Peonies have layered petals like roses, but without the thorns.

Arrangements

Use your flower-drawing skills to make bunches, bouquets or basket arrangements.

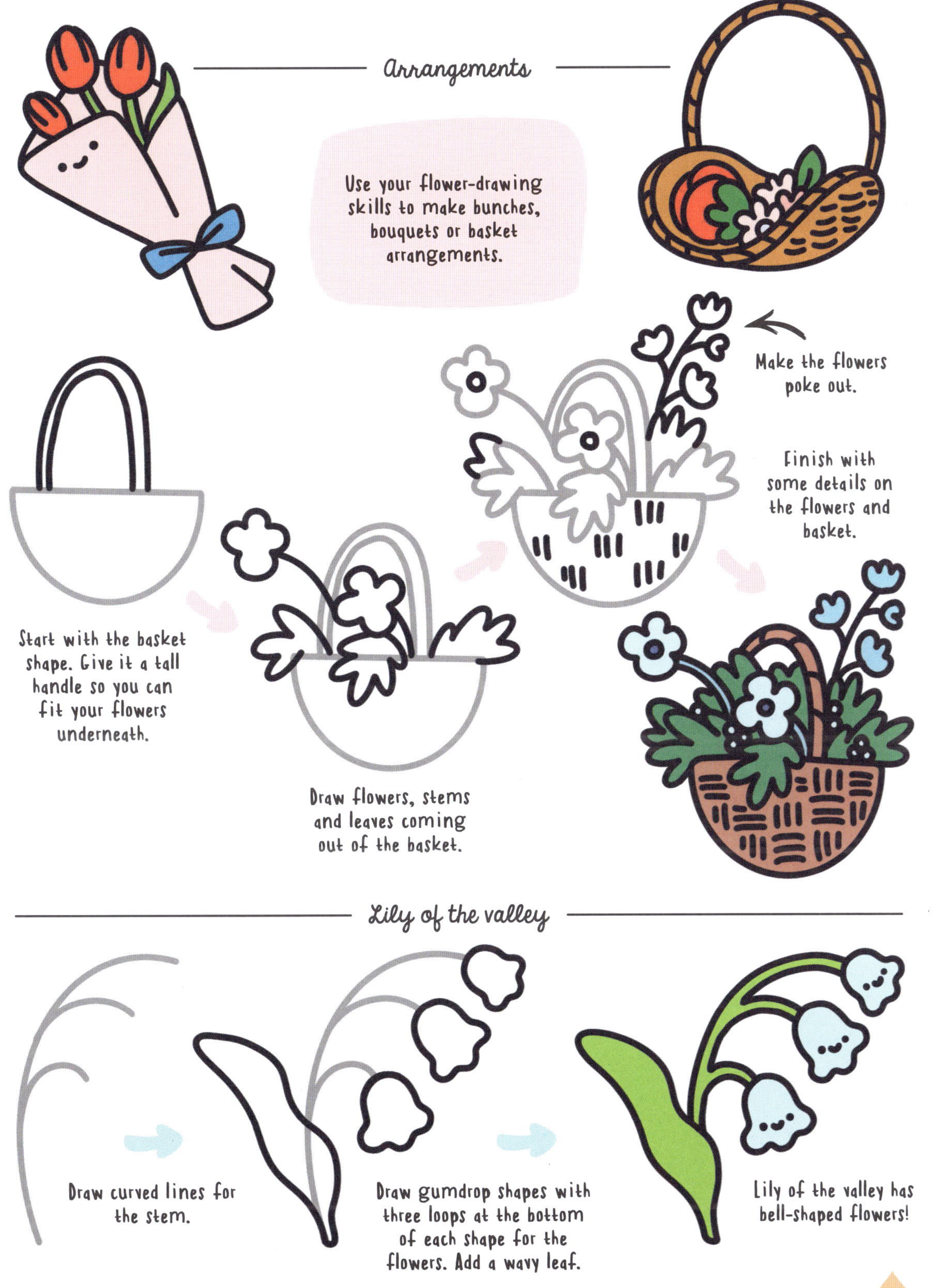

Lily of the valley

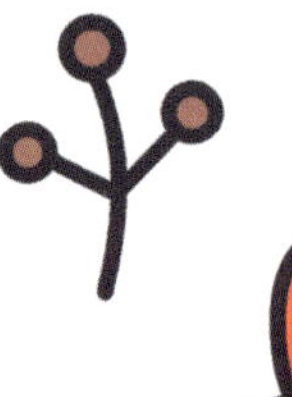

LEAVES

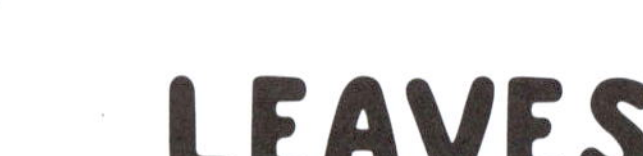

Leaves are little blades that come in many colours depending on the plant type or season of the year. Here are different shapes to draw.

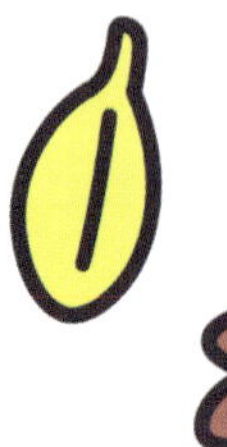
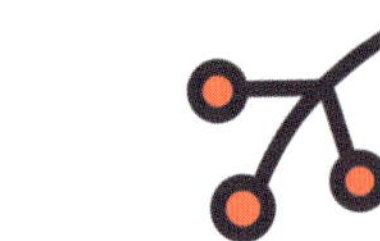
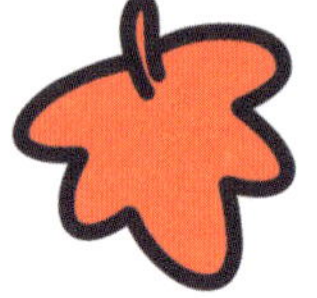
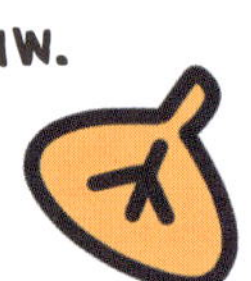
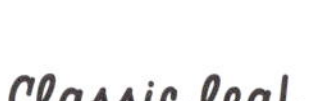

Classic leaf

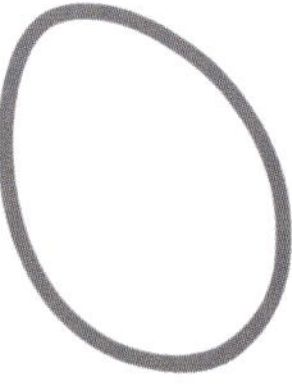

The most simple leaf is an egg-shaped oval.

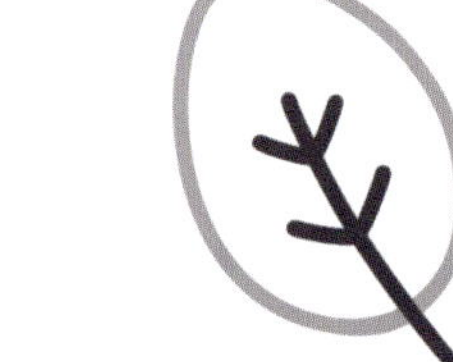

The stem is a line at the centre of the egg with a few veins on each side.

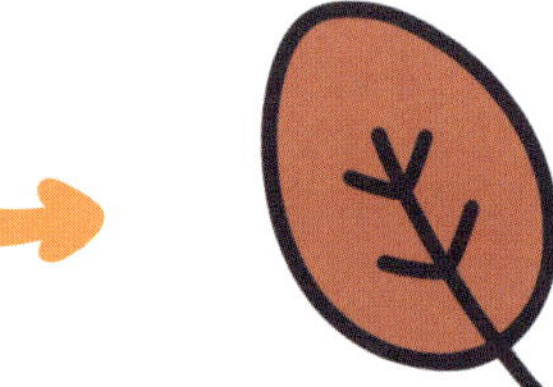

Colour in your leaf at the end!

Jinko leaf

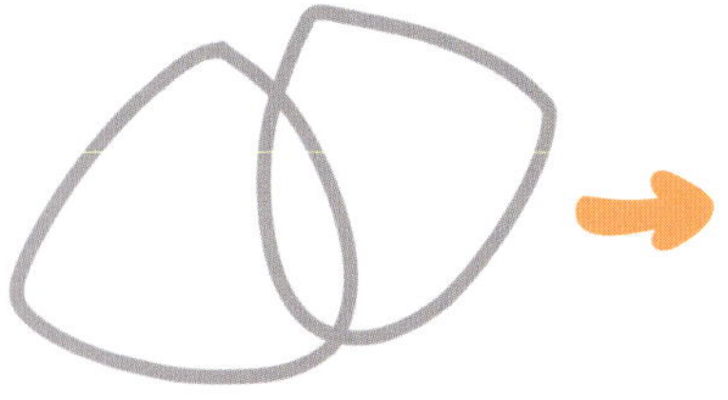

A ginkgo-shaped leaf is made of two triangles.

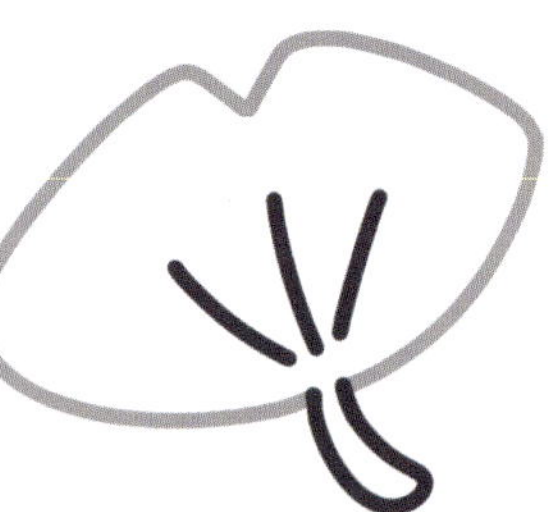

Connect the triangles. Then add a stem at the bottom.

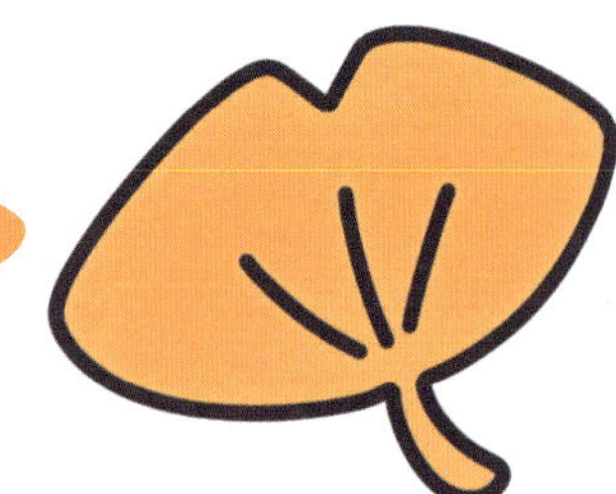

They start out green and change into yellow!

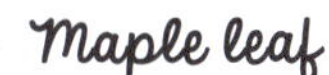

Maple leaf

Draw three rounded triangles.

Add two more larger triangles at the bottom.

Complete the drawing with a stem.

Poison leaf

Start with two lines that cross each other.

Add the leaves at the end of the lines.

Three leaves usually means it could be poisonous and itchy!

Large leaf

Begin this leaf by drawing three round bumps.

Complete the bottom with four more bumps.

Draw in a line at the centre for the stem.

BUSHES

Under the trees in the forest you can also find lots of different plants, including flower and berry bushes.

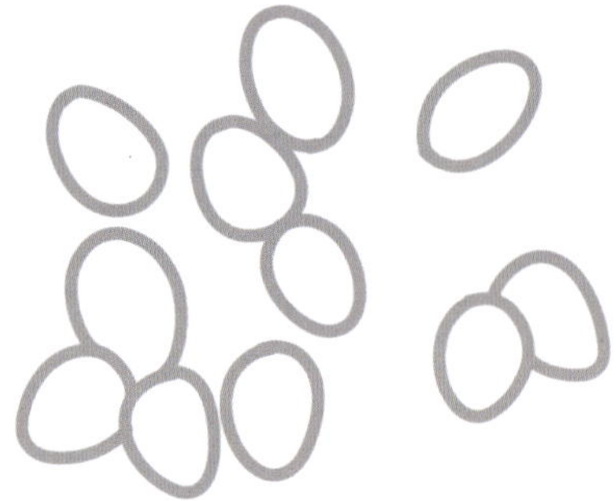

Give yourself a guideline for drawing strawberry leaves by starting out with a group of ovals.

Then draw pointy lines around the circles. This creates the leaf outlines.

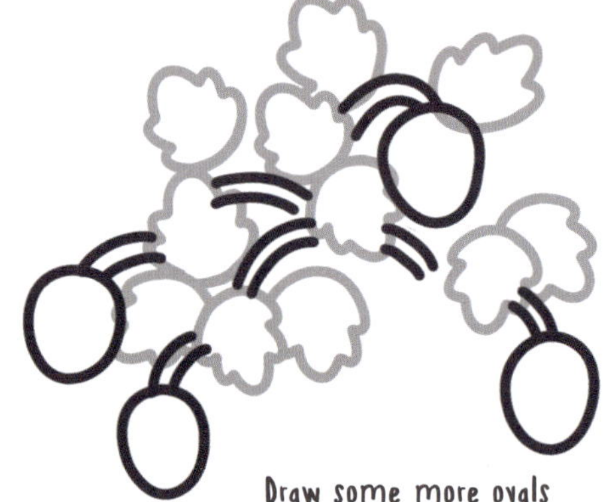

Draw some more ovals and stems in between the spaces to create the strawberries.

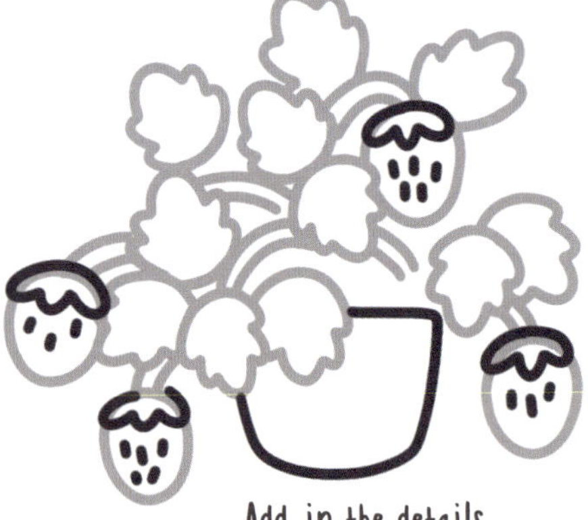

Add in the details of the strawberries, like the dot seeds and leaves on top.

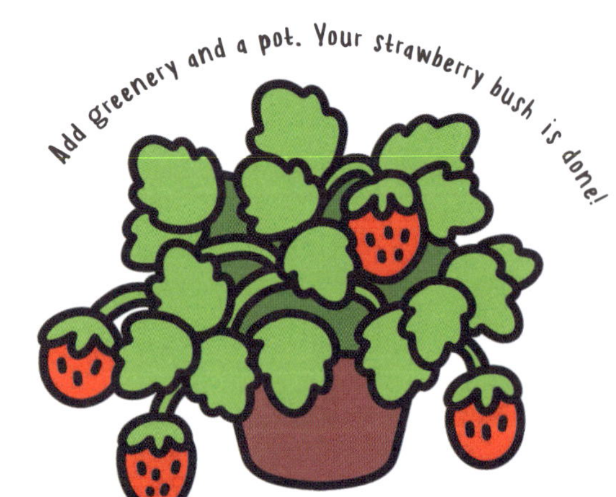

Add greenery and a pot. Your strawberry bush is done!

One way to draw bushes is to start with a circle that you can add leaves, flowers and berries to.

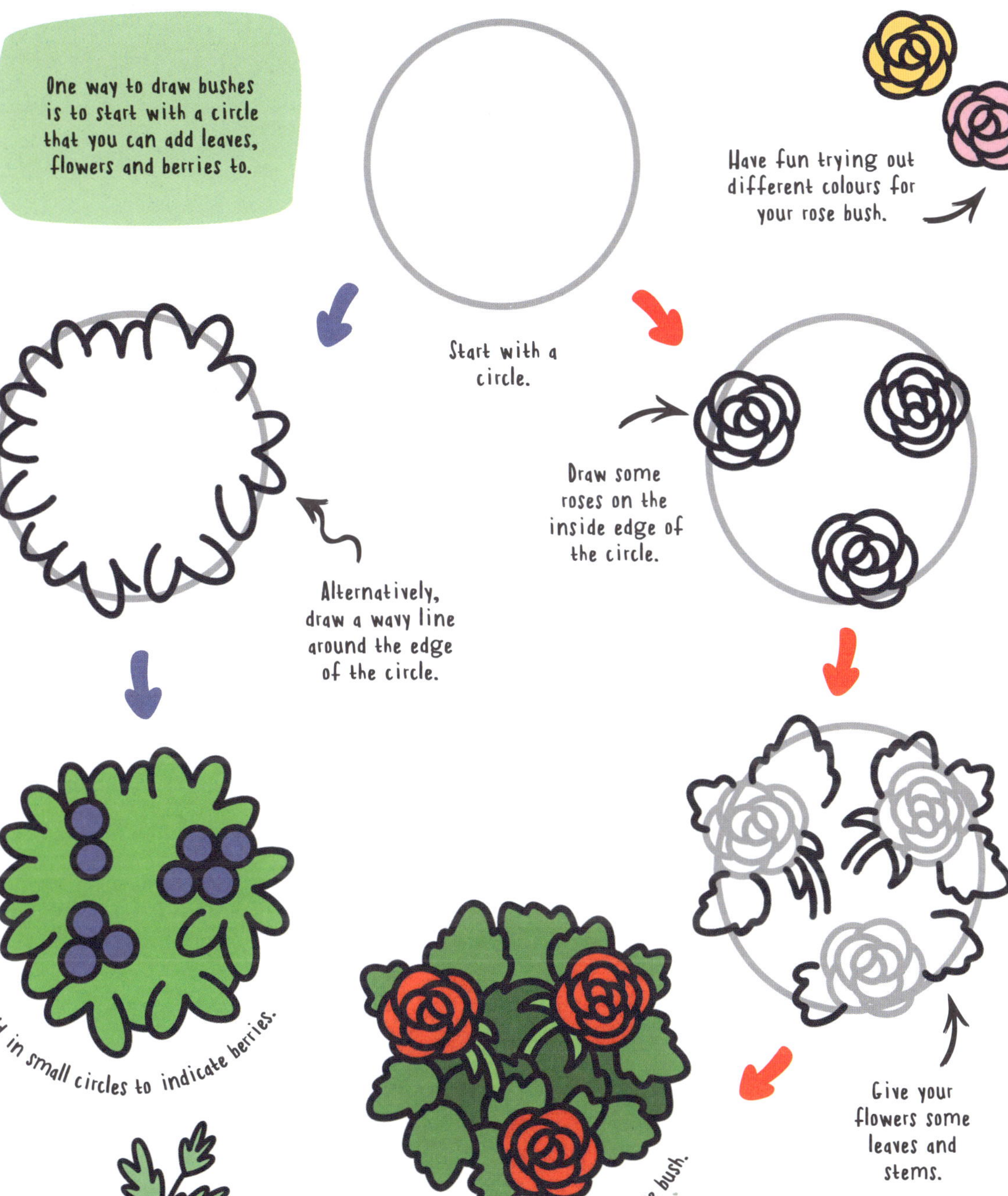

Your shrubs can also fan out from a central stem or pot. Draw your leaves and stems growing in different directions.

ACORNS, PINE CONES AND CONKERS

These are the three essential seeds for your woodland world. They are perfect for decorating around your home or making into cute little creatures.

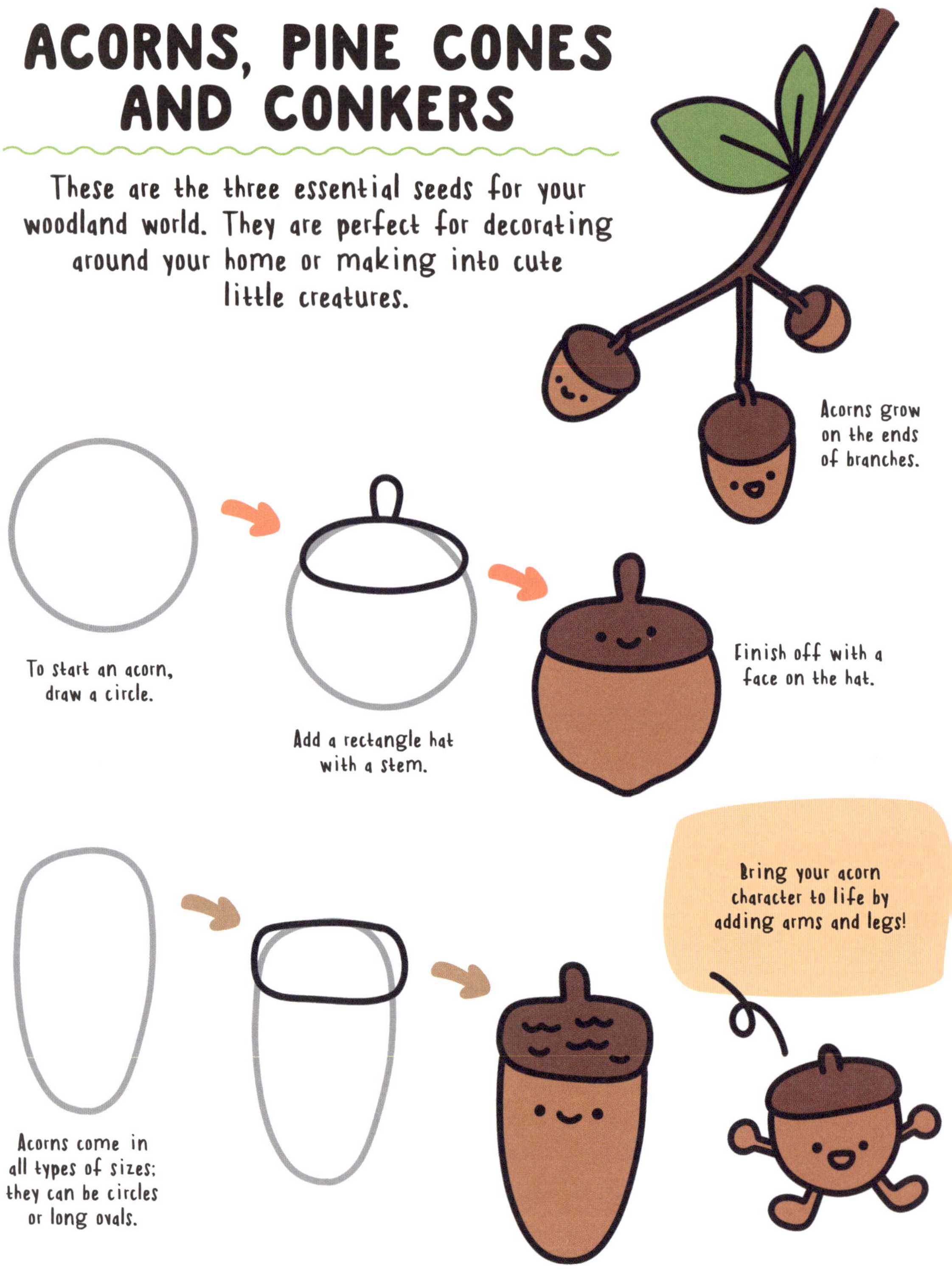

Pine cones

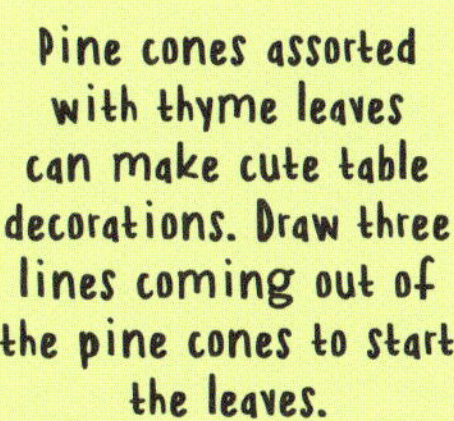

Pine cones assorted with thyme leaves can make cute table decorations. Draw three lines coming out of the pine cones to start the leaves.

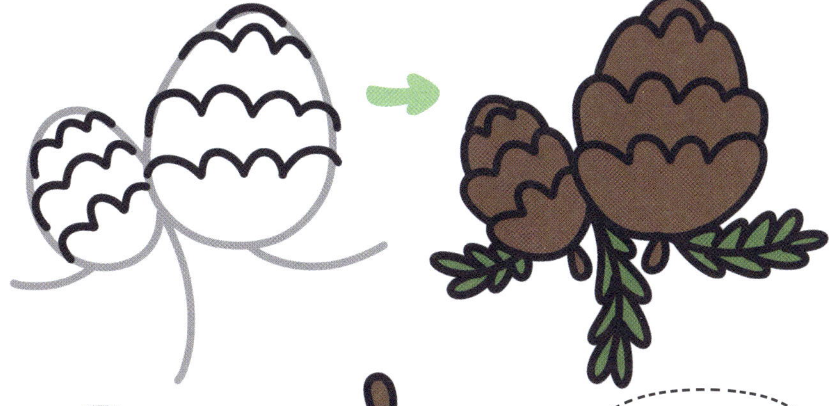

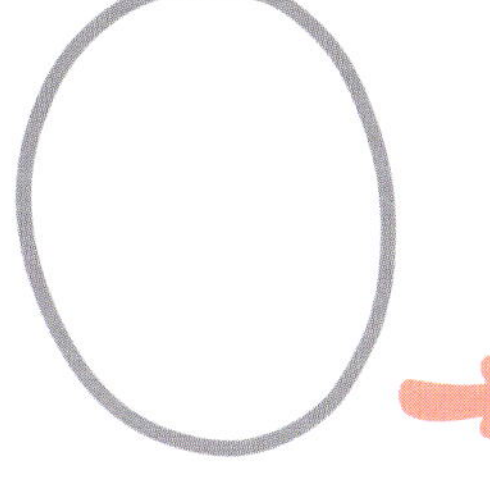

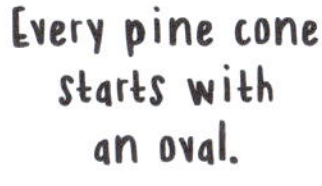

Every pine cone starts with an oval.

Draw bumpy lines around the oval to make the pine cone pattern.

I would look great in a wreath! (See page 122.)

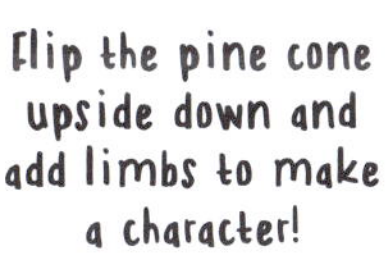

Flip the pine cone upside down and add limbs to make a character!

Conkers

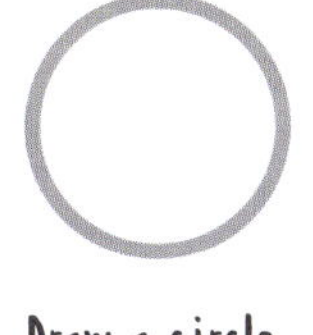

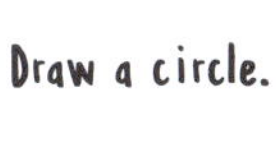

Draw a circle.

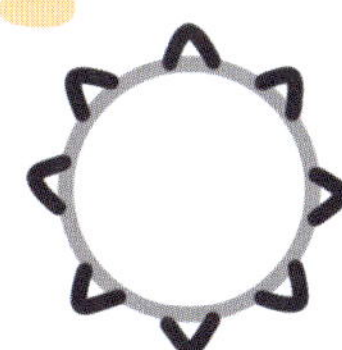

Add triangles around the circle.

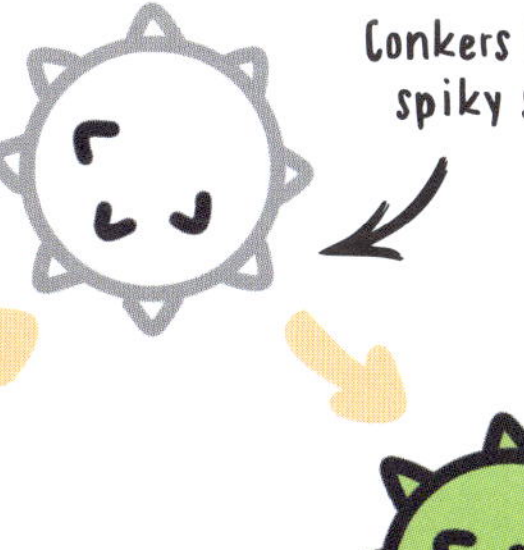

Conkers have a spiky shell.

Keep the mouth close to the eyes to make it even cuter.

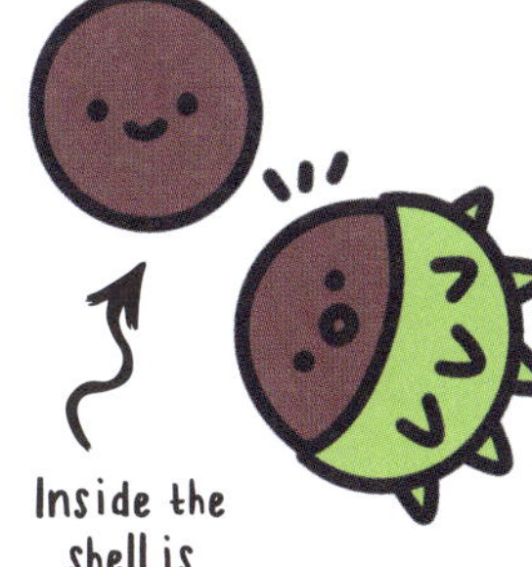

Inside the shell is the seed!

MOUNTAINS

Mountains are my favourite scenery type. They are simple to draw because the bases are always made up of triangles, and you can add fun features like trees or water.

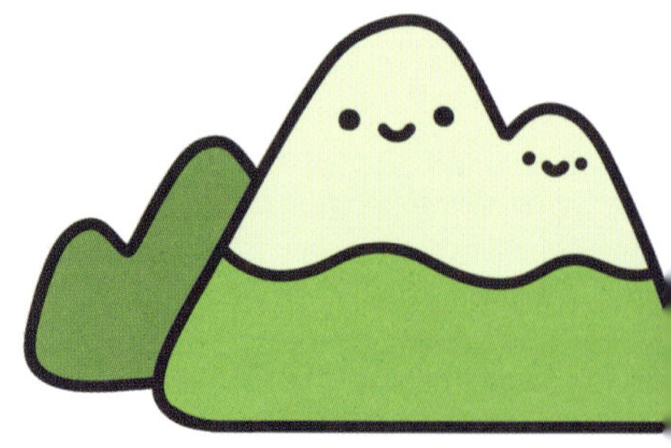

Mountains are lighter in colour on the top because they usually have snow up there.

Draw two overlapping triangles.

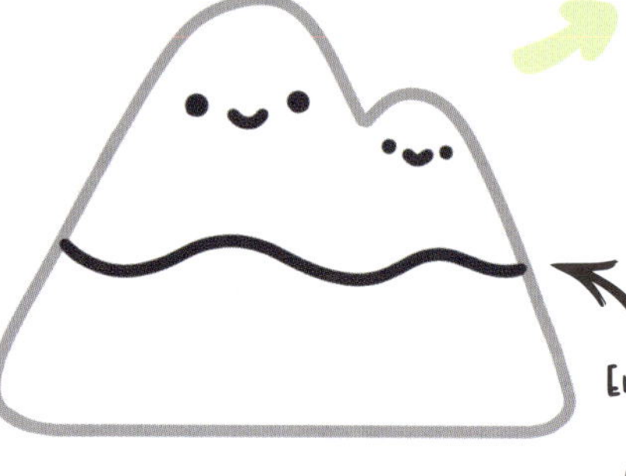

Erase the lines that overlap. Draw in the mountain details like the face and squiggly snow line.

In the clouds

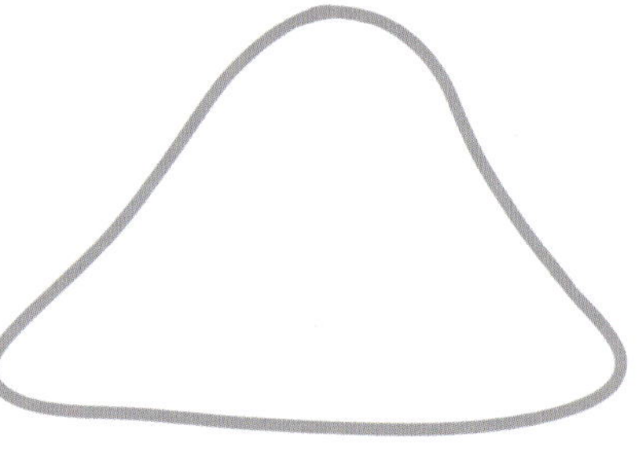

Draw a triangle with rounded corners.

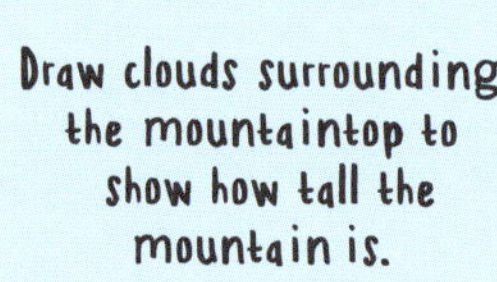

Draw clouds surrounding the mountaintop to show how tall the mountain is.

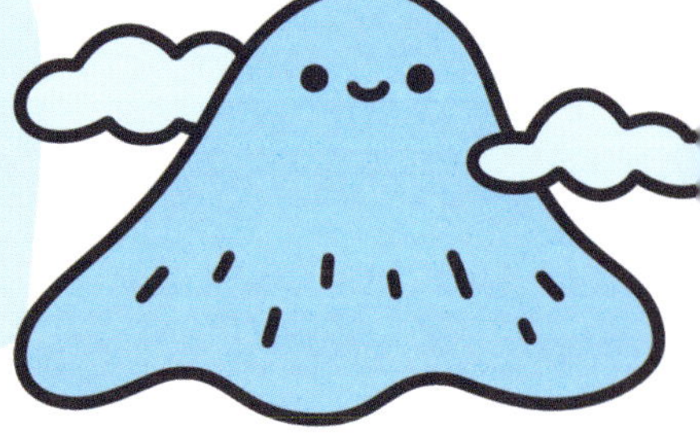

Draw a wavy line along the base of the mountain, and squiggly shapes for the clouds.

Mountain falls

Water on top of mountains comes from melted snow or rain. A pool of water can add a fun element to your mountain drawing.

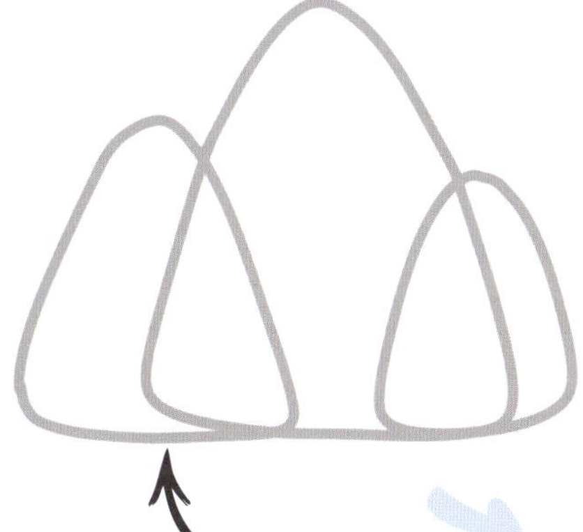

Draw three overlapping triangles.

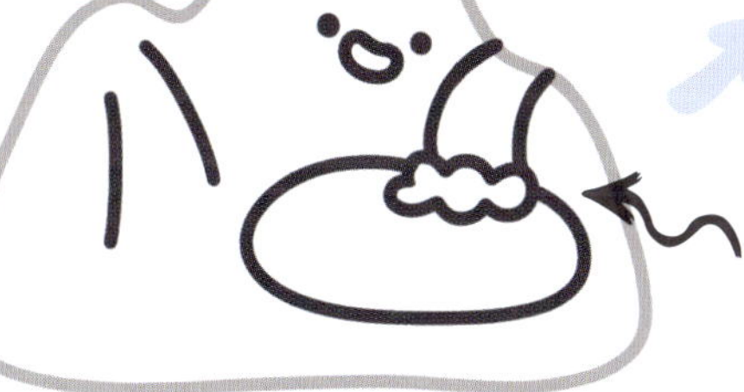

Draw an oval for the pool of water and add a waterfall that fills it.

Draw a cloud shape where the falling water crashes into the pool.

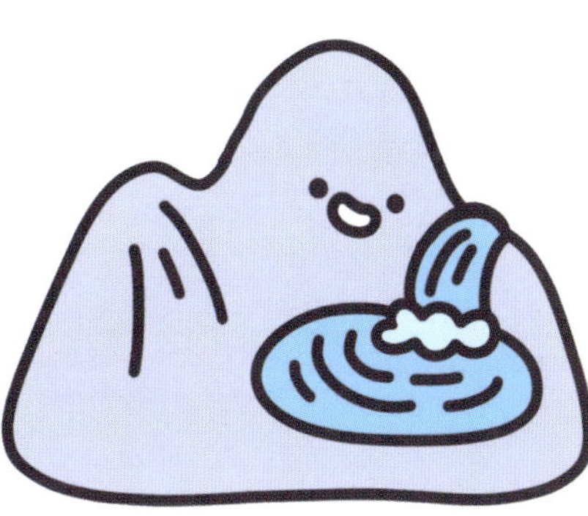

Tall and wide

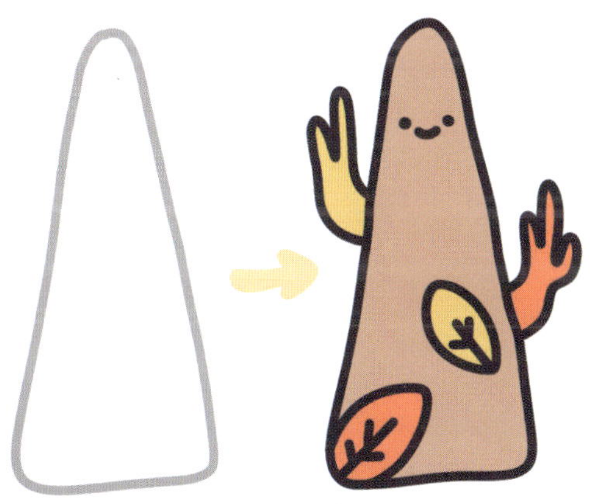

Your mountain could be tall and thin. This one is like a tree, with leaves and branches.

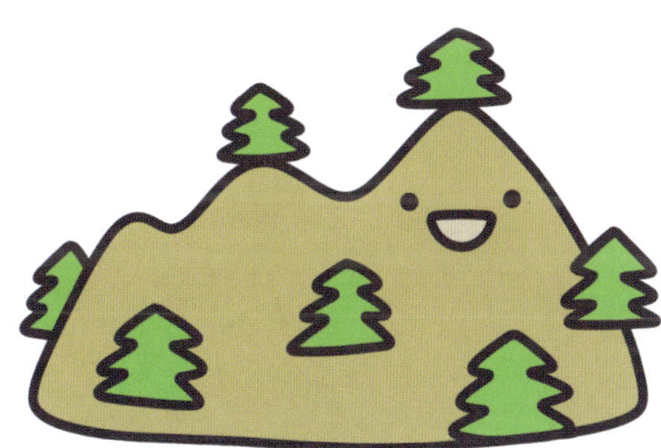

To make your mountain range wide, simply draw more triangles side by side.

ROCKS AND BOULDERS

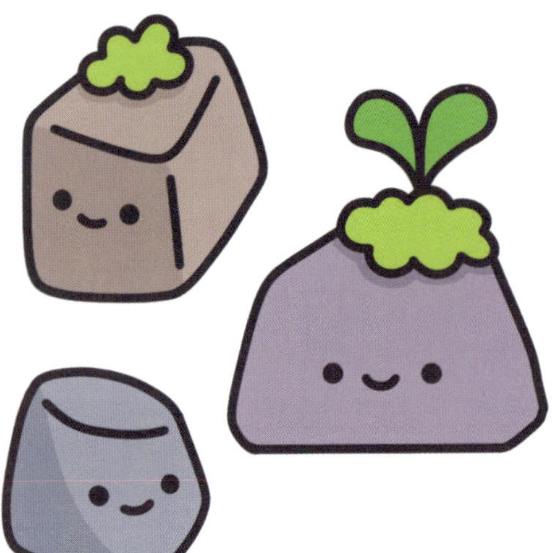

Something as simple as a rock can be transformed into a super-cute character! With just a face and some added features, you can draw your own rock creatures.

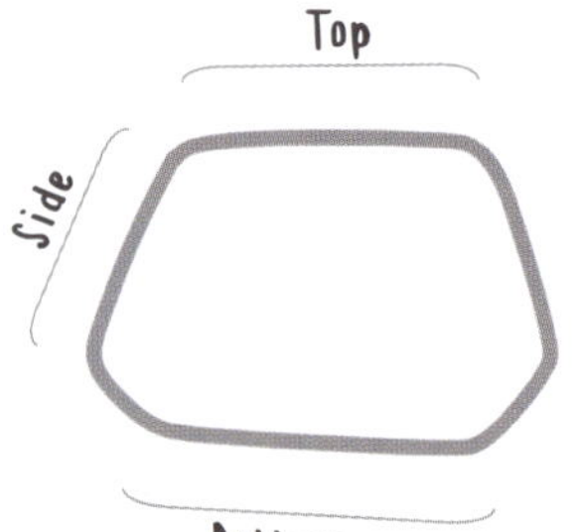

Start with any angular shape that has a top, bottom and sides.

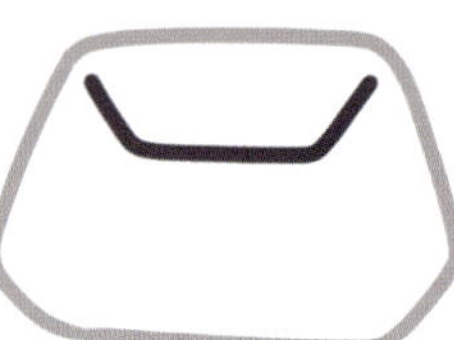

Now draw straight lines inside the basic shape to make your rock appear three-dimensional.

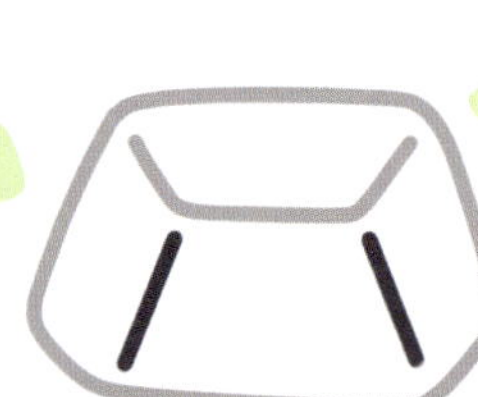

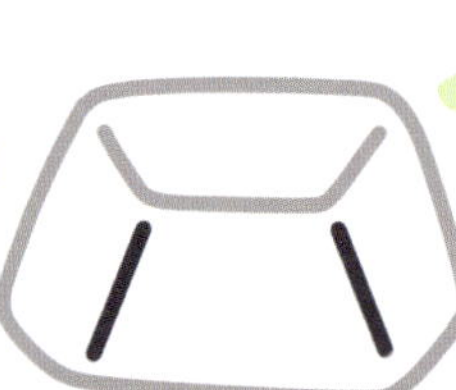

Add lines that echo the main rock shape.

Finish with a face.

Play with shapes

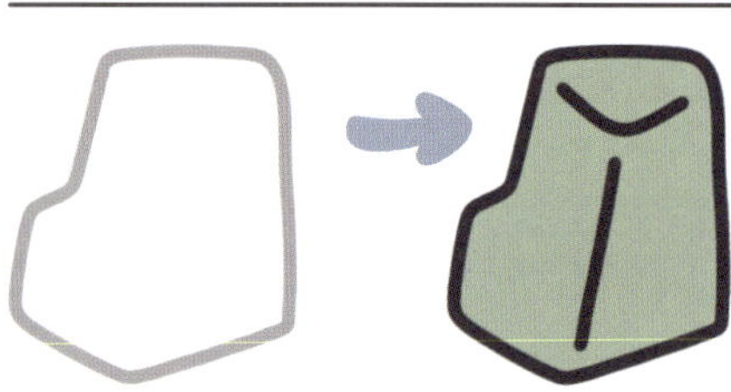

You can transform any two-dimensional shape into a three-dimensional rock . . .

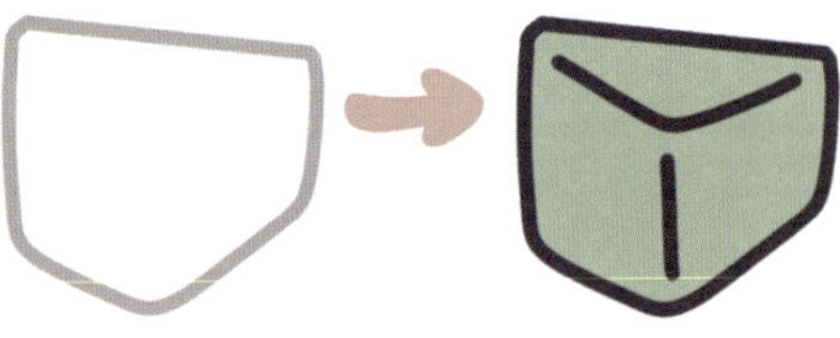

. . . using the same techniques.

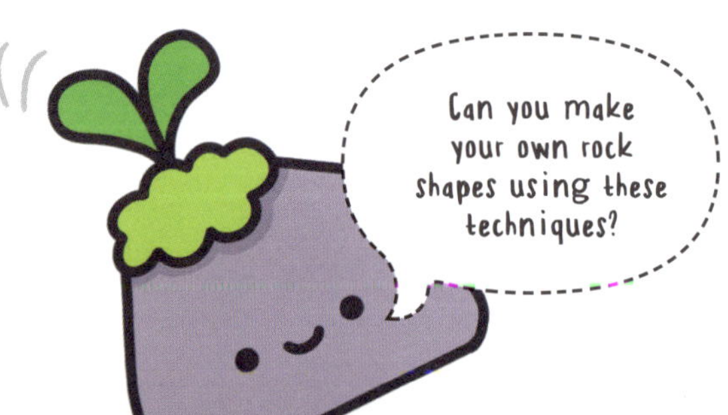

Can you make your own rock shapes using these techniques?

Plant rock

Draw the base shape for your rock and add ovals a short distance above.

Use curved lines to connect the ovals to the rock and make mushrooms. Add a wavy line for the moss growing on top of the rock.

Rock creatures

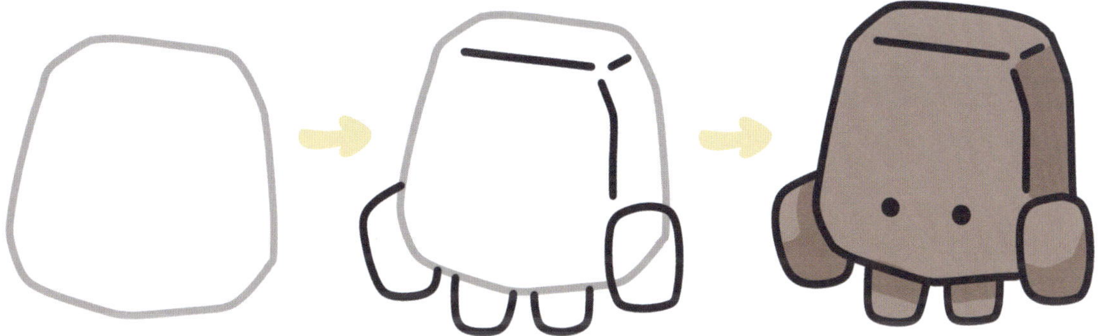

To draw a rock creature, start by drawing the rock base.

Add lines that make up the sides. Then draw the limbs.

The limbs are like smaller rectangle rocks.

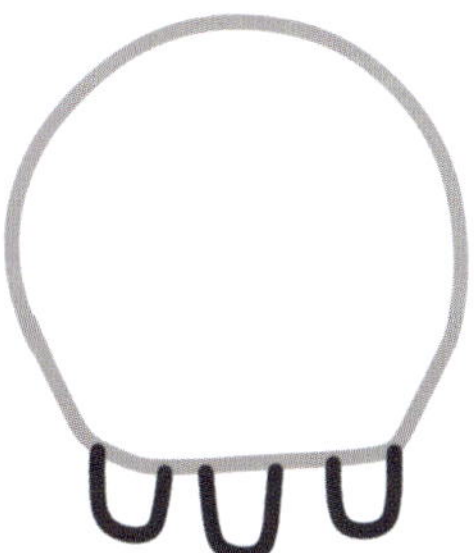

This rock creature has a rounded base shape and curved limbs.

Draw a wavy line all around the top of the rock for the moss.

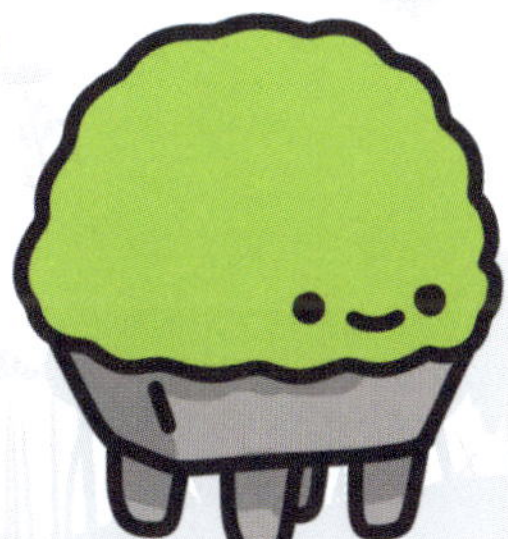

Make your rock creature wave its arms in the air while it is running to show excitement!

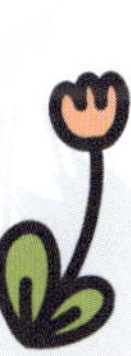

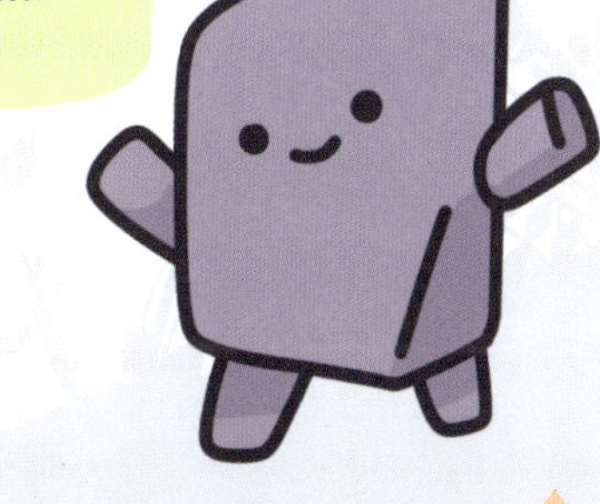

CRYSTALS

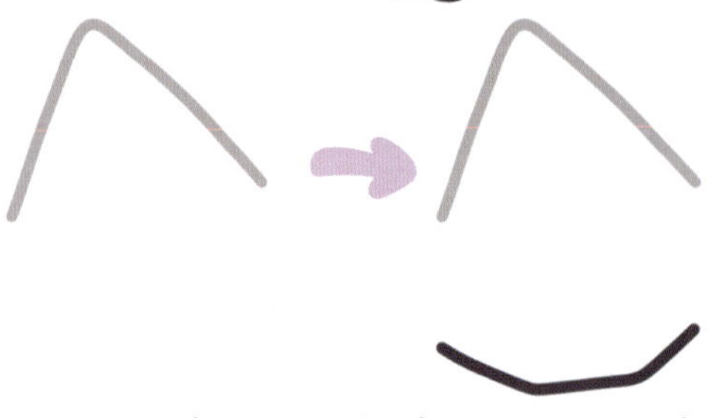

Crystals form naturally from melted rock or vapour. They start small and multiply into large, beautiful formations.

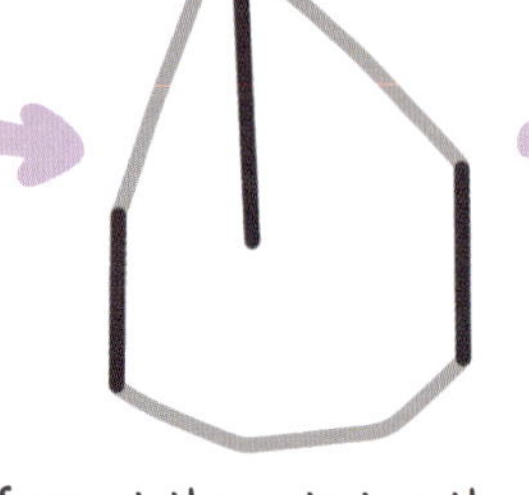

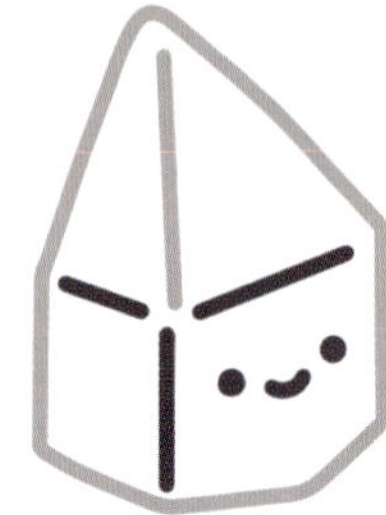

Draw two lines like the tip of a triangle.

Add lines in an angular formation a short distance below the first lines.

Connect the parts together and add a vertical line inside the shape.

Add a face and a few more lines to draw a three-dimensional crystal.

To give your crystals a shiny effect, add white lines when colouring.

You can draw different formations by adding more lines.

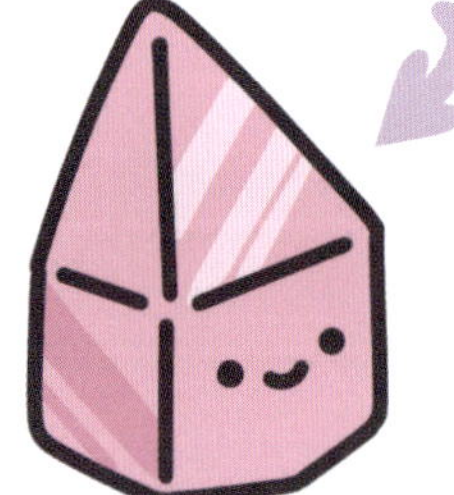

Rock crystals

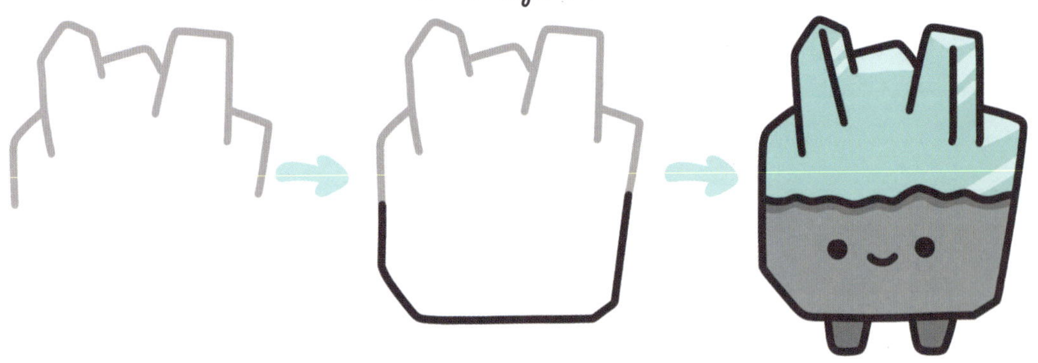

Crystals can grow on top of rocks. Draw a cluster of crystals.

Add the rock shape underneath the crystal formation.

Colour the top as a shiny crystal and the bottom as grey rock.

Crystal formations

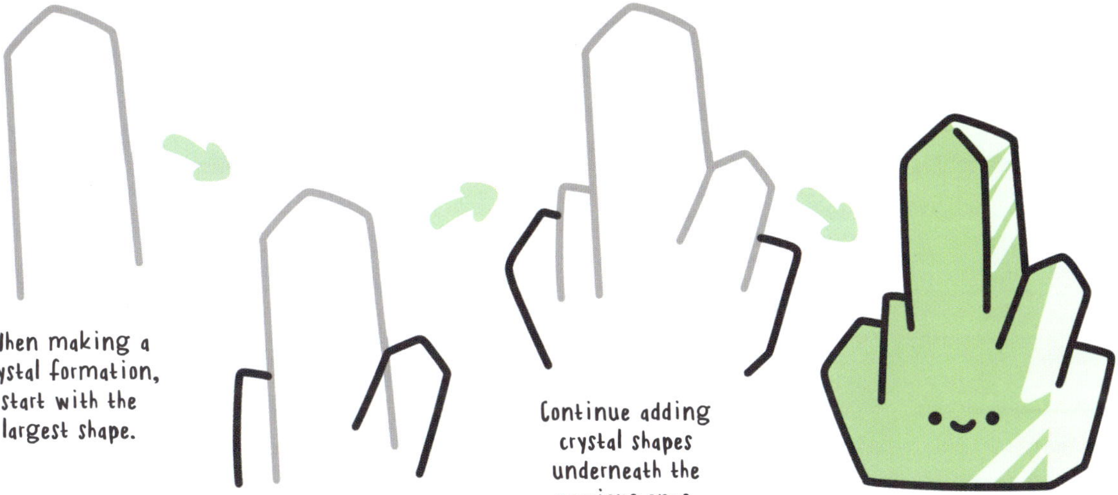

When making a crystal formation, start with the largest shape.

Add smaller crystal shapes under the first one.

Continue adding crystal shapes underneath the previous ones.

When you're happy with your formation, close the bottom with a horizontal line.

Crystal creature

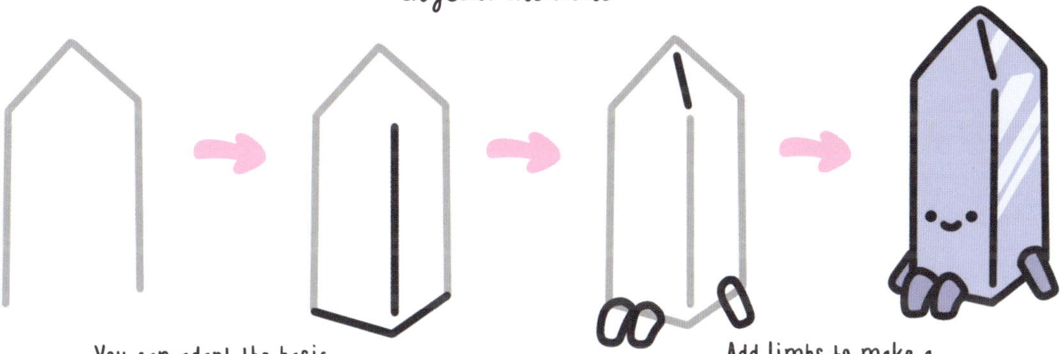

You can adapt the basic crystal shape really easily. This is a tall crystal.

Add limbs to make a crystal creature.

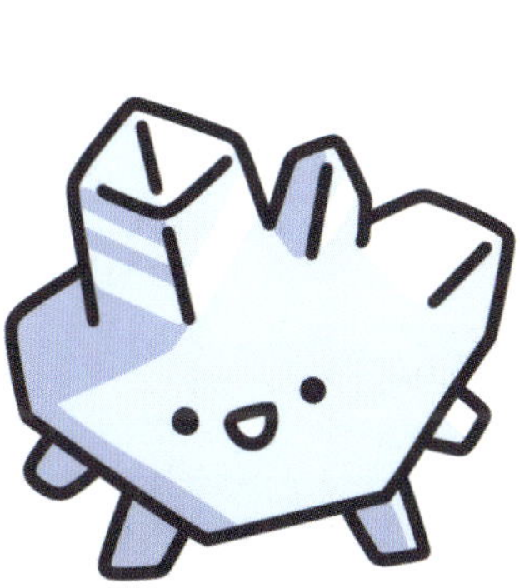

You can be creative with your crystal formations by giving them ears or limbs. Play around with their colours too.

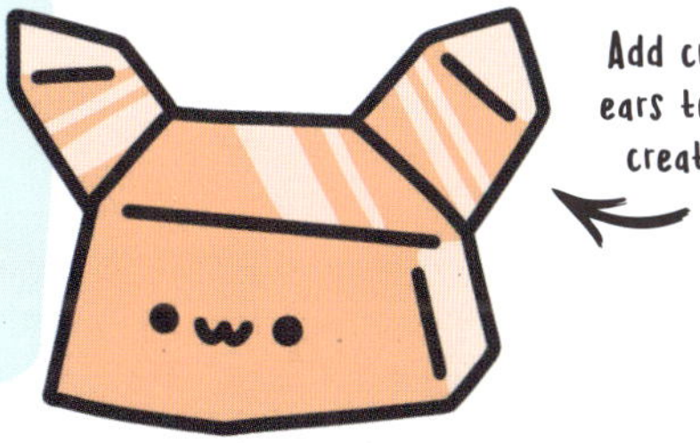

Add crystal ears to this creature.

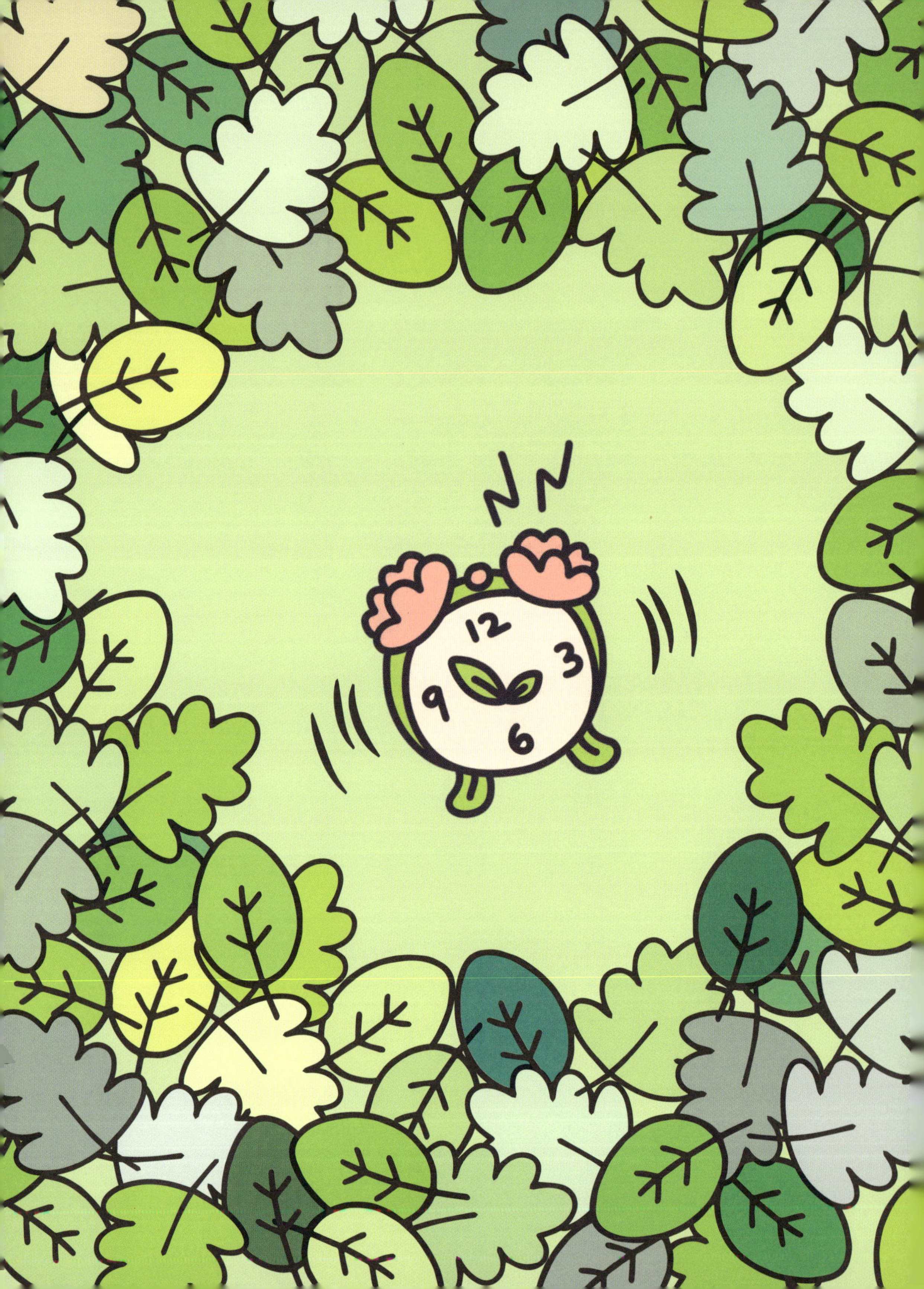
12
3
9
6

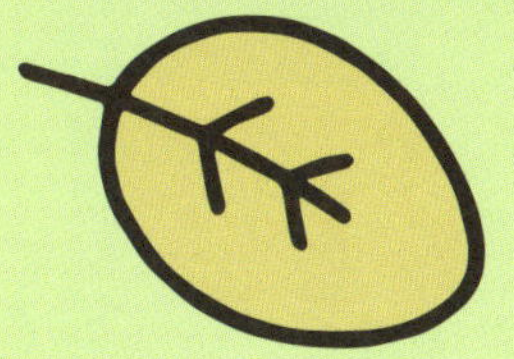

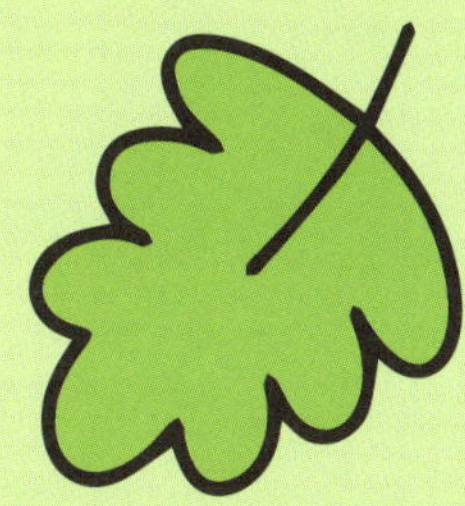

Chapter five

FOREST LIVING

Everything can be cute! To complete your woodland world, you need to give a woodland twist to inanimate objects, from houses to vehicles and everything in between.

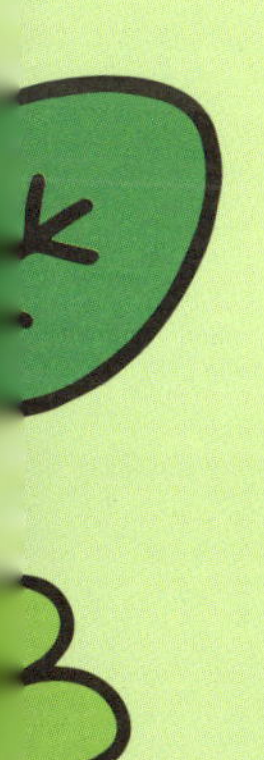

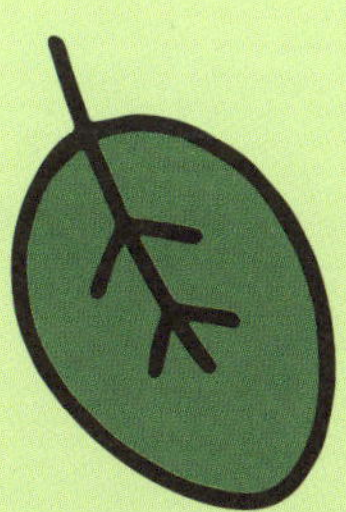

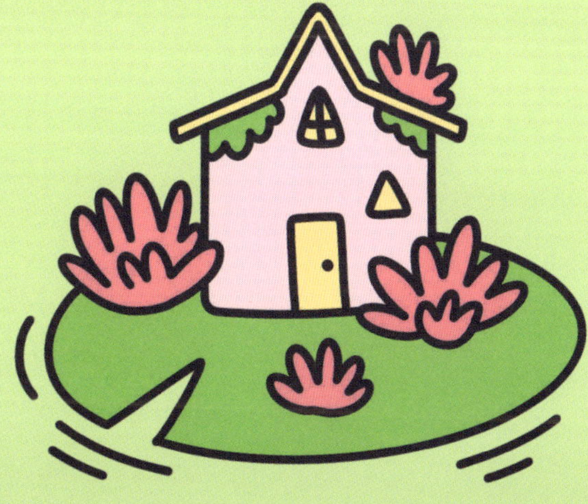

HOMES

When it comes to drawing homes for your woodland folk and forest creatures, you can be really creative. Build homes in the trees, on water or even out of the natural forest landscape.

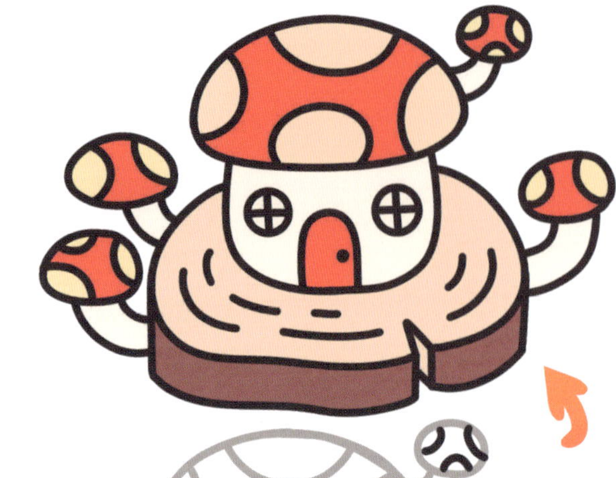

This is a mushroom house with lots of extensions! Draw a mushroom base.

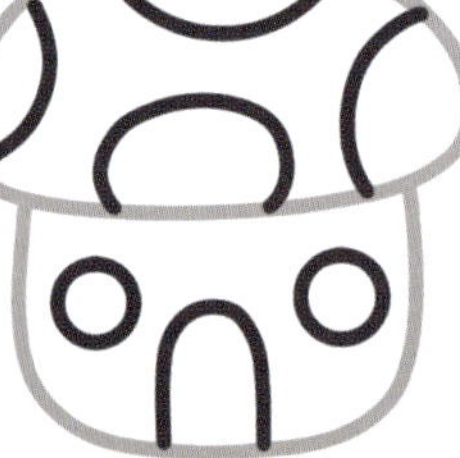

Draw circle windows, an arched door and circles on the roof.

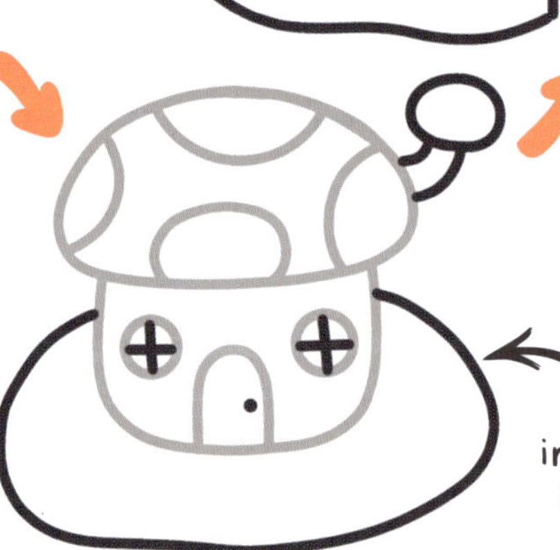

Draw a circle to indicate the log that the house sits on.

Fill out the log and add mushrooms sprouting out from it.

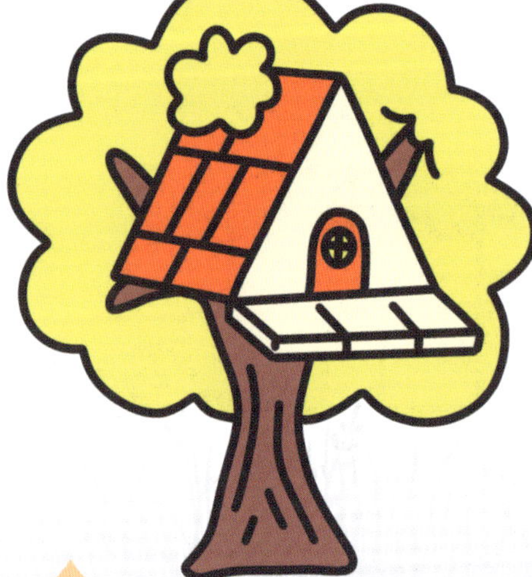

To draw a tree house, start with a tree, then add the house nestled in the branches.

Lily pad home

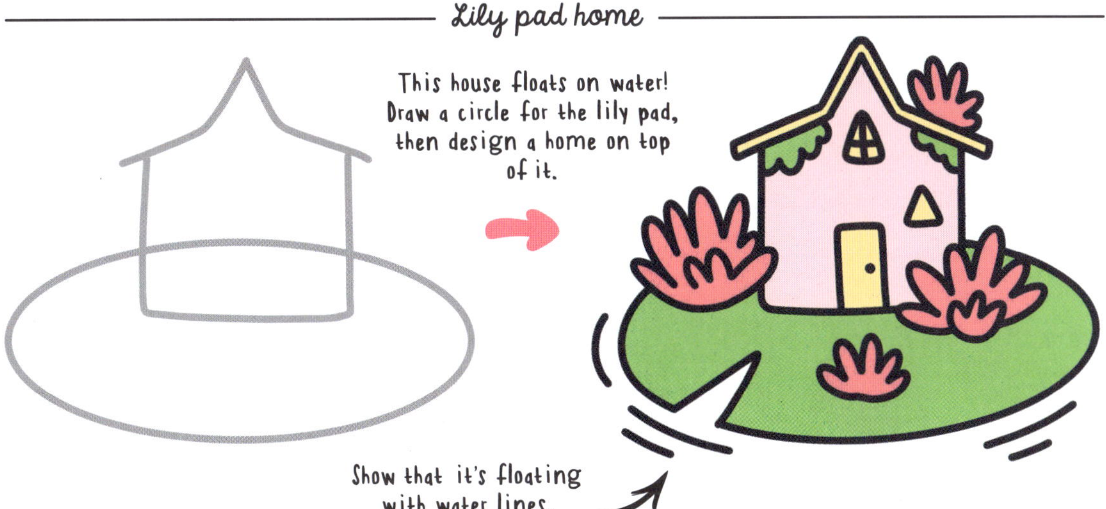

Bush garden home

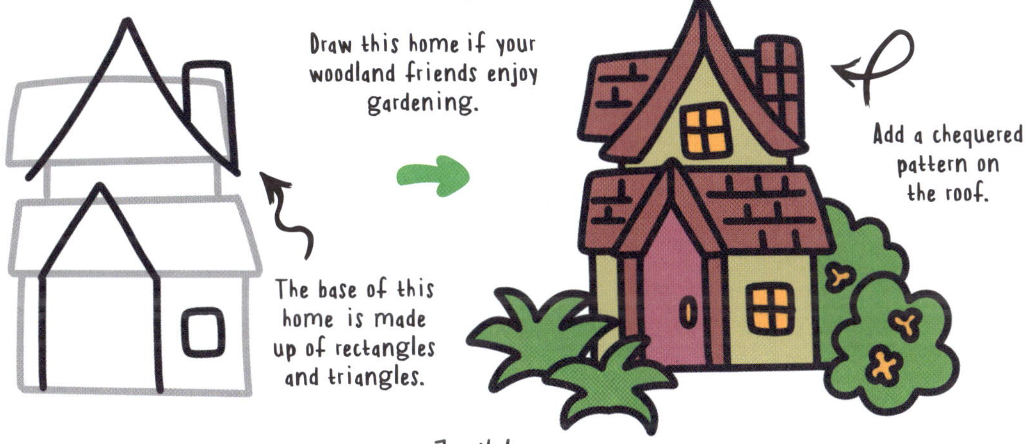

Fruit home

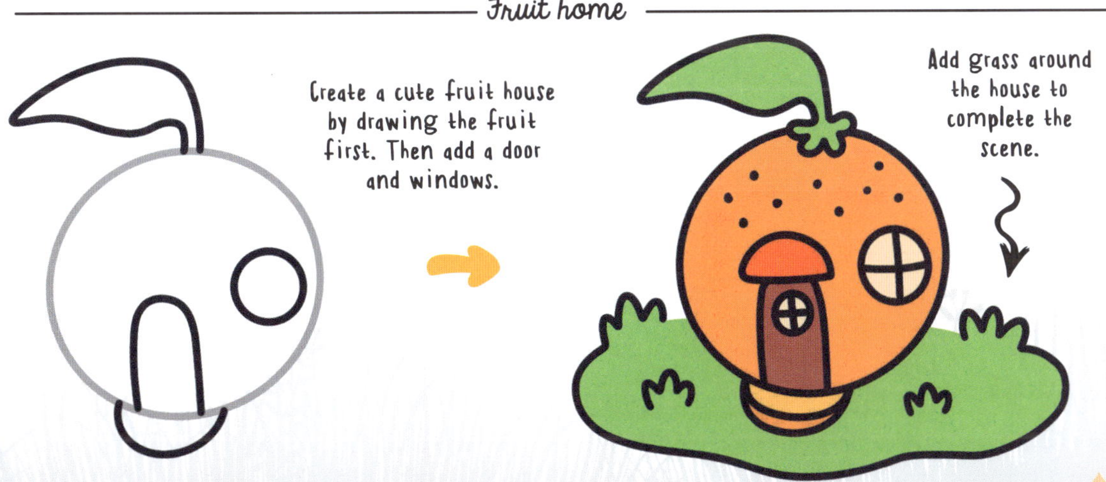

FURNITURE

Fill your forest homes with chic woodland furniture. Here are some pieces that I think you will like.

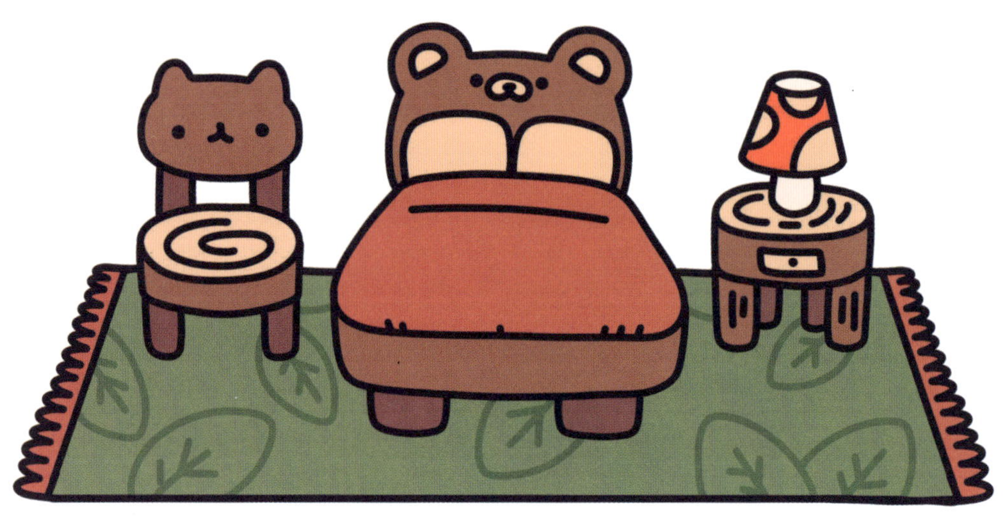

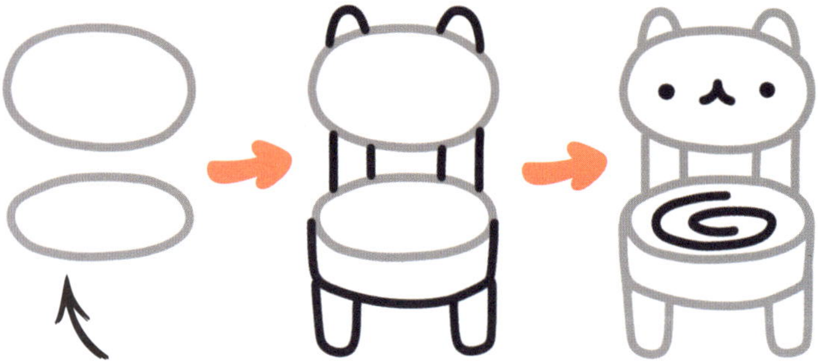

The bear chair starts with two ovals.

Add legs, back struts and all the bear details.

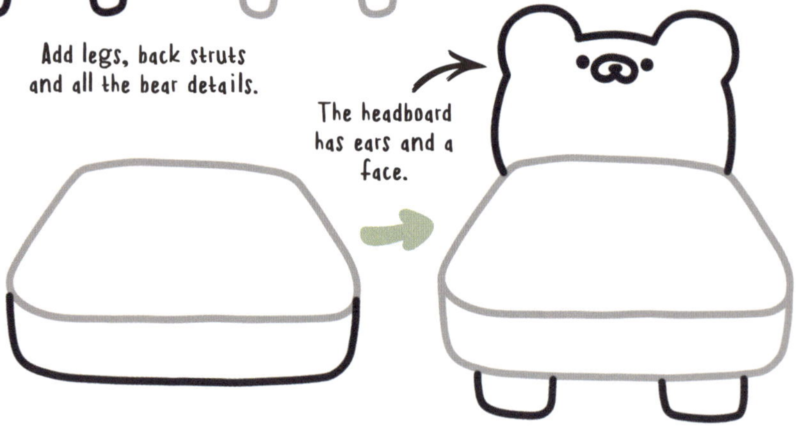

This room set is inspired by bears. Think about the woodland animals or plants that you can draw inspiration from.

The headboard has ears and a face.

To draw a bear bed, start with the mattress.

Froggy furniture

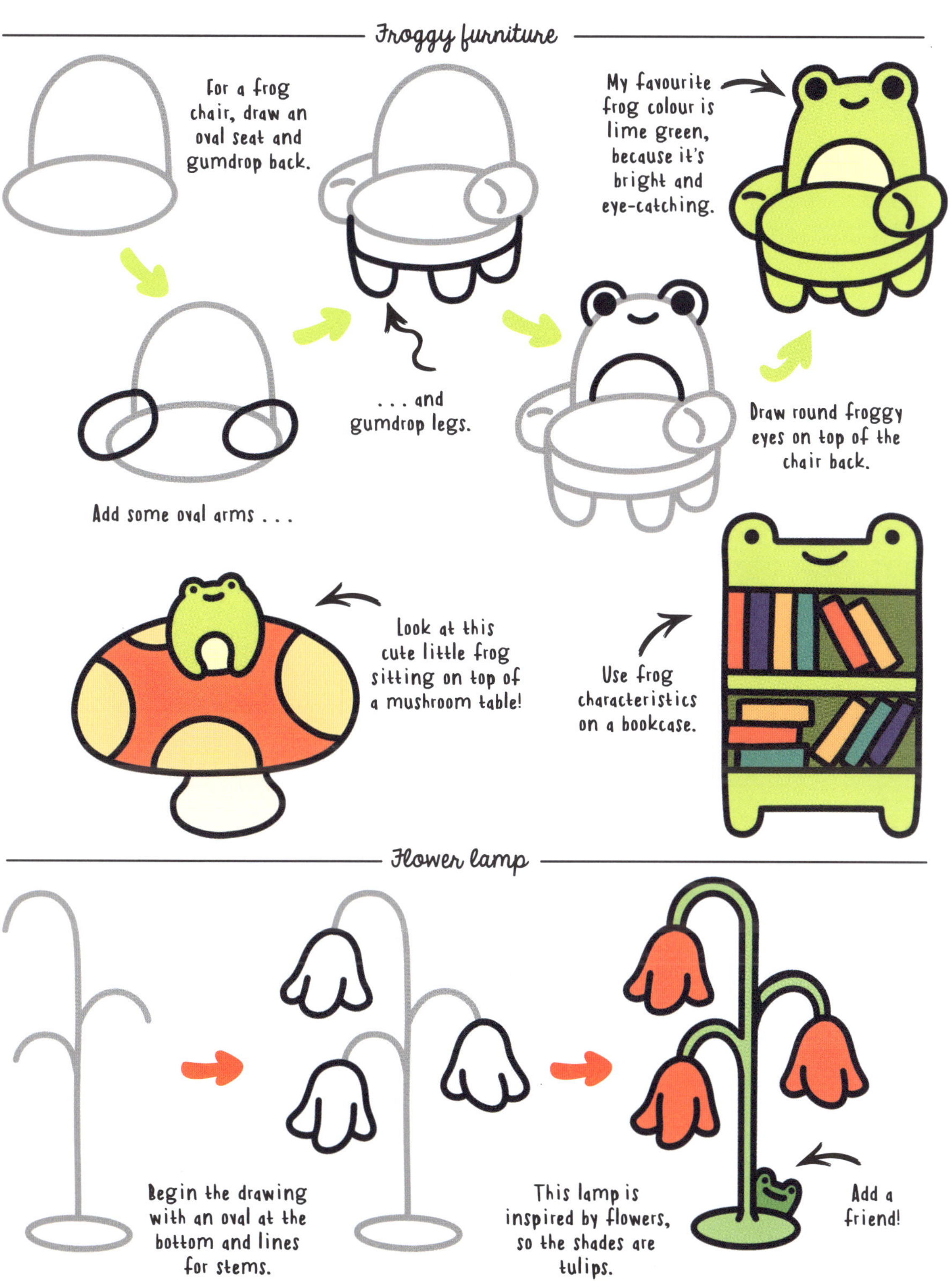

HOUSEPLANTS

Having houseplants is like bringing the forest indoors with you. Plants can brighten up any home, and bring in more oxygen.

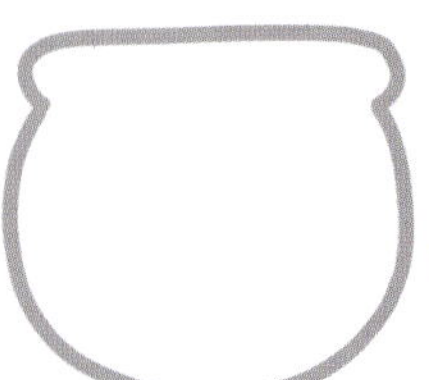

Draw a plant pot. This one is like an upside-down gumdrop.

Pilea plants have circle leaves.

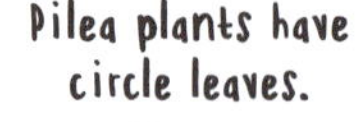

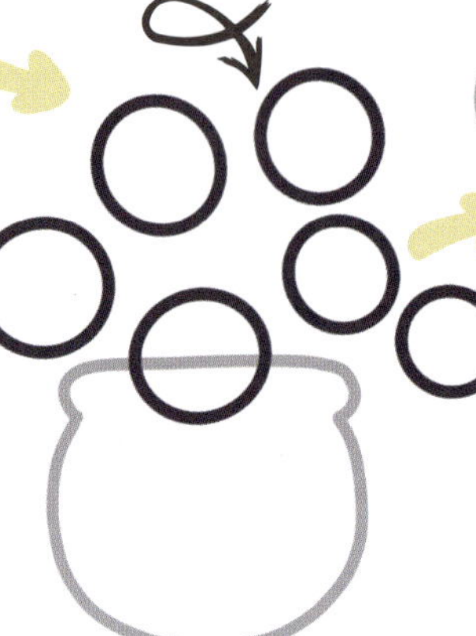

Draw circles of different sizes all around the top.

Connect the circles to the pot by drawing stems.

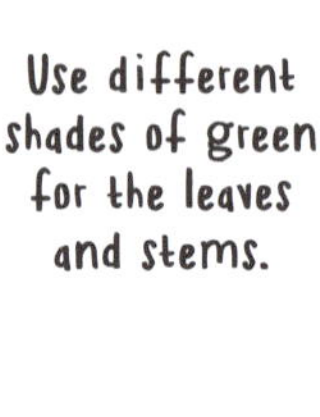

Use different shades of green for the leaves and stems.

The number of leaves that your houseplant has is completely up to you! I keep adding leaves until I feel like my drawing is full.

Leaves on leaves

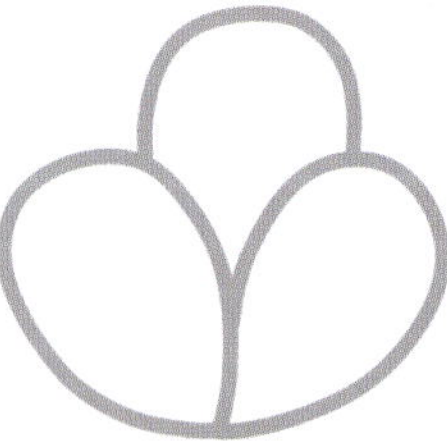

Sometimes I like to start by drawing leaves instead of the pot.

Keep adding leaves on top of one another.

Add leaf veins. Draw the pot at the bottom and then add a face.

Spiky

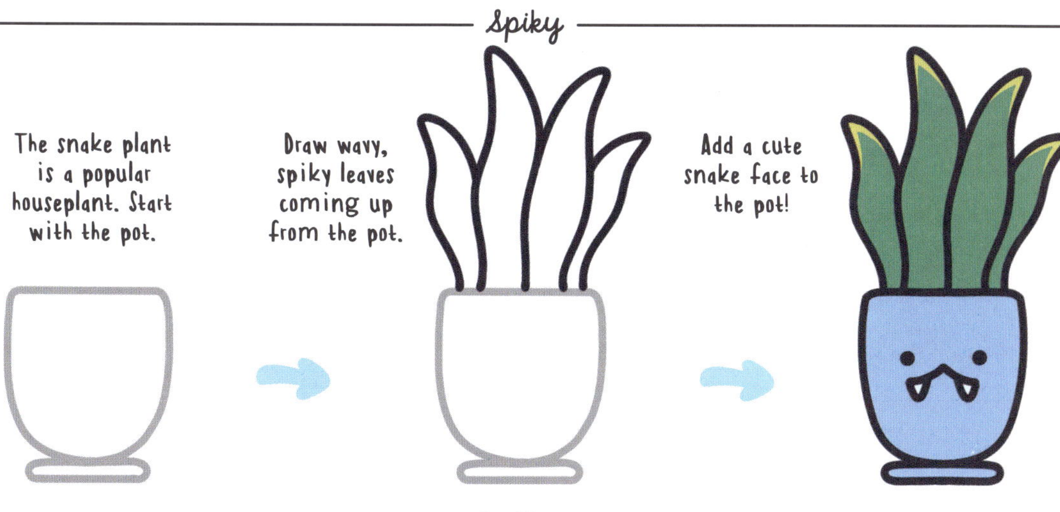

Frilly

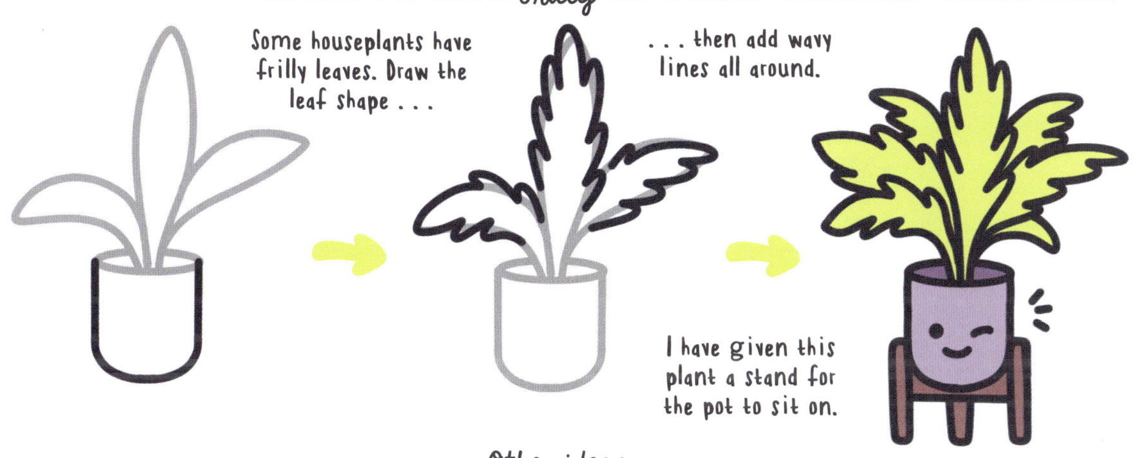

Other ideas

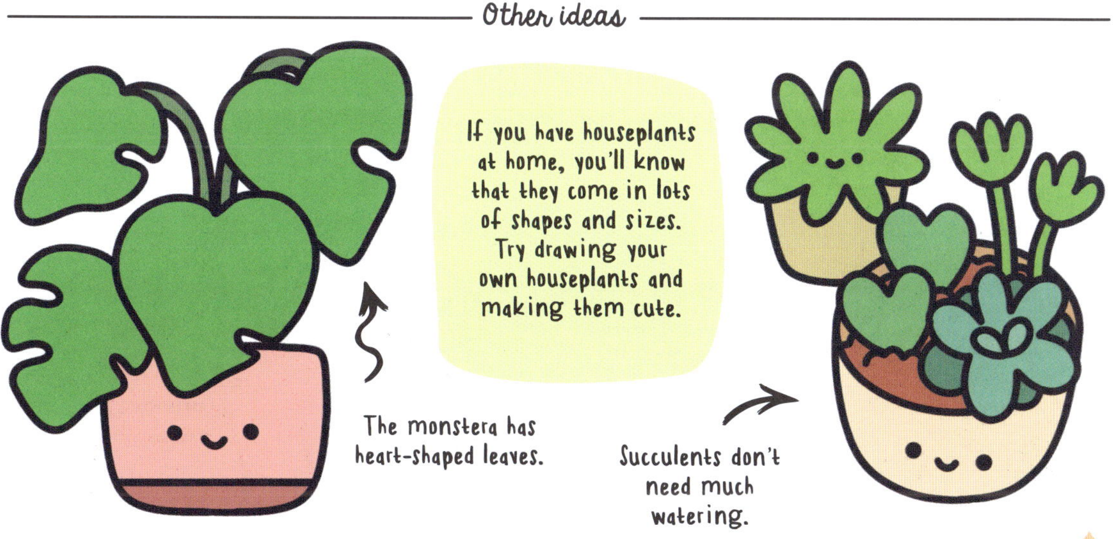

EVERYDAY OBJECTS

Willow-woven baskets can be filled with all sorts of objects.

Decorations and accessories inspired by woodland themes are the icing on the cake for your cute character and environment drawings. There are endless possibilities to combine everyday objects with forest themes, and I've given just a few examples here.

Woodland wreath

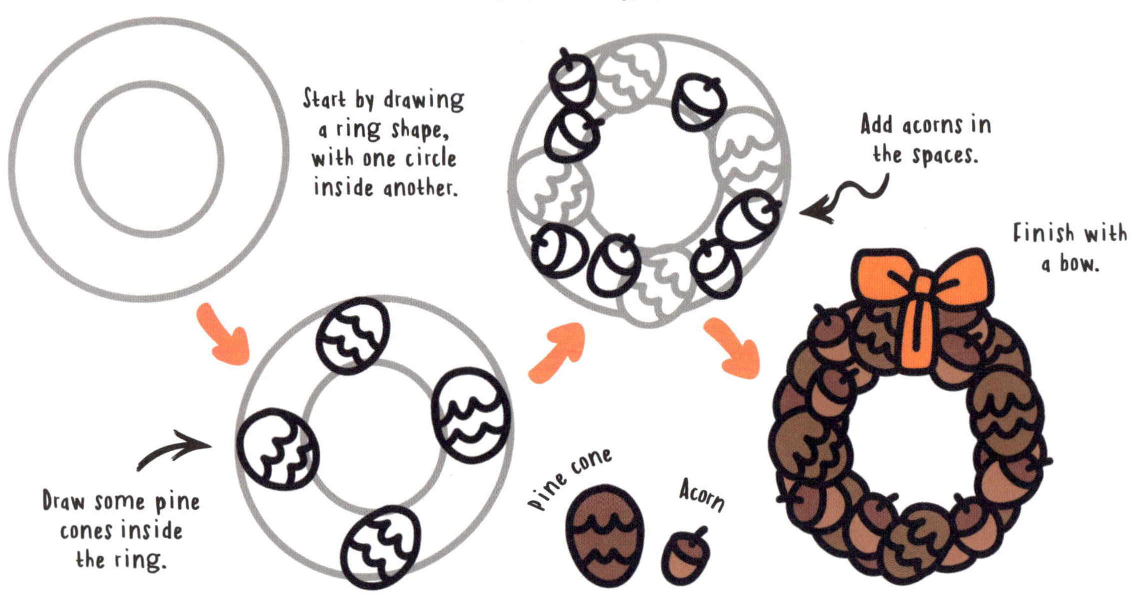

Home accessories

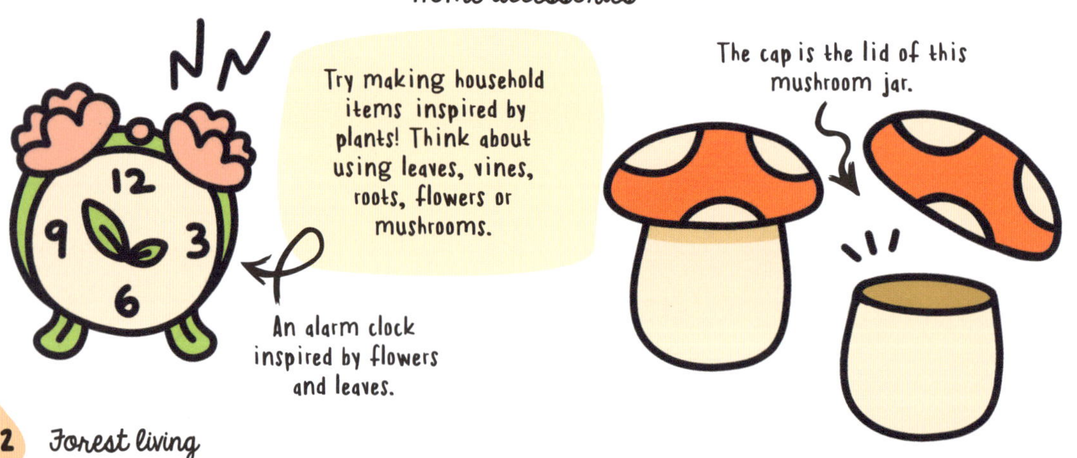

Try making household items inspired by plants! Think about using leaves, vines, roots, flowers or mushrooms.

An alarm clock inspired by flowers and leaves.

The cap is the lid of this mushroom jar.

Character accessories

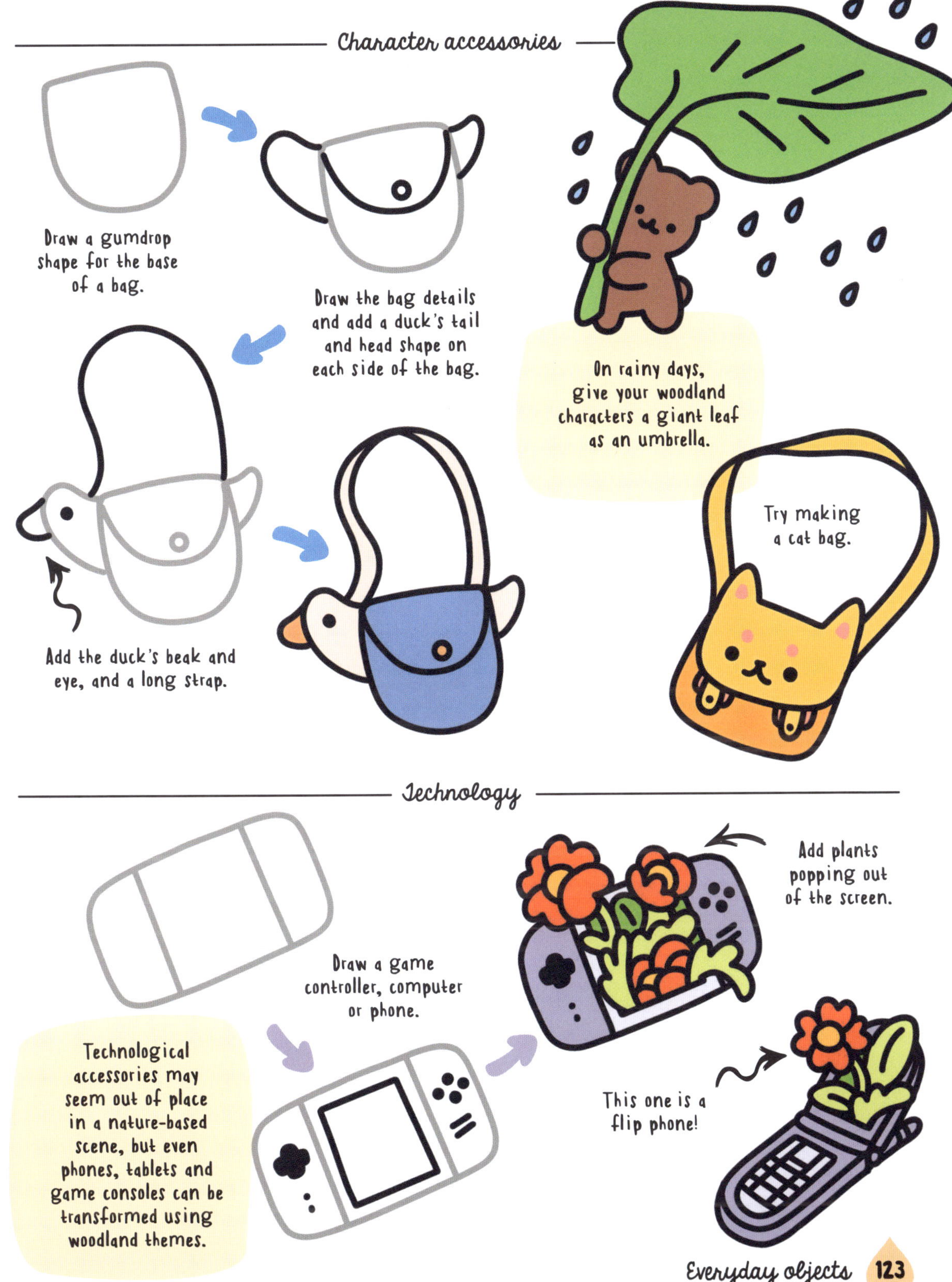

Technological accessories may seem out of place in a nature-based scene, but even phones, tablets and game consoles can be transformed using woodland themes.

FOOD AND DRINK

When creating woodland food, think of nature-inspired designs or fresh ingredients that can be found at farmers' markets. You can decorate dishware with plant patterns, or even give your food animal characteristics.

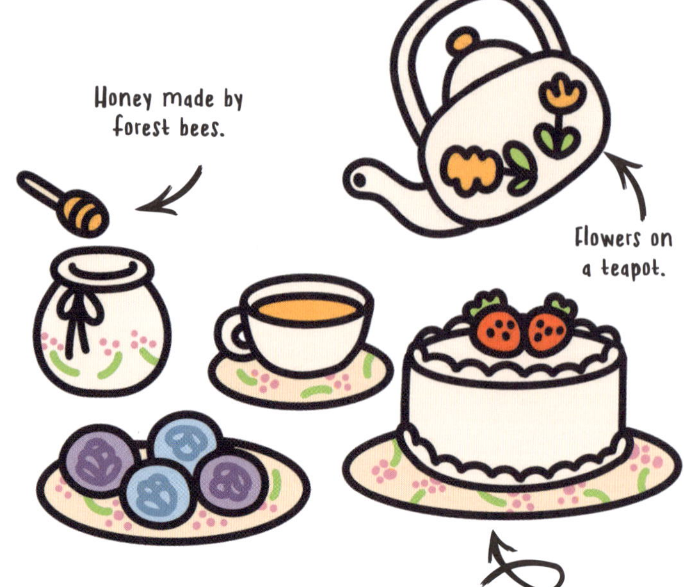

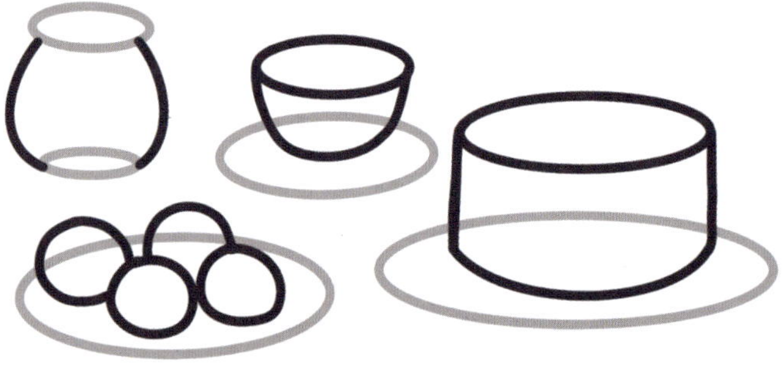

Lay the table with oval plates. Then start adding the food.

This is a cute teatime scene, with lovely treats. You could add triangle sandwiches or round biscuits.

Have fun adding the foodie details.

Fresh ingredients

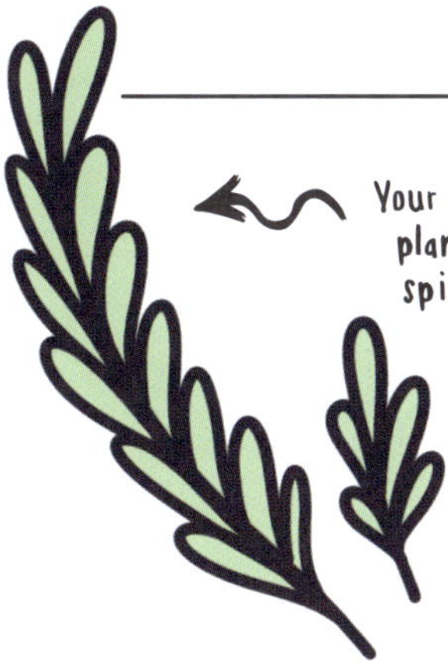

Your characters can forage plants like rosemary to spice up their recipes.

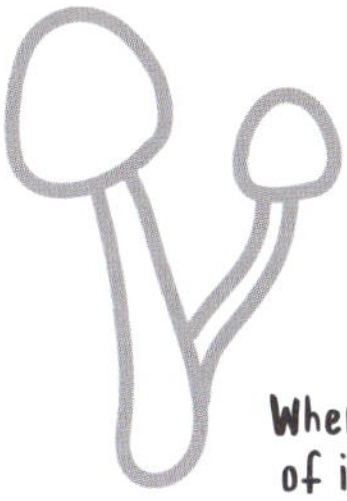

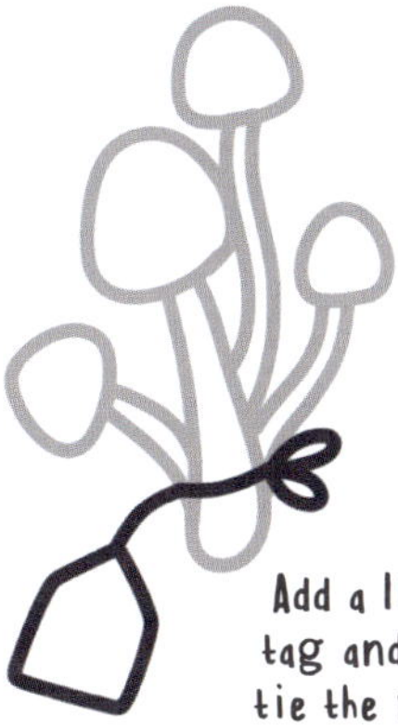

Add a little price tag and string to tie the mushrooms together.

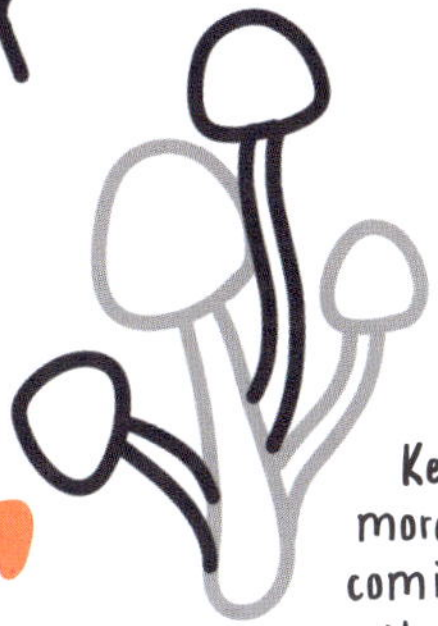

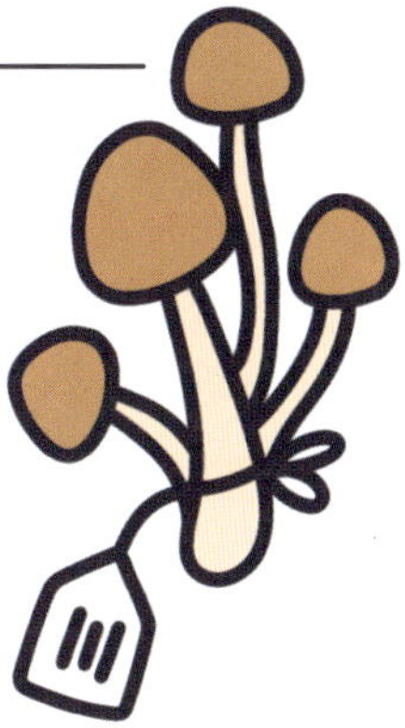

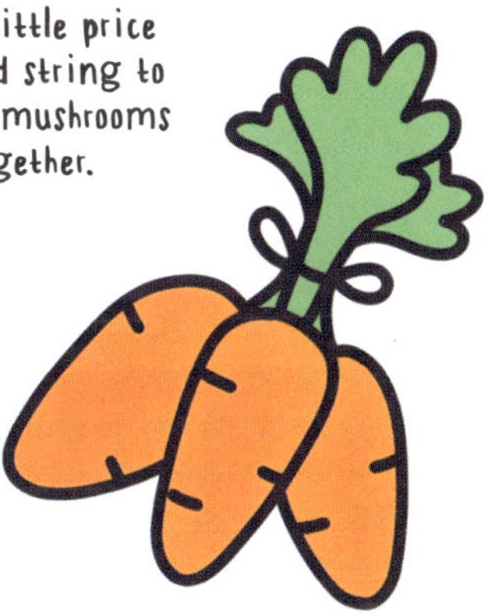

Keep adding more mushrooms coming out from the first ones.

When drawing a batch of ingredients, start out slow and just draw one or two.

Here's a bunch of carrots. Overlap the stems.

Beary bread

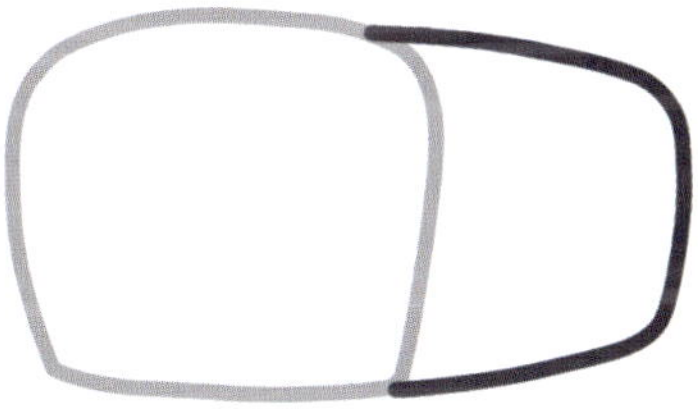

Draw a face and bear ears at the front of the loaf.

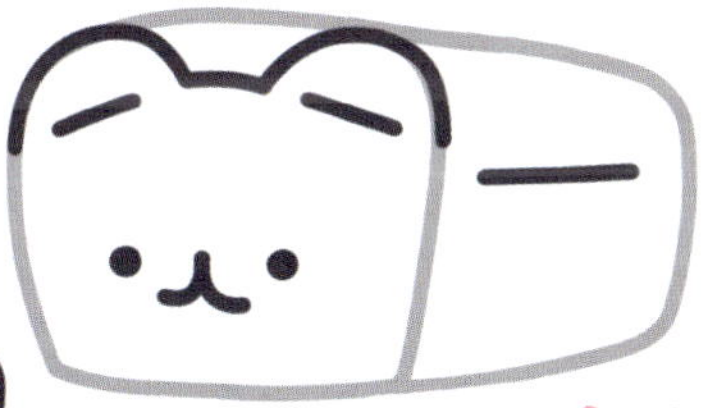

Colour the face a light cream and the sides a darker brown.

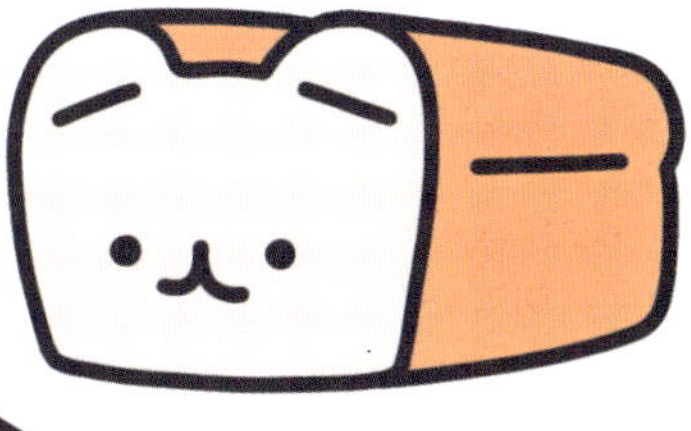

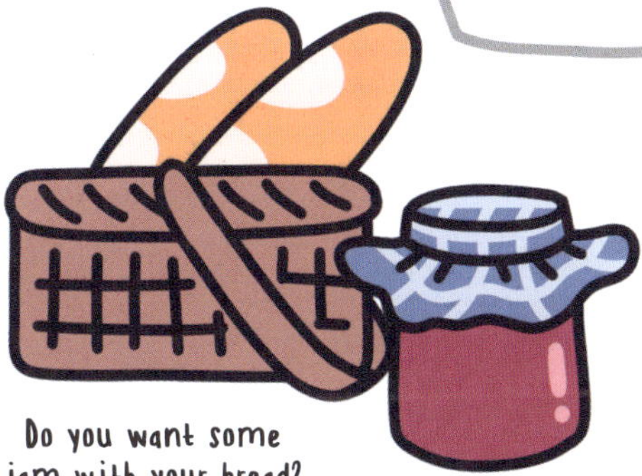

Draw a fresh loaf of bread by starting out with rounded rectangles.

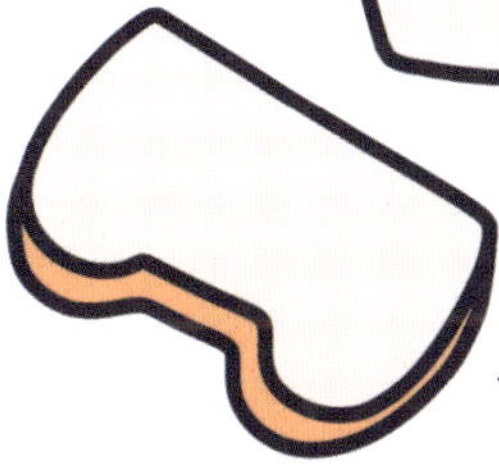

Draw a slice of toast on the side.

Do you want some jam with your bread?

VEHICLES

It is so much fun to make transportation for your characters by combining vehicles with woodland-themed elements.

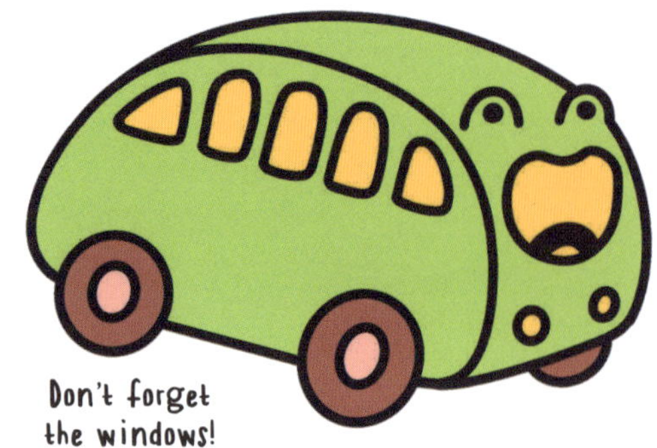

Don't forget the windows!

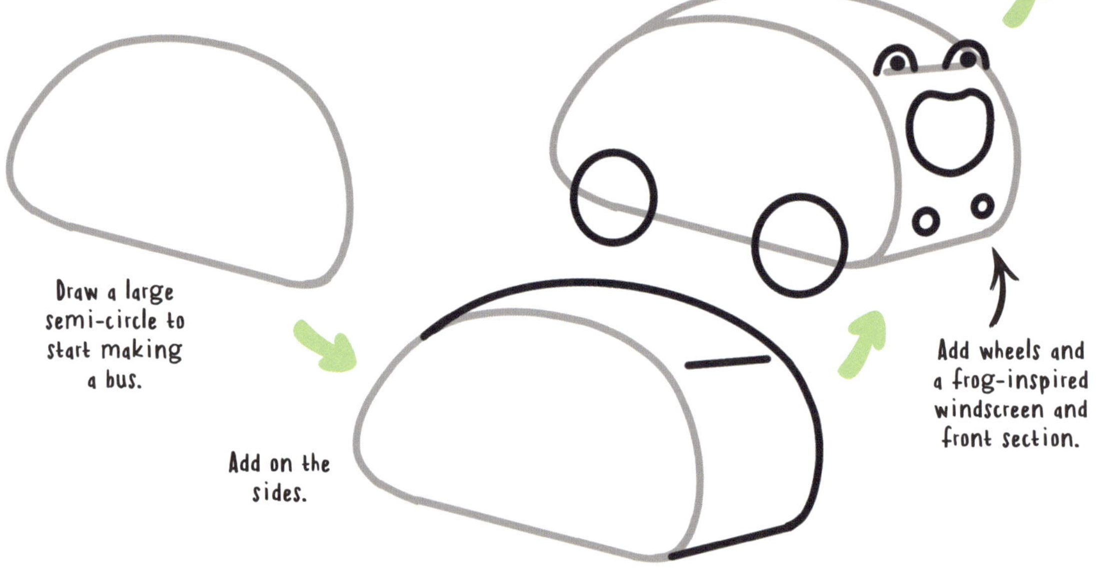

Draw a large semi-circle to start making a bus.

Add on the sides.

Add wheels and a frog-inspired windscreen and front section.

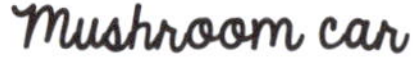

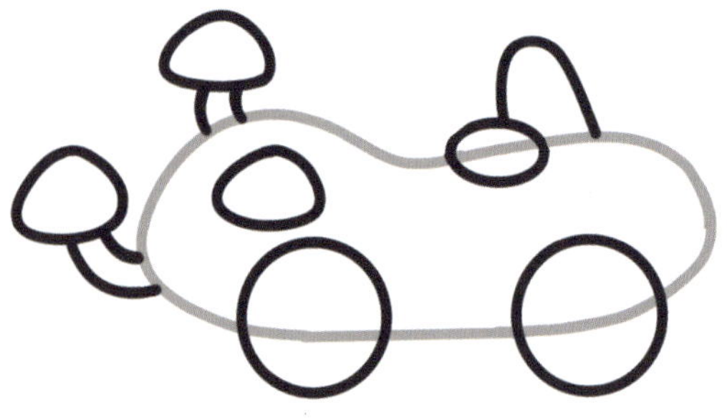

The base of this car is a jelly bean shape. Add wheels, a windscreen and some mushrooms.

This bunny loves their mushroom car!

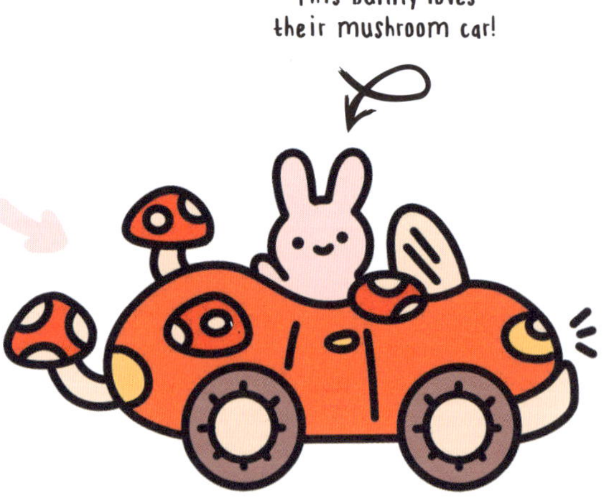

Helicopter bug

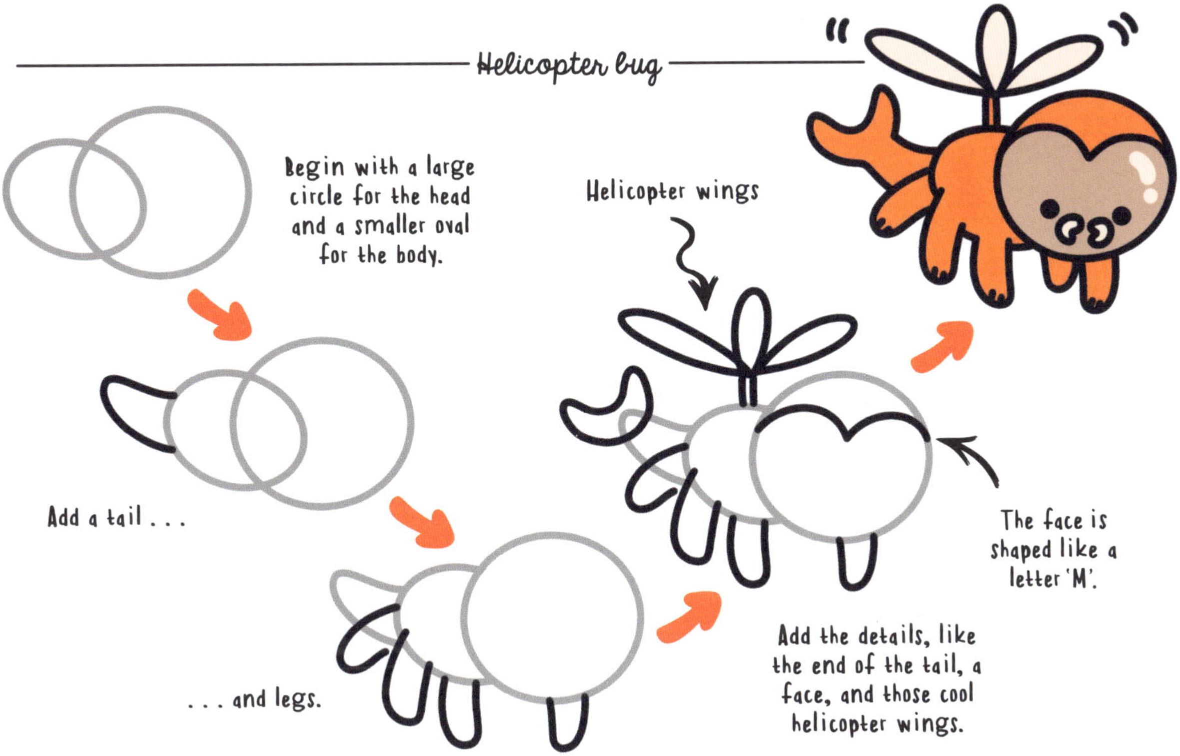

Begin with a large circle for the head and a smaller oval for the body.

Helicopter wings

Add a tail . . .

. . . and legs.

The face is shaped like a letter 'M'.

Add the details, like the end of the tail, a face, and those cool helicopter wings.

Flower motorcycle

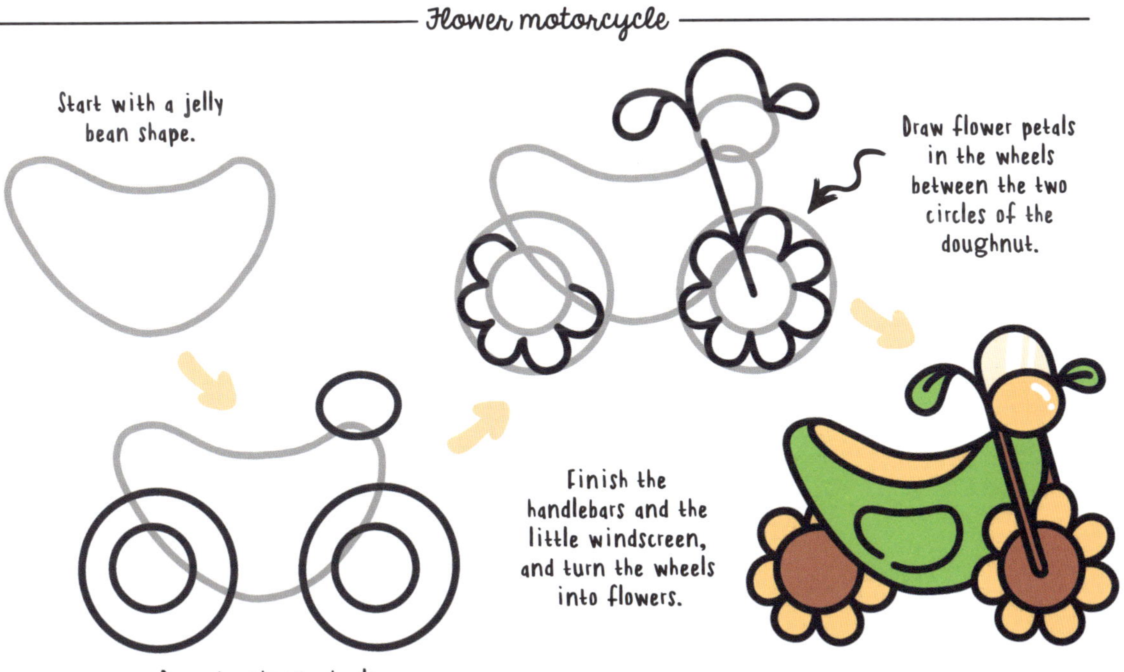

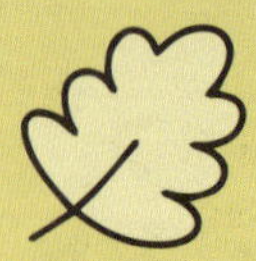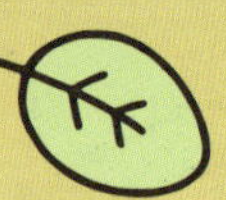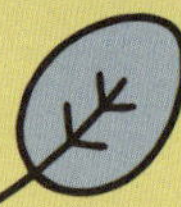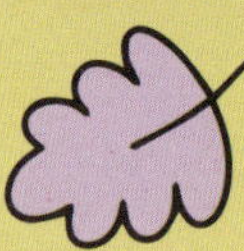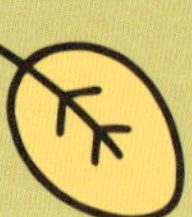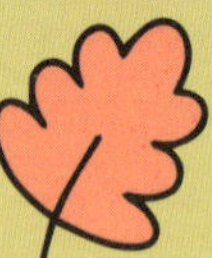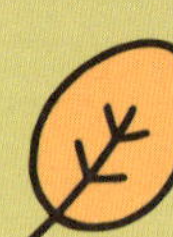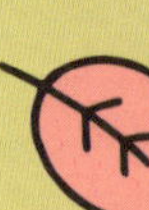

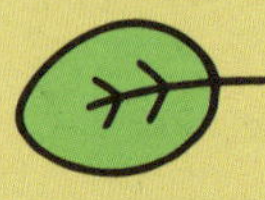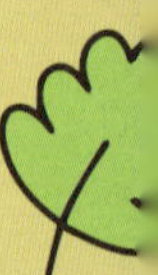

Author Acknowledgements

To the Quarto editing and publishing team, thank you for entertaining my random book ideas and being with me through all of these years. Special shout out to Kate, Claire, Martina, India and all of the behind-the-scenes team.

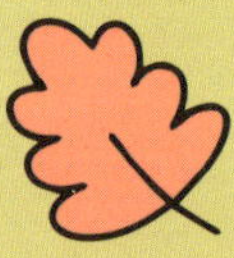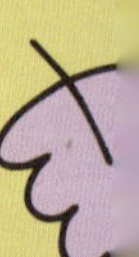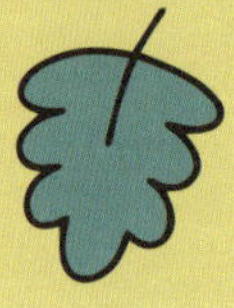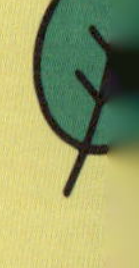

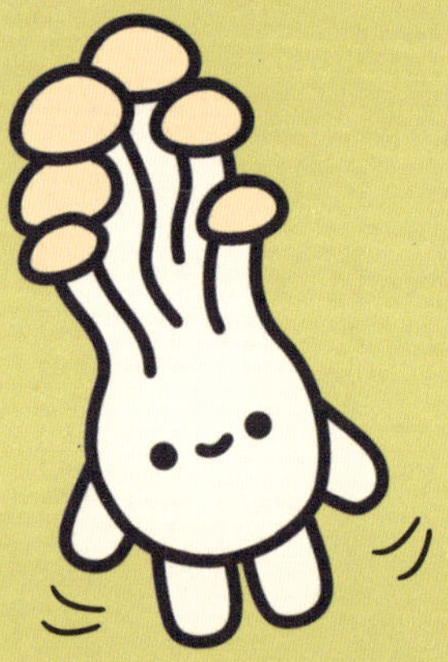

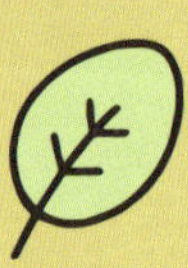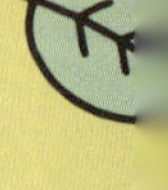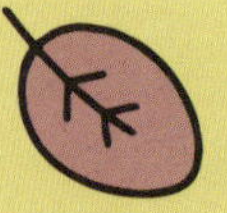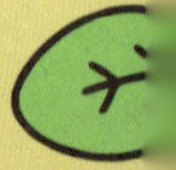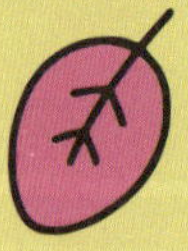

Picture Credits

Basileus/Shutterstock.com; ClareM/Shutterstock.com; FineArtSSThai/Shutterstock.com; Fona/Shutterstock.com; Jirawatfoto/Shutterstock.com; KenshiDesign/Shutterstock.com; Mallmo/Shutterstock.com; Martin Spurny/Shutterstock.com; Nai_Pisage/Shutterstock.com; Orientalprincess/Shutterstock.com; Panacea Doll/Shutterstock.com; Puckung/Shutterstock.com; Quayside/Shutterstock.com; r.classen/Shutterstock.com; SpicyTruffel/Shutterstock.com

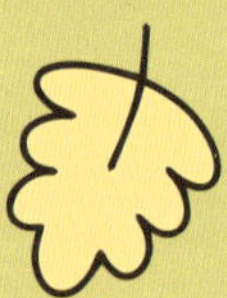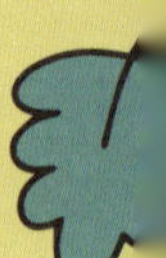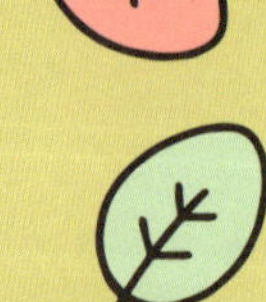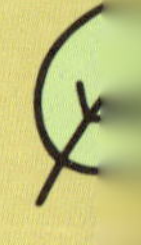

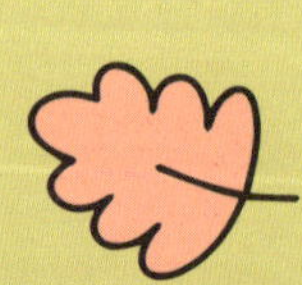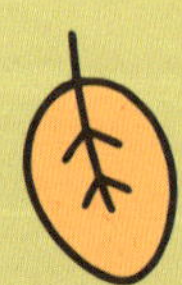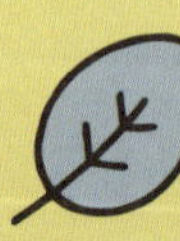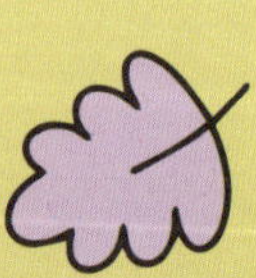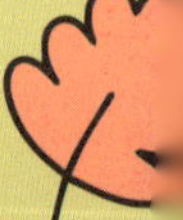